HISTORY OF
Mutual Savings Banks in Northampton, Massachusetts

KATHERINE FINNEY

MORNINGSIDE HEIGHTS · NEW YORK
KING'S CROWN PRESS
1945

Printed in the United States of America

KING'S CROWN PRESS
is a division of Columbia University Press organized for the purpose of making certain scholarly material available at minimum cost. Toward that end, the publishers have adopted every reasonable economy except such as would interfere with a legible format. The work is presented substantially as submitted by the author, without the usual editorial attention of Columbia University Press.

This is a War Time Book

FOREWORD

The relatively stable interest rates charged by the banks of Northampton, Massachusetts, a small city with few lending agencies, constituted the original stimulus to this inquiry. In economic analysis, interest rates command much attention but emphasis is usually placed upon rates in financial centers rather than upon those in small communities. It is believed that the factors found to be present in Northampton, a New England city with both manufacturing and agricultural interests and a city that has been rather stable in population and economic conditions, are typical of those found in small banks in many American communities.

This study inquires into the rates of interest charged and paid by the mutual savings banks of Northampton from 1876 to 1938 and indicates the factors determining these rates and the effects of the rates upon the accumulation of savings and upon the local demand for savings bank funds. In such a discussion it is necessary to describe the actual course of the investments and deposit liabilities of the savings banks and to consider elements which, in addition to interest rates, have influenced the accumulation of deposit balances and the utilization of those deposit balances.

The first chapter, giving a brief account of Northampton itself, is followed by a description of the growth of the mutual savings banks. Emphasis is given to the changes in their loans and investments and to the rise and activity of their deposit accounts. Various factors influencing the development of the banks are subsequently indicated. These include the competition of other savings and mortgage loan institutions, changes in interest rates, legal regulations, and economic fluctuations within the community. A summary chapter concludes the discussion.

Throughout the preparation of this study, the suggestions and criticism offered by Professor B. H. Beckhart have been most helpful, and I wish to express my deep appreciation of his advice and encouragement. I am grateful, also to Mr. Ralph

E. Harlow, Mr. Percy F. Spencer, and Mr. Sterling R. Whitbeck, as well as others connected with the various financial institutions in Northampton, who were generous in discussing with me the operations of the banks and in making available certain unpublished information. The Forbes Library of Northampton and the Cleveland Public Library rendered much assistance, especially in facilitating the use of the early volumes of the annual report of the Commissioner of Banks.

Katherine Finney

New York City
April, 1945

TABLE OF CONTENTS

Charts

Tables

Chapter I

THE CITY OF NORTHAMPTON

A. LOCATION

Northampton is located in the central part of western Massachusetts in the lowlands of the Connecticut River Valley. The valley itself is a broad expanse of fertile river flats and rich meadowland bordered by wooded hills and mountains. On the Northampton side of the Connecticut River these hills are the beginnings of the Berkshire Mountains. Flowing through Northampton is the small Mill River.

Early means of communication were provided by roads and by the Connecticut River and canals. Railroads, however, have furnished transportation facilities since the middle of the nineteenth century. The Boston and Maine and the New York, New Haven, and Hartford railroads maintain lines into Northampton.

Within a radius of about a hundred miles are the cities of Boston, Hartford, New Haven, and Albany. In the immediate vicinity lie the manufacturing centers of Springfield and Holyoke. Although agriculture is of great importance in the surrounding territory, there is considerable manufacturing in Northampton on a rather small scale.

B. POPULATION

From 1875 to 1940 the population of Northampton[1] grew slowly but rather steadily. In 1875, at the beginning of the period under study, the population numbered slightly more than eleven thousand, as shown in Chart 1. By 1925 the size of the popula-

[1] In the New England system of local government the town is of chief administrative importance. The town corresponds somewhat to the township found in other parts of the United States and represents an area for government rather than a center of population. Thus, towns often include much farm land and woodland as well as closely settled areas. In 1876 Northampton was such a New England town and included about thirty-five square miles, much of which was farming land. When Northampton was incorporated in 1883, the city retained the boundaries of the former town.

Chart 1

POPULATION OF NORTHAMPTON

At Five Year Intervals, 1875-1940

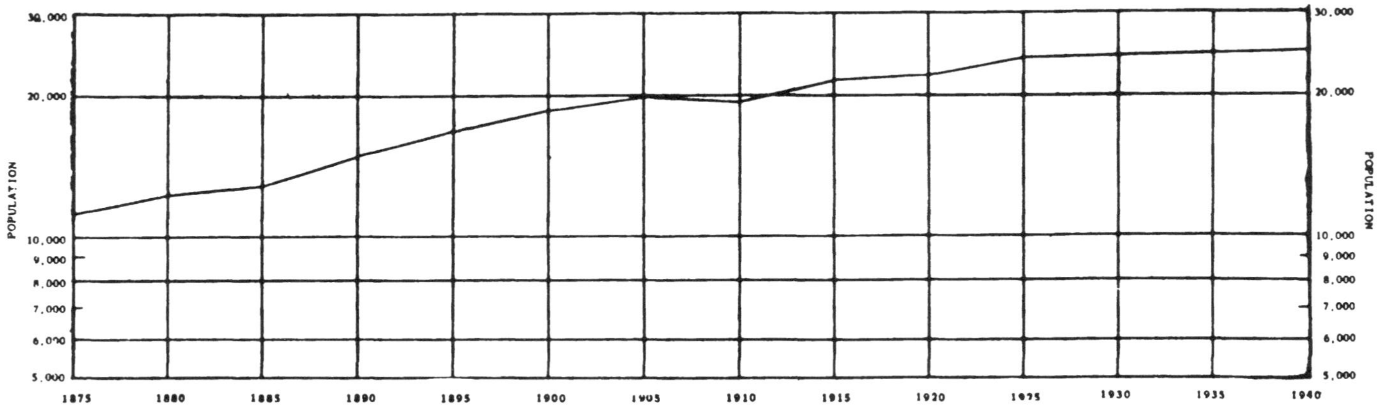

Source: Mass. *Decennial Census*. 1925, 1935.
U. S. Bureau of the Census. *Census of Population*. 1940.

tion had more than doubled, and small increases occurred from 1925 to 1940.

A considerable part of the population of Northampton is of foreign birth. Since 1875, census reports show the foreign born to be about 25 per cent of the total population. In the early years natives of Ireland, Canada, and England constituted almost the entire foreign born population, and this group has remained large. In 1895 a few persons who had been born in Poland or Russia were living in Northampton. This group, chiefly Polish, increased in size until in 1915 it was as numerous as the Irish, and the two groups, Irish and Polish, made up more than half of the foreign born population. Since then the Irish, Canadian, and Polish people have constituted the three largest groups of those born on foreign soil.

From the standpoint of the number of persons engaged, manufacturing has been the chief occupation of the inhabitants of Northampton and it has been of much greater importance than farming. According to the Massachusetts census report of 1875, more than two thousand persons were at that time employed in manufacturing and about five hundred were engaged in agriculture, either as farmers or as farm laborers. Thus, in 1875 about four times as many people were employed in manufacturing as in agriculture, and the predominance of manufacturing increased with the passage of time. Although the number engaged in farming remained about the same from 1875 to 1915, the number whose occupation lay in manufacturing increased during those years, and by 1915 more than four thousand persons were employed in the manufacturing industries. The Federal census of 1920 reported fewer employed in agriculture than in 1915, while the number engaged in manufacturing had increased slightly. Census data since 1920 are not available, but manufacturing has continued to overshadow farming as an occupation in Northampton.

Considerable numbers have found employment in trade, since Northampton serves as a buying center not only for those in the city itself but also for those in near-by parts of the county. The fact that Northampton is the county seat, furthermore, attracts legal and other business to the city.

Much employment has, also, been given by hospitals and schools and by the college located in Northampton. The largest of the educational institutions is Smith College, which opened in 1875. It grew from that time until in 1938 it had reached an enrollment of over two thousand students. About four hundred people are connected with the college as members of the teaching and office staffs and they form permanent residents of the city. The college, furthermore, employs several hundred local people to maintain the buildings and grounds and to assist in the dormitories. In addition, among the schools, there is to be found the Clarke School for the Deaf, which has been open since 1867. Several preparatory schools for girls existed during the period under study.

The Northampton State Hospital for the insane was opened in 1858. The growth in its capacity is shown by the fact that in 1895 it accommodated five hundred patients and by 1938 about two thousand patients. The United States Veterans' Administration also maintains a large hospital in Northampton, and the county operates a sanatorium.

C. MANUFACTURING

The earliest manufacturing in Northampton clustered along the Mill River since the river provided power for the operation of the mills and factories. By 1900 water wheels were still furnishing an important part of the power used by the Mill River plants, but steam was more widely used. Since 1900 electrical energy, generated with the abundant water power of the Connecticut River, has largely replaced the older sources of power.

Except for power, the area offers little to encourage manufacturing. There are no raw materials or minerals of economic importance. It seems to have been chiefly this factor of power which gave the original impetus to manufacturing in Northampton. Once factories were in operation, other industries were started because of the experience and interests of the men concerned in the management of the plants, because of capital accumulated from successful manufacturing, and because of the presence of an adequate and skilled labor supply.

Northampton has been characterized by great diversity of manufacturing; it has never been a one-industry town. The most important of its industries has been the manufacturing of silk, which began in the 1830's, when the attempt was made not only to manufacture silk but also to raise silk cocoons. Since that time silk manufacturing has remained of prime importance to Northampton, for the average number of wage earners employed in the industry has varied around 50 per cent of the average number of all wage earners employed in the community. In 1890, 53 per cent of the average number of wage earners employed in all Mill River industries were employed by silk concerns; in 1900, 43 per cent; in 1920, 48 per cent; and in 1930, 64 per cent.[2]

Cutlery plants have also been an important element in the industrial life of Northampton although they have never approached the importance attained by the silk companies either in number employed or in value of product. In 1938 several cutlery factories were still operating.

A concern which maintained itself over a long period of years is the Pro-phy-lac-tic tooth brush company -- the sole representative of the brush industry in Northampton. It was incorporated in 1866 as the Florence Manufacturing Company, the successor to a daguerreotype case company, and brushes soon became its chief product. Its history showed almost continuous expansion until 1927, and in 1930 it was the largest non-textile factory in the Northampton area.

From time to time there have been other industries in Northampton. There were factories for making sewing machines, oil stoves, caskets, barrels, wagons, buttons, paper, filter equipment, baskets and drums, and tacks.

In 1938 the chief industries consisted of a hosiery mill, three cutlery plants, and the Pro-phy-lac-tic Brush Company. In each of these, several hundred workers were employed. A pulp plant, a casket shop, a plant making filters, and a hattery were also operating, but each employed fewer than one hundred workmen. Smaller shops were making baskets, boxes, cabinets, and bottle caps.

Northampton industries, which were largely initiated and developed by local men and with local capital, continued to

2 Computed from data given in: Agnes Hannay, *A Chronicle of Industry on the Mill River*, pp. 129, 131. The data here include manufacturing in both Northampton and Williamsburg, a small center near Northampton.

operate under local control until after World War I. In the nineteenth century and in the early part of the twentieth century, there was a particularly enterprising group of men in Northampton able to turn their interests to the development of a wide range of industrial production. Northampton industries escaped for the most part from the wave of consolidations that swept the country around 1900. Although there were a few mergers before the War of 1914, most of the plants were operated by local men. In the period after the first World War this condition was somewhat changed and all of the silk companies became parts of larger organizations. The old Nonotuck Silk Company combined in 1921 with an outside firm, the Brainerd and Armstrong Company, to form the Corticelli Silk Company. The Belding Brothers company, which had long operated a silk plant in Northampton, was consolidated with the Hemingway company in 1926. The Belding Hemingway Company, in turn, combined with the Corticelli company in 1932. The assets of the McCallum company, another silk firm, were acquired by the Propper Company of Long Island in 1930. In this movement toward consolidation in the more recent years, the International Silver Company opened a branch in Northampton and the Pro-phy-lac-tic brush concern was merged with the Lambert Company.

As a consequence, in part, of this tendency toward ownership and management by local men and also because of the rather small size of the establishments, the labor policies pursued have for the most part been friendly. The companies have usually been interested in maintaining pleasant personal relationships with their employees. Many of the companies set up definite policies directed toward keeping their workmen in their employ for long periods of service. There have been few serious labor disturbances. The workers are not crowded into congested districts such as those often found in large industrial areas, but they live for the most part in small one-family houses.

Fluctuations in business throughout the United States as a whole are reflected to a considerable degree in manufacturing in Northampton, as shown in Chart 2. From the late 1890's to 1907, Northampton industries enjoyed a period of almost continuous prosperity and expansion, although there was a slight lull in the Spring of 1900. Business grew slack in 1907 and

Chart 2

MANUFACTURING ACTIVITY IN NORTHAMPTON, 1886-1938

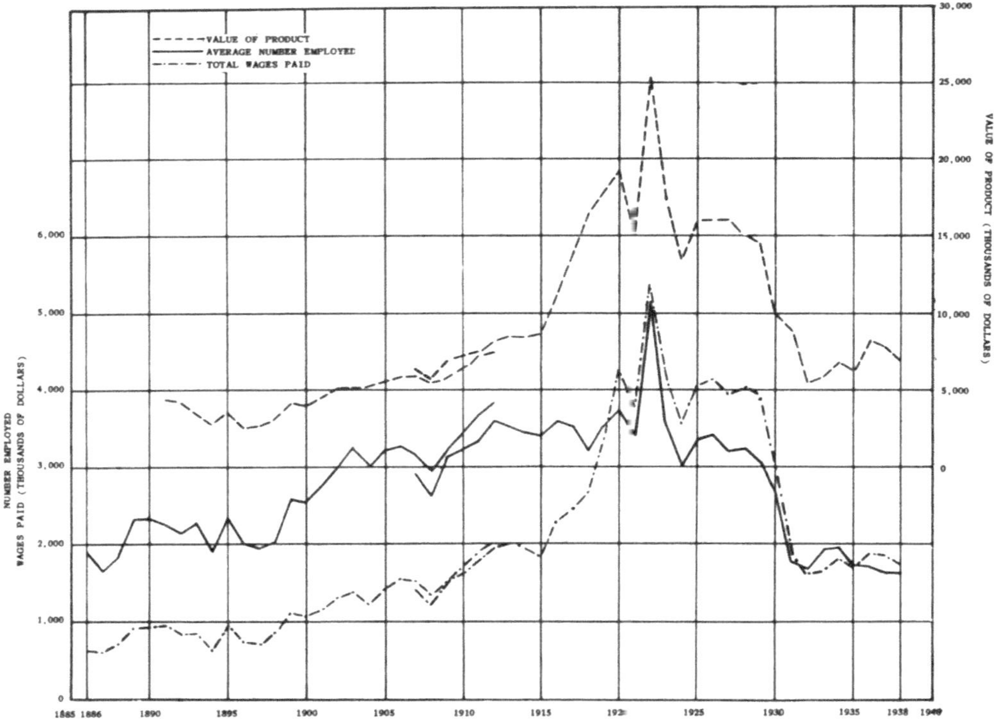

Sources: 1886-1912. [illegible] Northampton and Williamsburg, as given in Hanney, *op. cit.*, p. 129.
1907-1938. Mass. Dept. of Labor and Industries, *Annual Report on the Statistics of Manufactures*, 1907-1921, and *Statistics of Manufactures, 1920-1938*.

continued at a low level in the early part of 1908. All shops in the city were affected and were running on part-time schedule, and in many cases they were discharging employees. Business revived in 1908, however, and from 1909 to 1913 was active. In 1914 there was a period of lessened activity which continued into 1915.

The first World War provided a great stimulus to manufacturing in Northampton. The industries experienced a period of enormous activity both before the United States entered the war and during the time when the country was actually participating. The value of manufactured products increased from $8,581,000 in 1914 to $16,249,000 in 1918. The silk industry was extremely active because of the disruption of foreign textile industries and because of increased demand. One Northampton firm was supplying the Government with silk powder bags. A filter plant was making gun carriages. Even the tooth brush factory increased its production and worked on a three-shift day.

Although the armistice brought the cessation of Government orders in 1918 and the cancellation of many orders already placed, the Northampton plants continued operations at a high rate in 1919 and in the early months of 1920. The product of manufactures reached $19,265,000 in 1920, and employment and payroll payments were likewise high. Late in 1920 manufacturing activity declined and the plants continued to feel the depression into 1921. Most of the firms were operating only a few days a week.

The expansion in manufacturing was resumed in 1921 and culminated in an all-time peak in 1922. The value of product reached $25,269,000 in 1922 and the average number of wage earners employed in manufacturing increased to 5,189, by far the greatest volume of employment attained in Northampton. Production continued at a high level through 1929. The Pro-phy-lac-tic company continued to expand until about 1927 and the cutlery plants maintained their production.

The silk industry in the entire country had expanded so greatly during the war, however, that it suffered from much competition when the war was over. The industry, furthermore, complained of rapid changes in fashion with which it was difficult to keep pace. As a result of these two factors the Northampton silk industry operated on only a part-time schedule in 1924 and the following years.

In 1929 and in the next three years, the number employed in manufacturing, as well as the value of product, decreased continuously. Retrenchments were necessary, many concerns operated on greatly reduced schedules, and some factories closed permanently.

> Altogether the post-War shut-downs meant the loss of 43 per cent of the wage-earning positions, on the basis of 1920 figures, and 50 per cent of the production capacity measured in value of output.[3]

The most important of these shut-downs occurred in the silk industry. In 1931 and 1932, two of the plants closed permanently, leaving the Propper-McCallum Hosiery Company the sole representative of the silk industry in Northampton. For a few years another company manufactured rayon at the Belding Hemingway plant but it discontinued operations in 1936.[4] Employment in manufacturing in Northampton dropped from 3,088 in 1929 to 1,697 in 1932 and the value of the manufactured products fell from $14,582,000 to $5,415,000. There was some improvement thereafter but in 1938 the average number employed had again dropped to the 1932 level and the value of product was $6,738,-000.

D. AGRICULTURE

Many kinds of farm and market garden products are grown in the Northampton area. The lowlands along the Connecticut River are unusually fertile but the soil in the hilly country lying farther back from the river is thin and poorly suited to cultivation. In the hilly regions dairying is carried on; it has been, and still is, of great importance both to Northampton and to Hampshire County, in which Northampton is located. Because of the importance of dairying, a great deal of hay is raised. Poultry and eggs as well as milk have been important farm products. Many Irish potatoes are grown, and corn is the most important of the cereals. Tobacco and onions were impor-

[3] *Ibid.*, p. 122.
[4] *Ibid.*, p. 121n.

tant farm products in the earlier years under consideration. Within recent years they have not been of importance in Northampton, itself, although they still make up a large portion of the agricultural output of Hampshire County.

Farms in Northampton are relatively small, averaging about forty or fifty acres in size, and almost all of them are operated by full or part owners.

E. SUMMARY

Thus the city of Northampton has shown only gradual changes in population and economic conditions. In the early years of this study a great variety of manufacturing was carried on, and the first World War further stimulated industry. Although activity was high after the war, manufacturing in Northampton did not share in the great expansion that took place in the country as a whole. A gradual movement of industry away from Northampton occurred. Partially offsetting this movement was the stability provided by the various institutions located in Northampton and by the fact that the city served as a shopping center for the surrounding area.

Agriculture is of secondary importance in Northampton. The farms, which are rather small, have specialized in dairy and poultry products and in onions, potatoes, and other small crops. Tobacco, which was important in the earlier years, declined in importance, except for a slight increase in the early 1920's.

The population, which has been engaged primarily in the manufacturing industries, has grown slowly throughout most of the period included in this study. A considerable part of the population is foreign born, Canadian, Irish, and Polish people making up the largest of the foreign born groups.

Chapter II

THE ASSETS OF THE SAVINGS BANKS

The savings banks of Northampton have always been mutual savings banks, that is, they are banks operated for the benefit of the depositors or savers. Except for that part of income used to build up the reserve funds required by law, all of the earnings of mutual banks are distributed to the depositors in proportion to the size of their deposits. The management of each mutual savings bank in Massachusetts is under the direction of a self-perpetuating board of trustees, whose members have for the most part assumed their responsibilities as a community service. Of the Northampton men earlier referred to as leaders in manufacturing activity in the late nineteenth and twentieth centuries, many served as savings bank trustees.[1]

There are now three mutual savings banks in Northampton. Two have served the community continuously throughout the entire period from 1876 to 1938. The larger and older of these is the Northampton Institution for Savings, which was organized in 1842. The other is the Florence Savings Bank, organized in 1873 and located in the secondary business center of Northampton known as Florence. The third bank at the present time is the Nonotuck Savings Bank, which opened in 1899. In the preceding year occurred the closing of the Hampshire Savings Bank, which had operated continuously from 1869 to 1898.[2] Thus, with

1 Hannay, *op. cit.*, p. 82. Later, Calvin Coolidge served as president of one of the banks, the Nonotuck Savings Bank.

2 The Hampshire Savings Bank was placed in receivership by the Board of Commissioners of Savings Banks in 1898 because of a defalcation, originally estimated at about $300,000. The treasurer, or executive officer, of the savings bank also served as president of the Hampshire County National Bank and the two banks occupied the same bank room. Certain bonds were used as assets of both banks and the records were falsified in order to show large deposits by the savings bank in the national bank at the time of state examination of the savings bank. Further difficulty was created by the keeping of mortgage notes that had already been paid and by the failure to write off loans on personal security that had no realizable value. The Hampshire Savings Bank eventually paid a total of 79.1 per cent on its deposit liabilities. (Mass., *Annual Report of the Board of Commissioners of Savings Banks*, Part I, 1898, pp. xiii-xvi; *ibid.*, 1899, p. xvii; *ibid.*, 1900, p. xii).

the exception of one year, there were three savings banks operating in Northampton at any given time during the period under discussion. The comparative sizes of the banks are indicated in Chart 3, which shows the total assets in each year from 1876 to 1938.

The savings bank data included in this study are taken largely from the Annual Reports of the Massachusetts Commissioner of Banks and relate to the holdings as of the thirty-first of October of each year. When reference is made to changes in the year 1906, for example, the changes actually occurred between October 31, 1905, and October 31, 1906, rather than during the calendar year.

This chapter describes the various types of investments in which the Northampton banks have placed their funds and the changes in importance of the major forms. Definite shifts in the kinds of assets held by the banks have resulted from changes in the local community served, movements in the general investment market, and variations in the legislative regulations pertaining to mutual savings banks.

Investment of funds held by the savings banks of Massachusetts has been subject to extensive and detailed regulation by the state. In the early years savings banks were chartered by individual acts, but in 1834 a general law was enacted to permit mutual savings banks to be incorporated without individual legislative action. This law also limited the manner in which savings banks could invest their funds. Although the economic development of the United States and the growth of deposits in the savings banks have brought many changes in the regulations governing investments, the aim has always been to provide maximum safety of deposits and so to encourage thrift on the part of people of small resources. The banks are organized primarily for the purpose of serving people who desire security of principal with whatever income can be derived rather than the possibility of greater income combined with greater risk of losing their savings. The mutual savings banks of Massachusetts seem to have fulfilled their purpose well, for the amount of loss to depositors has been but a very small proportion of the total amount placed on deposit in the banks.

Chart 3

TOTAL ASSETS

Northampton Savings Banks, October 31 of Each Year, 1876-1938

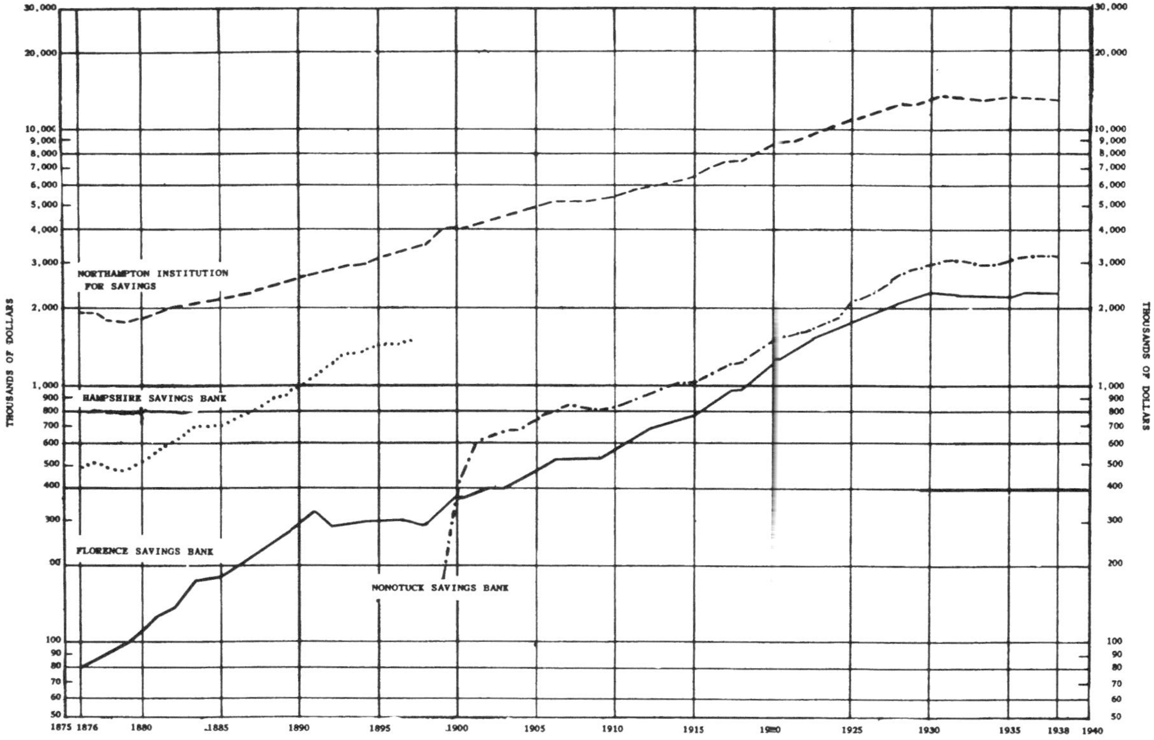

Source: Mass. Commissioner of Banks. *Annual Report*. 1876-1938.

PART I. LOANS

A. MORTGAGE LOANS

The savings banks of Massachusetts have been permitted to own securities, both bonds and bank stock, and to extend loans secured by mortgages or other collateral. Each of these kinds of earning assets is discussed in detail in the following pages. In the Northampton banks, loans have been the most profitable class of investment and the largest one, accounting for well over half of the total assets. Of the loans, those based upon real estate mortgages have generally been of greater importance than those based upon other kinds of security.

1. Legal Regulation

Loans on mortgages were permitted under the earliest regulation. In 1876 the law permitted investment of funds in loans on first mortgages of real estate situated in Massachusetts if the amount loaned was not more than 60 per cent of the value of the property. A report by two or more members of the board of investment of the bank concerning the value of the property was required. The aggregate amount of such loans could not exceed 70 per cent of the total amount of deposit in the bank.[3]

The law remained unchanged until 1908, when provisions were made concerning the revaluation of mortgaged property and the maximum that could be loaned on unimproved real estate.[4] Revaluation of property which served as security for a loan was required at intervals of not more than five years, and, if, at the time of revaluation, any loan was found to be in excess of the maximum percentage of value, the amount loaned was to be reduced. Although the old requirement of 60 per cent of value was retained for other mortgage loans, not more than 40 per cent of the value of the property was to be loaned in the case of unimproved and unproductive real estate. These changes were made in order to increase the efficiency of the real estate loan business of the savings banks

The next change in mortgage loan provisions was made in 1933, when it was required that no loan on mortgage should be made

[3] Mass. Acts 1876, c. 203, sec. 9, cl. 1st.
[4] Mass. Acts 1908, c. 590, sec. 68, cl. 1st.

for a period longer than three years and the maximum interval for revaluation was reduced from five to three years.[5]

In order to facilitate the transfer of real property, it was later provided that a new first mortgage could be accepted from the purchaser of real estate upon which the bank already held a first mortgage. The new loan in such a case was not to exceed the amount due on the existing mortgage together with the accumulated interest and accumulated taxes and municipal liens.[6]

The increasing competition for good real estate loans after the depression of 1932 induced the banks to seek changes in the regulations. As a result, savings banks were permitted after 1937 to make loans on improved or productive real estate for a period greater than three years provided the terms of the note required quarterly amortization at a rate of 2 per cent a year, or more. Such a loan was not to exceed 60 per cent of the value of the property if the rate of amortization was 2 per cent, or 70 per cent of value if amortization took place at 3 per cent.[7] Thus the savings banks might compete the better with cooperative banks (sometimes called building and loan associations), which were allowed to extend mortgage loans for terms longer than three years and for amounts up to 80 per cent of the value of the property.

When the various Federal agencies were established to assist in the home loan market, the savings banks were authorized to make use of their services. The savings banks could become members of the Federal Home Loan Bank and invest in its stock. When the Home Owners' Loan Corporation began operations, the Massachusetts savings banks were permitted to accept its bonds in exchange for any home mortgage or for real estate held as a result of foreclosure.[8] By act of 1935 the banks were permitted to make such advances of credit as were insured according to the National Housing Act, Title I, section 2, and to obtain such insurance and to make mortgage loans insured under Title II of the National Housing Act. In 1937 the law was amended to allow the making of loans insured by the Federal Housing Ad-

[5] Mass. Acts 1933, c. 334, sec. 22.
[6] Mass. Acts 1936, c. 191.
[7] Mass. Acts 1937, c. 180.
[8] Mass. Acts 1933, c. 46 and c. 343.

ministrator, although such investment was authorized only until July 1, 1939.[9]

2. Description of Loans

a) Type of Real Estate

The Northampton banks have loaned chiefly upon the security of home mortgages and the few loans that they have made upon business and multiple-dwelling units have proved less satisfactory than the home loans.

The Florence Savings Bank seems to have adhered closely to the policy of making no loans on business houses or apartment houses; in 1938 it had only one loan on a business house and none on an apartment building. It made very few loans on farms in the later years. Thus, practically all of the real estate loans of the bank have been on homes, either one-family or two-family houses. The loans of the Nonotuck Savings Bank have also been home loans for the most part. As was true of the other banks, the Northampton Institution for Savings has made its loans chiefly on homes, but it has extended loans also upon farms and upon apartment and business houses. It is perhaps to be expected that this bank, which is considerably larger than the other two, should be forced into making loans on commercial buildings because of the greater amount of its funds seeking investment.

Mortgages on homes, especially those on one-family houses, have proved to be the most satisfactory type of mortgage security. Their own home is one of the last things that people will relinquish when they are in financial distress and, consequently, losses on home loans have been smaller than those on loans upon commercial buildings.

b) Location of Real Estate

The banks have placed their real estate loans, for the most part, in Northampton itself although in the 1920's their loans included a somewhat larger area. The Florence Savings Bank, located in the industrial community of Florence, has not gone into the main part of the city but has confined itself chiefly

9. Mass. Acts 1935, c. 162; Acts 1937, c. 240.

to loans upon real estate situated in Florence and in Leeds, a community adjacent to Florence. However, it did extend loans in near-by Springfield in the 1920's, and in 1938 many of its loans were based upon property located there. The other two banks also made loans in Springfield, although their loans came somewhat later than those of the Florence bank. In the late 1920's real estate in Springfield was booming and most of the banks in western Massachusetts extended some loans there at that time. The Northampton banks made no loans at a greater distance than Springfield.

The general experience of the Northampton banks, and of all savings banks,[10] has indicated that greater difficulty is encountered with loans made upon property located at some distance from the bank than with loans based upon near-by property. The bank officers cannot know real estate conditions and trends in other areas as intimately as they know real estate values in their own community, nor can they know borrowers as well as those in their own city. The risks involved in loans on distant property are, therefore, greater. In addition, the loans at a distance involve more time and expense in supervision, or they require that the bank conduct its business through an agent.

c) Valuation of Real Estate

In the valuation of real estate the banks take into consideration a number of different factors: cost or purchase price, current market value, age and condition of the property, and location. In connection with location, not only the present value but also the trend in values in the neighborhood and the probable future of the neighborhood must be regarded. The possibility of using the site for other purposes may increase the value of the real estate. In general the banks seem to have followed a conservative course in the original valuations of property to be mortgaged.

[10] The advisability of restricting real estate loans to property located in the immediate vicinity was indicated by a special banking commission of Massachusetts in 1934. The commission recommended that no loan be permitted outside a radius of fifty miles of the lending bank and that certain other restrictions be placed upon the location of mortgaged property. [Mass. Sen. Doc. No. 100 (1934), pp. 38, 53.]

The banks have probably not adhered closely to the requirement that revaluation be made every three years and that the amount of the loan be adjusted if the loan exceeds the legal maximum. In 1938 there were many loans in excess of the 60 per cent or 40 per cent maximum. With the general low level of the real estate market this might be justified on the basis of the anticipation of a future rise in real estate values. In more extraordinary or special cases, as in 1936, when a flood caused severe and permanent damage to the lowlands, the banks reduced the valuation of property and, consequently, the amount of the loans made thereon. When the banks find that loans are in excess of the allowed percentage of valuation, they encourage borrowers to reduce the difference through quarterly payments on the principal.

d) Size of Loans

Since most real estate loans of the Northampton savings banks have been made on homes, the average size has been small. Chart 4 shows the variations in the average size of the mortgage loans outstanding in each of the banks from 1889 to 1938. The loans made by the Northampton Institution for Savings and by the Nonotuck bank are larger and show much greater variation in size than do those made by the Florence bank, which has pursued the policy of loaning almost exclusively on homes.

The average size of the loans of the Northampton Institution for Savings, slightly over $2,000 in 1889, increased to $3,800 in 1893 and remained over $3,000 until 1899, when the average dropped to about $2,000. From 1901 to 1929 the average size of loans showed a generally upward trend, reaching well over $6,000 in the period from 1927 to 1930. This increase indicates rising construction cost and value of homes, but it also suggests that, as the available funds of the bank increased, more and more of the loans were being placed upon business houses and multiple dwellings. After 1929 loans declined in size and by 1938 the average had fallen to about $5,400.

The outstanding loans of the Nonotuck bank fluctuated around $2,000 until 1920, after which their size rose rapidly until by 1933 they had reached their maximum average of about $4,500. In subsequent years the average was slightly smaller.

Chart 4

AVERAGE SIZE OF REAL ESTATE LOANS OUTSTANDING

October 31 of Each Year, 1889-1938

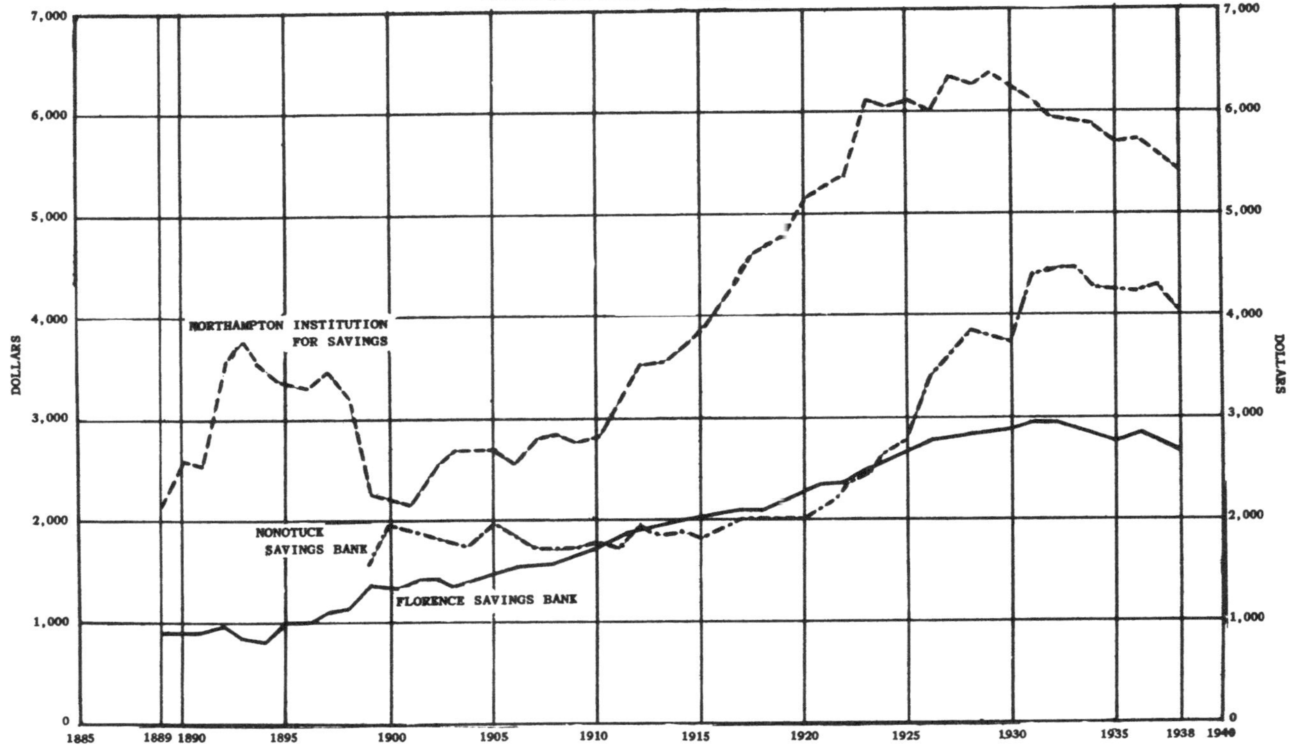

Source: Mass. Commissioner of Banks. *Annual Report*. 1889-1938. (Computed from data in this source, 1889-1906.)

The loans of the Florence bank showed a gradual but steady increase in size from $900 in 1889 to $2,900 in 1931, and then a decline to less than $2,700 in 1938. The loans were smaller than those of the other banks because they were based almost exclusively upon one-family or two-family houses and were extended chiefly within an area of rather modest dwellings.

The size of loans made by all the Northampton banks thus reflected the general rise in construction costs and in real estate values until the prolonged depression of the 1930's. The average size of loans differed in the three banks, however, because of differences in the nature of the property mortgaged.

e) Number of Loans

The total number of mortgage loans outstanding in the savings banks of Northampton showed an upward movement from 1889 to 1931, as indicated by Charts 5, 6, and 7. As the population of the city grew, the number of mortgage loans increased, and, in the prosperous years from 1905 to 1915 and from 1920 to 1930, the number of mortgage loans made by all of the savings banks increased much more rapidly than the population.

The long-time rates of increase in the mortgage loans of the Florence bank and of the Northampton Institution for Savings have been similar since 1889, the first year for which data are available. Little change occurred until 1899, when the number of real estate loans increased sharply. After a period of relative stability from 1900 to 1910, the number of loans was generally increasing until the interruption caused by the participation of the United States in the World War. The loans of the Nonotuck bank increased in number from the time of its organization in 1899 until 1912 and in the years immediately following 1912 little increase occurred. With American participation in the war the number of loans made by the Northampton banks decreased in 1918. In the post-war years, however, the number of mortgage loans increased as a result of the demand for loans arising during the expansion of building in the 1920's and as a result of the availability of funds in the Northampton savings banks brought about by the reduction of holdings of Treasury bonds. The number of loans continued to grow until after the collapse of 1929. Loans of one of the banks declined in number in 1931; the decline in the other two banks began in 1932.

Chart 5

NUMBER OF REAL ESTATE LOANS

Florence Savings Bank, October 31 of Each Year, 1889-1938

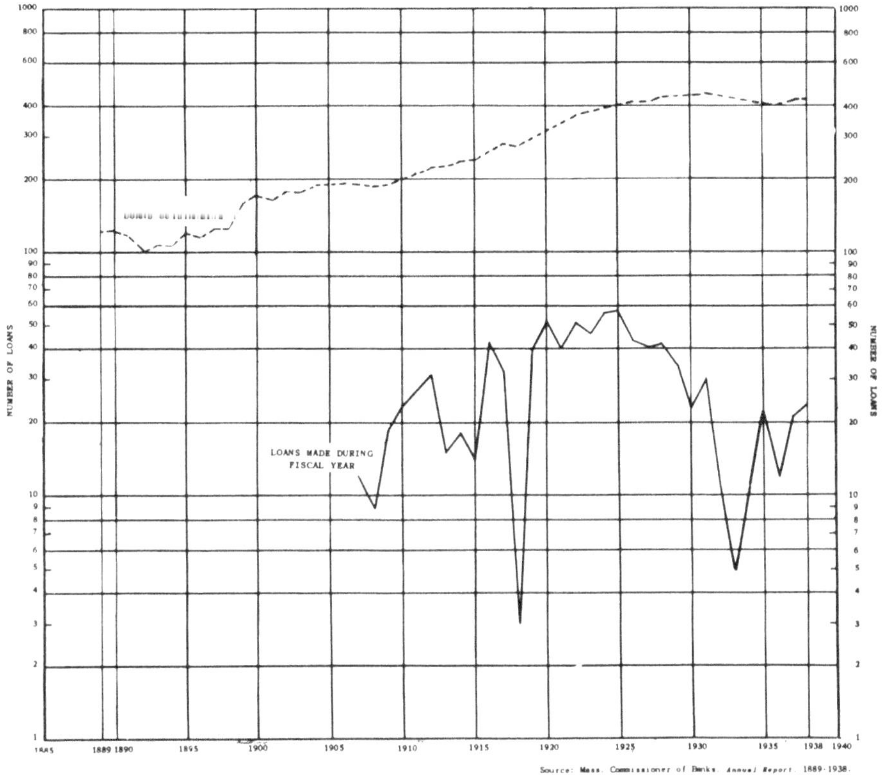

Source: Mass. Commissioner of Banks. *Annual Report*. 1889-1938.

Chart 6

NUMBER OF REAL ESTATE LOANS

Northampton Institution for Savings, October 31 of Each Year, 1889–1938

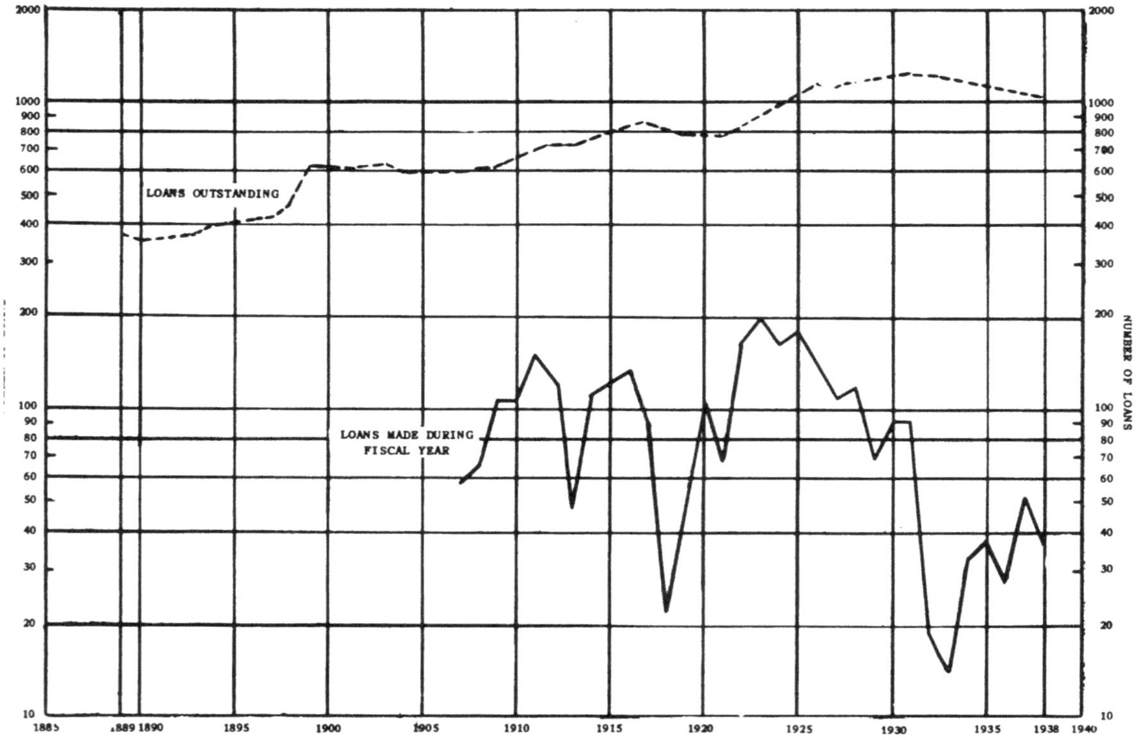

Source: Mass. Commissioner of Banks. *Annual Report*. 1889-1938.

Chart 7

NUMBER OF REAL ESTATE LOANS

Nonotuck Savings Bank, October 31 of Each Year, 1899–1938

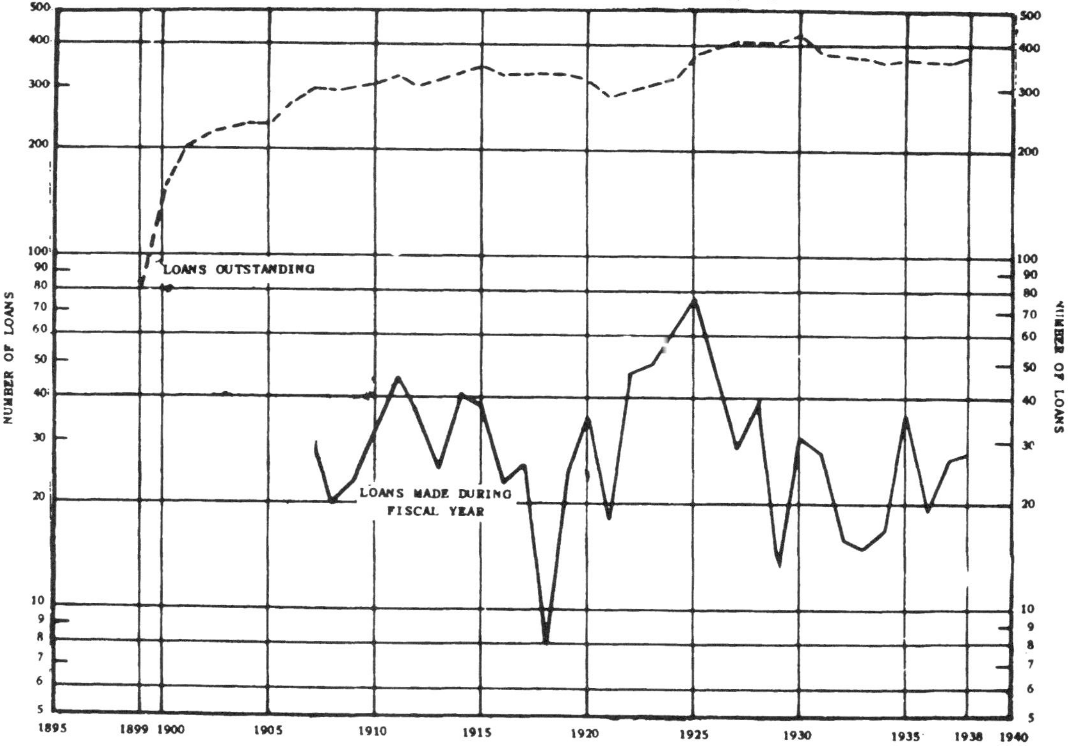

Source: Mass. Commissioner of Banks. *Annual Report*. 1899-1938.

The number of loans extended by the Northampton Institution for Savings exceeded the number made by the other two banks combined. They increased from three hundred or four hundred in the early 1890's to more than one thousand in the years from 1925 to 1938. The number of outstanding loans of the Florence bank during the same period increased from slightly over one hundred to more than four hundred, while those of the Nonotuck bank after 1910 ranged between three hundred and slightly more than four hundred.

The number of new loans made on real estate during the year showed similar variations in all of the banks (see Charts 5, 6, and 7, pages 21, 22, and 23). New real estate loans dipped sharply in 1913 and 1918 and slightly less sharply in 1921. In 1922 loans increased again and many new loans were made each year through 1925. Fewer were made in 1926 and the decline continued, with some interruption, until 1933, when the number of new loans reached the 1918 level. In the years following 1933 the number of loans was somewhat higher.

The extension of mortgage loans, therefore, reflected the degree of prosperity and the amount of building construction in Northampton. The number of loans increased promptly in response to improvement in economic conditions, but the rise during the fairly prosperous years halted before the downturn in business activity.

f) Term of Loans

All mortgage loans made by the Northampton banks throughout the period included in this study were payable on demand or one day from date. This resulted from the preference of the banks for that type of mortgage required in connection with demand loans rather than for that required for time loans, and, furthermore, time loans extended for short terms, such as those required by law during part of the period studied, involved the inconvenience of renewal at frequent intervals.

In actual practice, mortgage loans have customarily run for long periods of time, even thirty or forty years. Such loans frequently extend from the time of the purchase of real estate to the death of the borrower. While this may be safe enough if the general credit of the borrower remains high and the premises are kept in good repair, it may lead to difficulties. Because of depreciation brought by physical wear and by variation in architectural fashions and because of changes in the desirability of location, there is often great fluctuation in the degree to which loans are protected by the mortgaged property.

The position of the banks with respect to the requiring of a reduction in principal has been somewhat weakened by virtue of the fact that their loans have had no definite maturity date. When real estate loans are made for a stated term of three or five years, each borrower ordinarily renews his loan periodically, and it is relatively easy for the bank to force some reduction of the principal amount as part of the renewal process. Although the legislative provision relative to periodic revaluation of property might be expected to influence the banks to require a reduction of principal, it seems to have very little actual effect.

g) Amortization of Loans

The Northampton savings banks had not by 1938 availed themselves of the provision in the act of 1937 allowing them to grant amortized loans. In 1935 and 1936, however, they adopted a policy of required amortization. This is carried out through an informal agreement between the bank and borrower, an agreement not included in the terms of the note. Such an arrangement permits the banks flexibility in meeting the individual needs of the borrower. Amortization payments are usually made quarterly and are ordinarily at the rate of a 2 per cent or 3 per cent reduction in principal each year. One of the banks attempts to place its mortgage borrowers upon a rent-paying basis, that is, it encourages monthly "rent" payments which apply toward reduction of the principal of the loan.

All new loans made by the banks are on the basis of such informal amortization plans. Thus, a considerable portion of the loans, about 30 per cent or more in 1938, is being systematically reduced. This offers a twofold advantage to the banks. It encourages borrowers to retire their obligations and to retire them before the property has depreciated in value. In the second place, it provides the banks with a revolving fund which may be used for the making of new loans and investments.

3. Investment in Mortgage Loans

The total volume of real estate loans of the Northampton banks reflected the variation in real estate values in the city to a considerable degree. Both the value of the mortgage loans of all the savings banks and the assessed value of all real estate decreased from 1875 to 1880, as shown in Chart 8. This downward adjustment was necessitated by the inflation of values during and after the Civil War. From 1880 to 1930, however, there was an increase in the assessed values and loans grew even more rapidly,[11] increasing from 16 per cent of assessed value in 1880 to 43 per cent in 1930. The volume of loans was rising at a much greater rate than assessed values between 1920 and 1930. These were years during which Northampton banks extended loans in the city of Springfield, however, so that the more rapid growth of loans did not necessarily mean that a larger share of the real property of Northampton was being financed by the savings banks.

When the real estate loans of the individual banks are considered, similar downward changes appear in each of them from 1876 to 1880, but divergent movements occurred between 1880 and 1900. After 1900 the real estate loans of the banks show similar movements. These are apparent in Charts 9, 10, and 11, pages 28, 29, and 30, which show the volume of loans outstanding.

From 1880 until the time of its closing the loans of the Hampshire bank were generally increasing, and they were increasing more rapidly than the total assets of the bank, as indicated in Chart 12, page 32. The mortgage loans of the Florence bank likewise increased to 1885, when they amounted to $125,000 and constituted 68 per cent of the assets of the bank. From 1885 to 1895 they remained fairly stable in amount. Because deposits were increasing during those years, this stability of loans means that a decreasing proportion of the assets of the Florence bank took the form of real estate loans (see Chart 13, page 33). By 1895 mortgage loans made up 41 per cent of the assets. During these years when loans underwent

[11] The closing of the Hampshire Savings Bank caused an interruption in the growth of real estate loans in 1898.

Chart 8

ASSESSED VALUE OF REAL ESTATE AND REAL ESTATE LOANS OF SAVINGS BANKS
in Northampton, 1875-1940

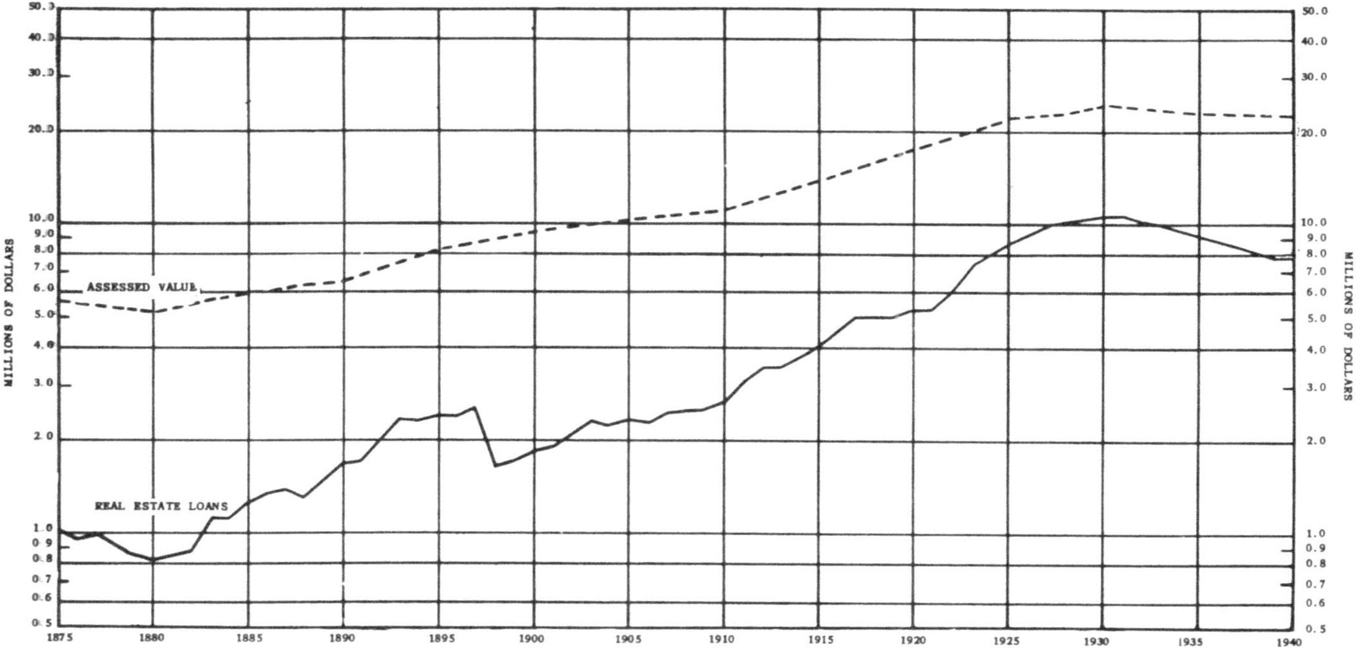

Sources: Assessed Values, at five year intervals: Mass. Commissioner of Corporations and Taxation. *Aggregates of Polls, Property, Taxes, Etc.* 1875-1940.
Real Estate Loans: Computed from data in the annual reports of the Commissioner of Banks.

Chart 9

LOANS OUTSTANDING

Florence Savings Bank, October 31 of Each Year, 1876–1938

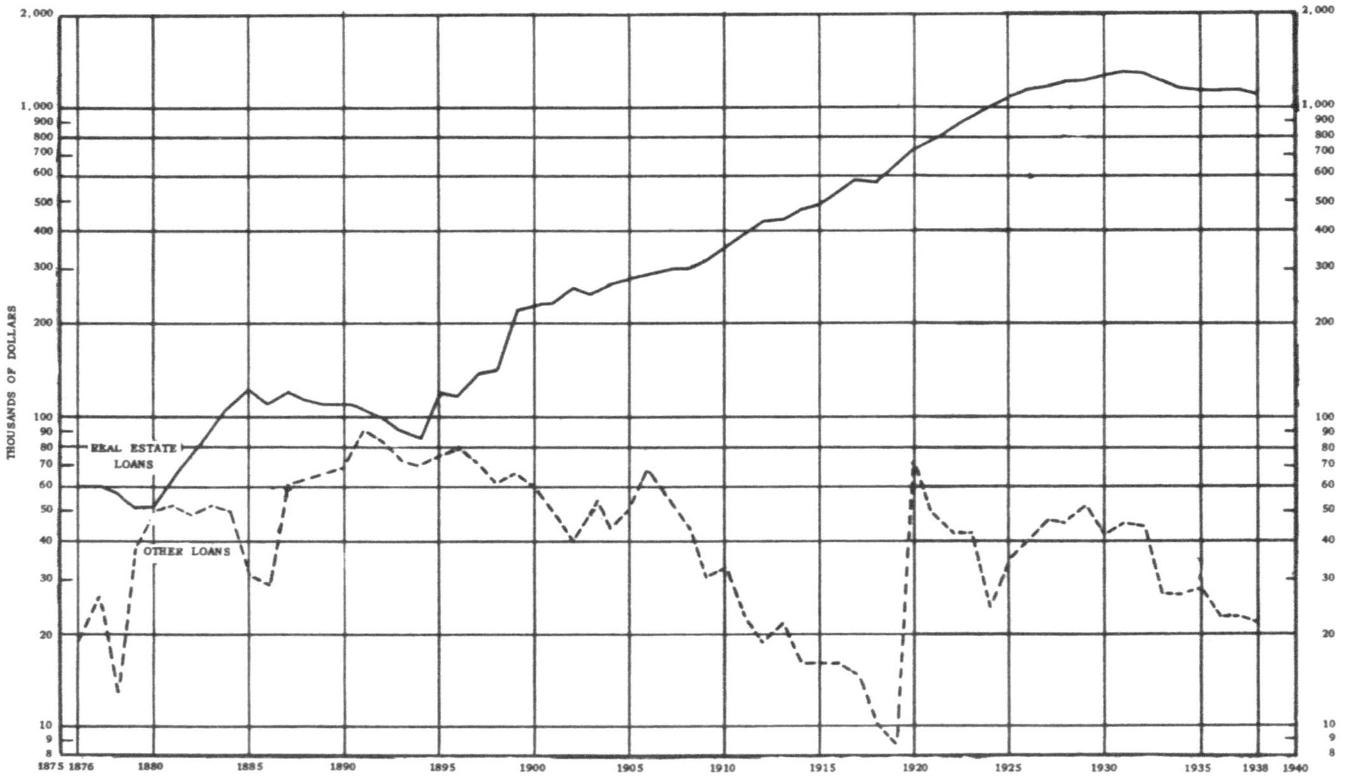

Source: Mass. Commissioner of Banks. *Annual Report*. 1876-1938.

Chart 10

LOANS OUTSTANDING

Hampshire Savings Bank, 1876-1897

Nonotuck Savings Bank, 1899-1938

October 31 of Each Year

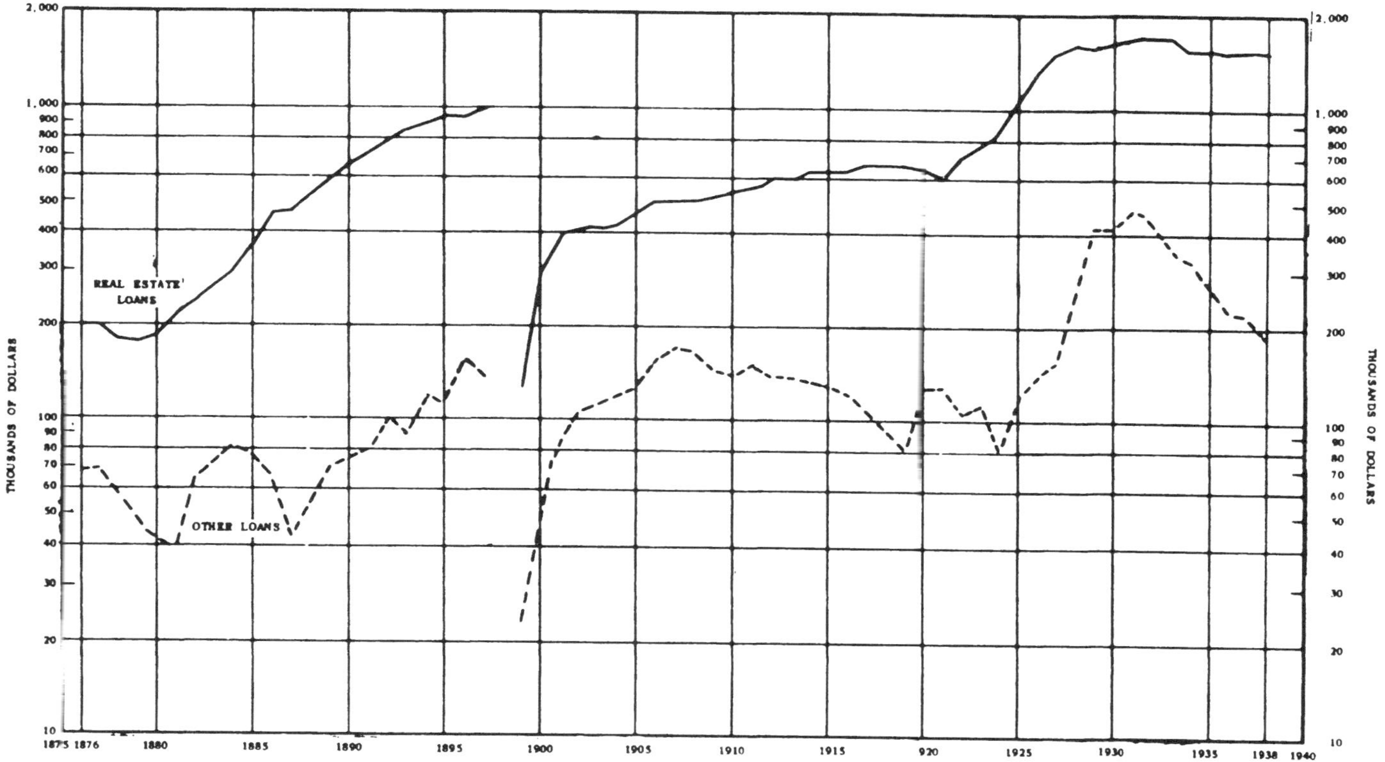

Source: Mass. Commissioner of Banks, *Annual Report* 1876 1938.

Chart 11

LOANS OUTSTANDING

Northampton Institution for Savings, October 31 of Each Year, 1876-1938

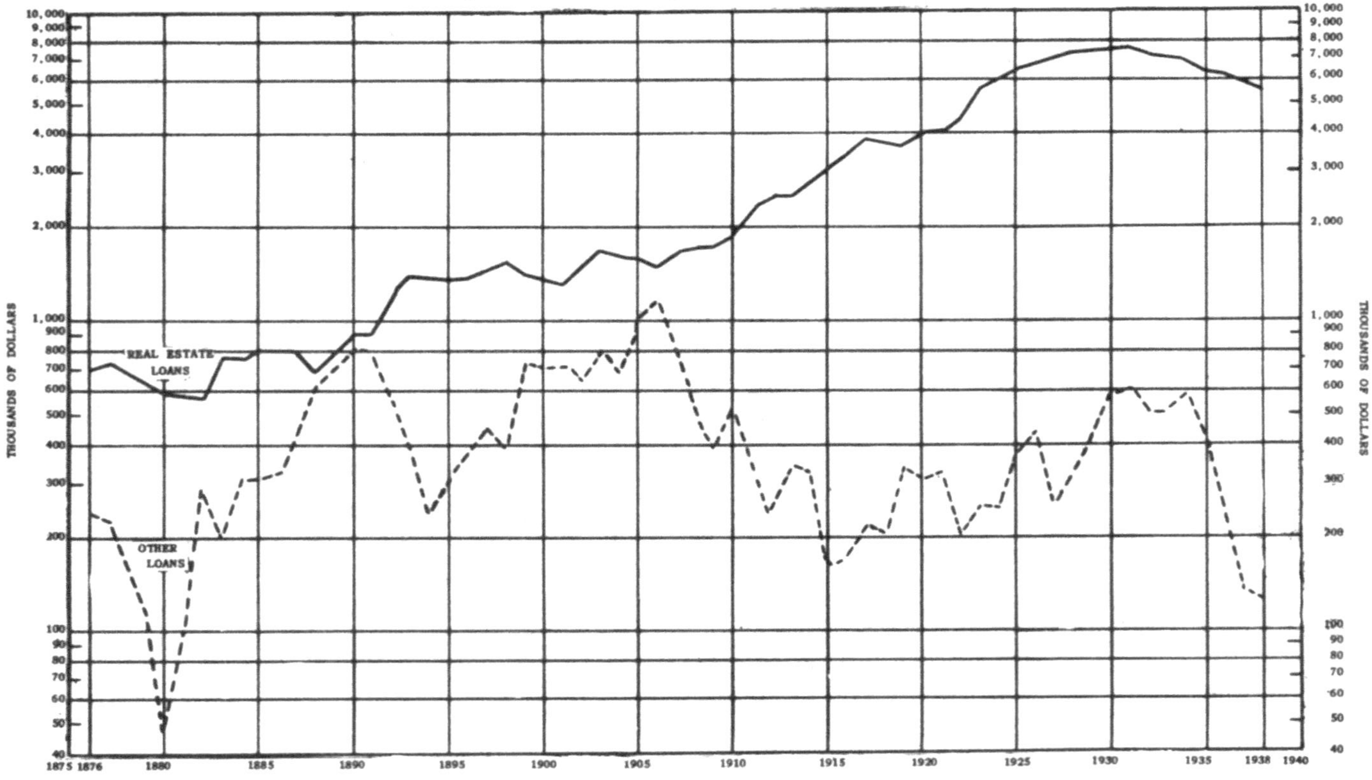

Source: Mass. Commissioner of Banks. *Annual Report*. 1876-1938.

little change, the Florence bank was beginning its investment in bonds and stock. From 1896 to 1900 the real estate loans of the Florence bank increased rapidly.

Contrary to the behavior of the loans of the Hampshire Savings Bank and the Florence Savings Bank, the mortgage loans of the Northampton Institution for Savings continued to decrease for a few years after 1880. They then rose, however, to 1885. During these years bond yields, especially those on Treasury obligations, were low, and funds set free by the withdrawal of the bank from public funds were invested first in loans on collateral other than mortgage and then in loans upon mortgage security. In the Northampton Institution for Savings the loans increased sharply from $787,000 in 1889 to $1,397,000 in 1893, but they were relatively stable from 1885 to 1889 and from 1893 to 1900. As indicated by Chart 14, page 34, the Northampton Institution for Savings invested a much smaller part of its total assets in real estate loans than the other two banks.

From 1900 to 1910 the loans in each bank increased but the rise was at such a rate that loans made up almost a constant proportion of total assets. This was a fairly prosperous period for Northampton and the total value of assessed real estate was increasing. The rising bond yields during these years, however, led to the expansion of bond investments by the banks, and the increase in real estate loans was therefore slow.

From 1910 to 1920 real estate loans grew somewhat more rapidly. There was great activity in business during these years, which included the period of the first World War, and real estate values rose rapidly.

Loans secured by mortgages grew swiftly from 1921 to 1927. Both the activity in the real estate market and certain difficulties in investing elsewhere contributed to the growth of real estate loans. During the prosperous twenties, building construction was resumed after its virtual cessation in the war years. Moreover, bond prices were rising so that it was less profitable to invest the growing funds of the banks in securities than in mortgage loans. In addition, many railroad bonds lost their status as legal investments during the early 1920's. From 1921 to 1927 the real estate loans of the Northampton Institution for Savings rose from about $4,122,000 to more than

Chart 12

LOANS OUTSTANDING
in Per Cent of Total Assets
Hampshire Savings Bank, 1876-1897
Nonotuck Savings Bank, 1899-1938
October 31 of Each Year

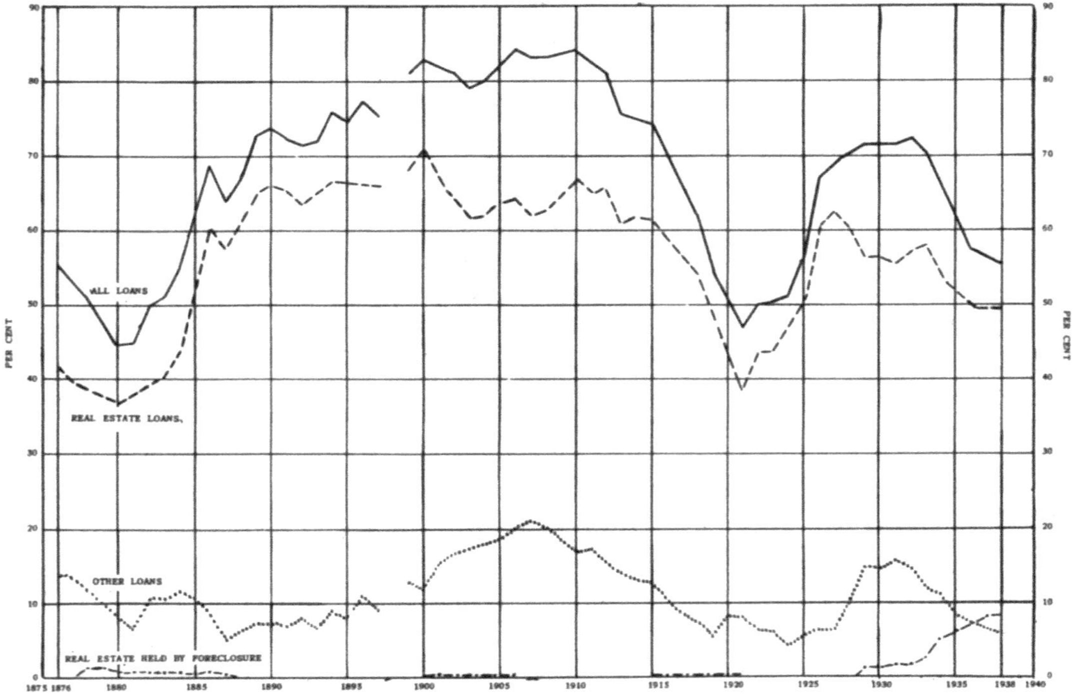

Source: Computed from data in the annual reports of the Commissioner of Banks.

LOANS OUTSTANDING
in Per Cent of Total Assets
Florence Savings Bank, October 31 of Each Year, 1876–1938

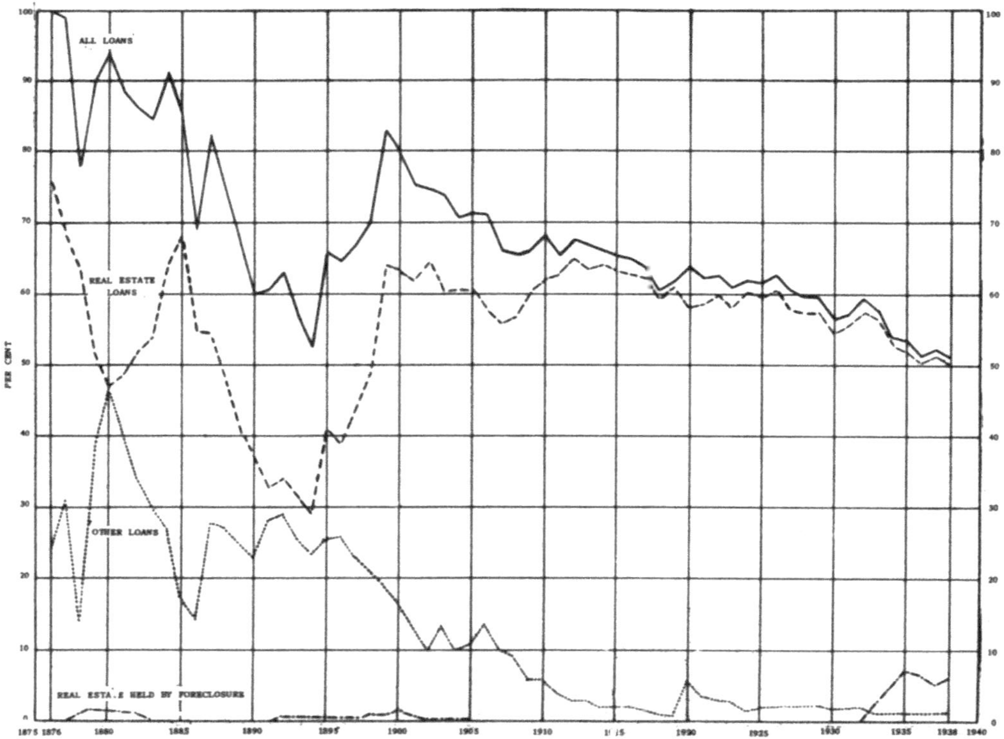

Source: Computed from data in the annual reports of the Commissioner of Banks.

Chart 14

LOANS OUTSTANDING

in Per Cent of Total Assets

Northampton Institution for Savings, October 31 of Each Year, 1876-1938

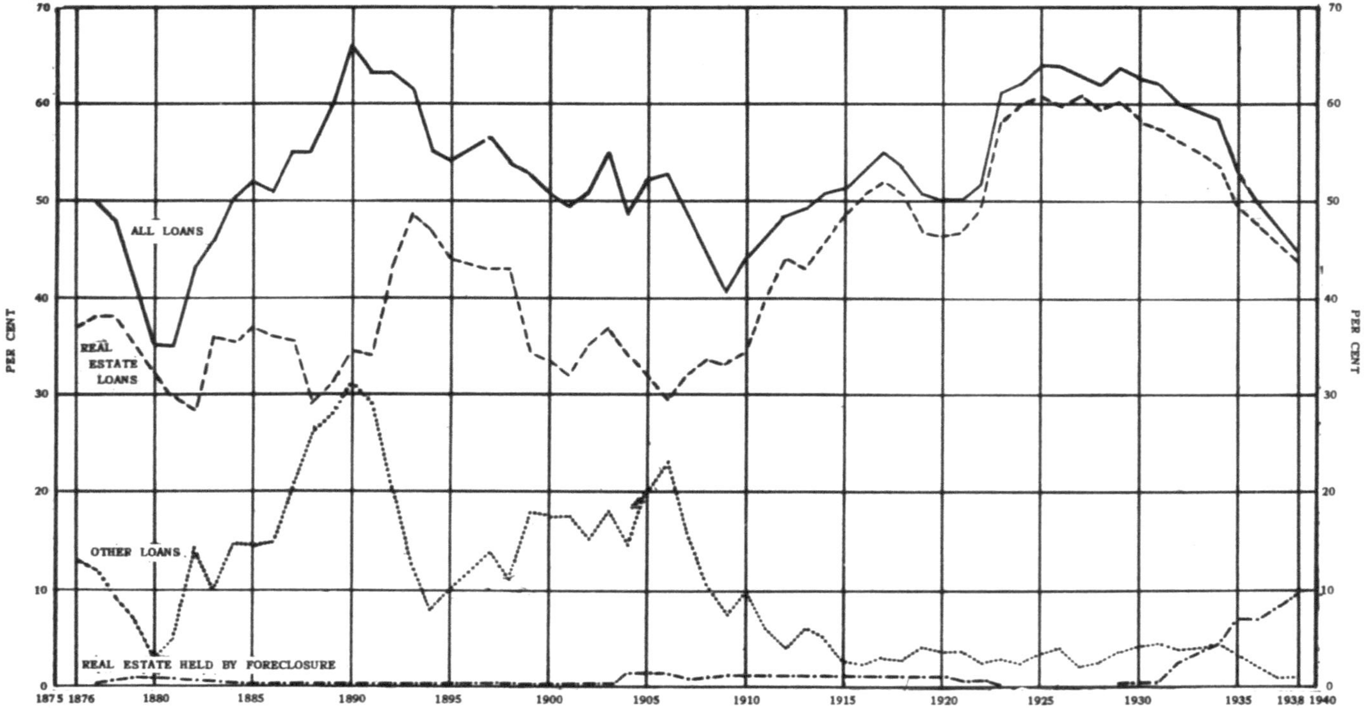

Source: Computed from data in the annual reports of the Commissioner of Banks.

$7,159,000. This involved an increase from 47 per cent to 61 per cent of assets. In the Nonotuck Savings Bank mortgage loans amounted to $606,000, or 39 per cent of assets, in 1921, and by 1927 they had risen to $1,508,000, or 62 per cent of assets. The Florence Savings Bank increased its investment in loans from $792,000 in 1921 to $1,172,000 in 1927. Since total assets had grown at about the same rate, however, the percentage of assets invested in mortgage loans continued to be about 60 per cent.

It was during this period of rapid expansion of real estate loans that the Northampton banks began to extend a large number of loans in the Springfield area. This was not only a consequence of the abundance of funds available for investment but also a result of the boom in the Springfield real estate market.

From 1927 to 1933 the volume of real estate loans of the Northampton savings banks underwent slight change, but in 1933 and the following years, depressed business conditions were reflected in declining loans on real estate. By 1938 the mortgage loans of the Northampton Institution for Savings had dropped to $5,607,000 and 44 per cent of assets. Although the volume of real estate loans in the Nonotuck bank did not show as great a drop, they declined to $1,531,000 or 50 per cent of the assets. The loans of the Florence Savings Bank likewise showed a smaller decrease than those of the Northampton Institution for Savings, but they fell from a peak of $1,311,000 in 1931 to $1,137,000, a fall from 56 per cent to 50 per cent of its assets.

Thus the fluctuations in the volume of mortgage loans of the Northampton savings banks responded to conditions in the real estate market, the general level of prosperity in the community, and opportunities for alternative investment in bonds and stocks.

4. Unsatisfactory Loans

The amount of real estate held by foreclosure is an indication of general business conditions in the community and of the quality of real estate loans at any particular period. Foreclosure comes as a last resort and usually after the bank has reduced interest rates and nursed the loan as long as there is any chance of recovery. Foreclosure in itself is an expensive procedure, costing about $100 directly and involving subsequent expenses of supervision and sale of real estate. Savings banks in Massachusetts are permitted to hold real estate acquired by foreclosure for five years, with possible further extensions of time by the Bank Commissioner. In 1908 banks were granted permission[12] to take a mortgage for the whole or part of the purchase price of any real estate acquired by foreclosure even though such loans exceeded the maximum percentage of value established for the usual mortgage loan.

Real Estate Acquired through Foreclosure in Relation to Total Assets. The amount of real estate taken over by the banks had never reached large proportions until the depression of the 1930's. For a few years around 1880, the real estate held through foreclosure amounted to about 1 per cent of the assets of each of the Northampton banks (see Charts 12, 13, 14, pages 32, 33, and 34). After 1887 the Hampshire Savings Bank held no real estate by foreclosure. From 1884 to 1891 the Florence bank reported no such item and the holdings of the Northampton Institution for Savings were only a fraction of 1 per cent of its assets. In subsequent years the banks either held no real estate which had been acquired through foreclosure or held amounts seldom reaching 1 per cent of assets.

In 1929 foreclosed property reappeared, and after 1932 it reached an alarming magnitude. In 1938 the Nonotuck bank and the Northampton Institution for Savings held a much larger proportion of their assets in the form of real estate by foreclosure than at any other time during the period studied. The Nonotuck bank held 8.4 per cent and the Institution for Savings held 9.6 per cent of its assets in foreclosed real estate. For the Florence bank, foreclosed property reached a maximum in 1935, when 7.2 per cent of assets were involved. The amount held in 1938 was large, however, being 6.2 per cent of all assets owned by the bank.

Even at its highest the amount of real estate held through foreclosure was not a large proportion of the total assets of the banks; nevertheless, it became large enough after 1930 to

[12] Mass. Acts 1908, c. 590, sec. 68, cl. 10th.

cause real concern. It is a symptom of generally unsatisfactory conditions and an item representing possible future loss, and it is ordinarily an asset yielding little income and requiring considerable care in management.

Real Estate Acquired through Foreclosure and the Volume of Real Estate Loans. In addition to the comparison with total assets, the amount of real estate acquired through foreclosure may well be compared with the volume of mortgage loans outstanding, as presented in Charts 15, 16, and 17, pages 38, 39, and 40. When the amount of real estate held by foreclosure is expressed as a percentage of outstanding loans on mortgages it gives an index of the soundness of loans made. This percentage may exaggerate the unsatisfactory condition of loans inasmuch as foreclosures are usually high at a time when the number of loans on real estate is low.

During most of the years until 1932 the amount of real estate acquired by foreclosure was less than 4 per cent of outstanding loans on mortgages and the percentage usually was much less than 4 per cent. The charts indicate that until the 1930's the bad years for mortgage loans in Northampton occurred around 1880 and in the early 1900's. During those years few of the loans of the Nonotuck bank had to be taken over. This probably resulted in part from the fact that it was a new bank and its loans therefore represented more recent appraisal of credit risk than did the loans of the other banks.

The severity of the depression of 1932 and the following years is reflected in the large amount of real estate held by foreclosure, which rose sharply in 1931 and 1932 and reached a high point varying from 14 per cent to 22 per cent of all loans on mortgages. The Northampton Institution for Savings with its larger loans and loans on non-home buildings shows the least satisfactory record. The continuance of the percentages at a rather high level in all of the banks indicates the slowness of the real estate market. Once a bank has had to take over real estate, it finds it difficult to dispose of the property or to dispose of it without taking a heavy loss.

Real Estate Acquired through Foreclosure and the Guaranty Fund. The relationship between the real estate held through

Chart 15

REAL ESTATE HELD BY FORECLOSURE AND TAXES AND INSURANCE PAID ON MORTGAGED PROPERTY
in Per Cent of Real Estate Loans
Florence Savings Bank, October 31 of Each Year, 1876-1938

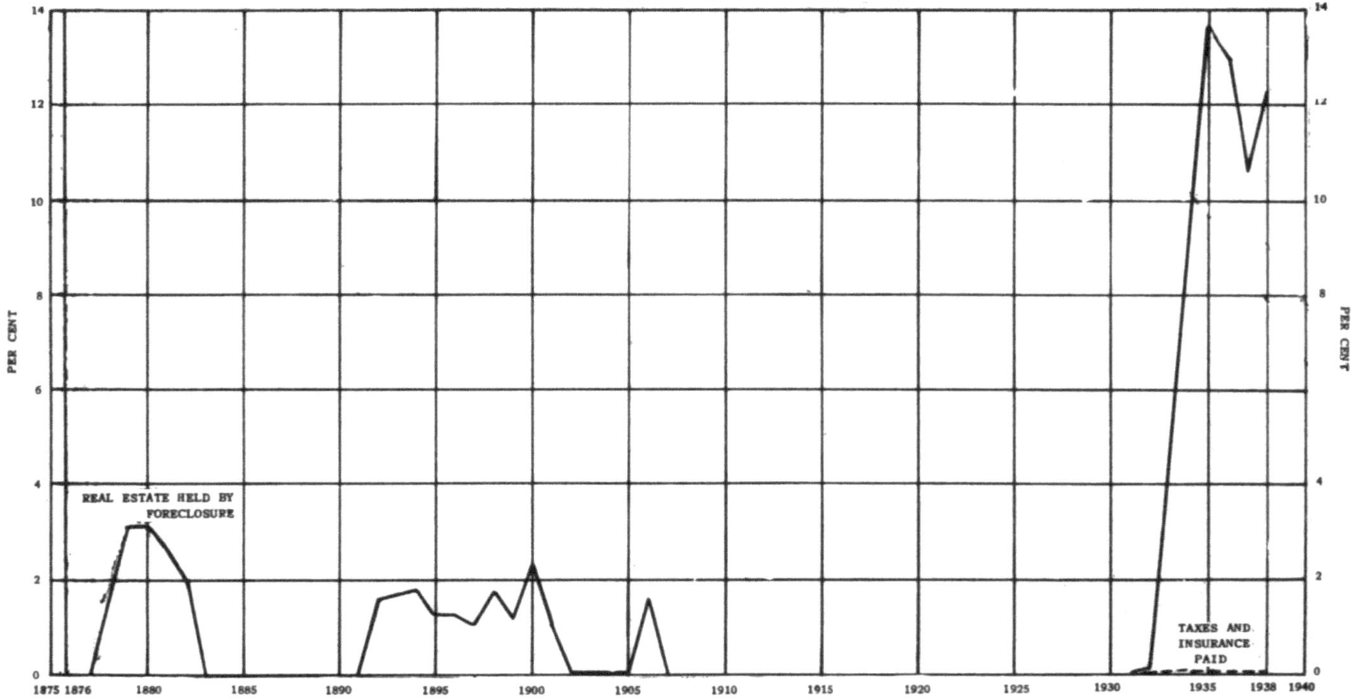

Source: Computed from data in the annual reports of the Commissioner of Banks.

Chart 16

REAL ESTATE HELD BY FORECLOSURE AND TAXES AND INSURANCE PAID ON MORTGAGED PROPERTY
in Per Cent of Real Estate Loans
Hampshire Savings Bank, 1876-1897
Nonotuck Savings Bank, 1899-1938
October 31 of Each Year

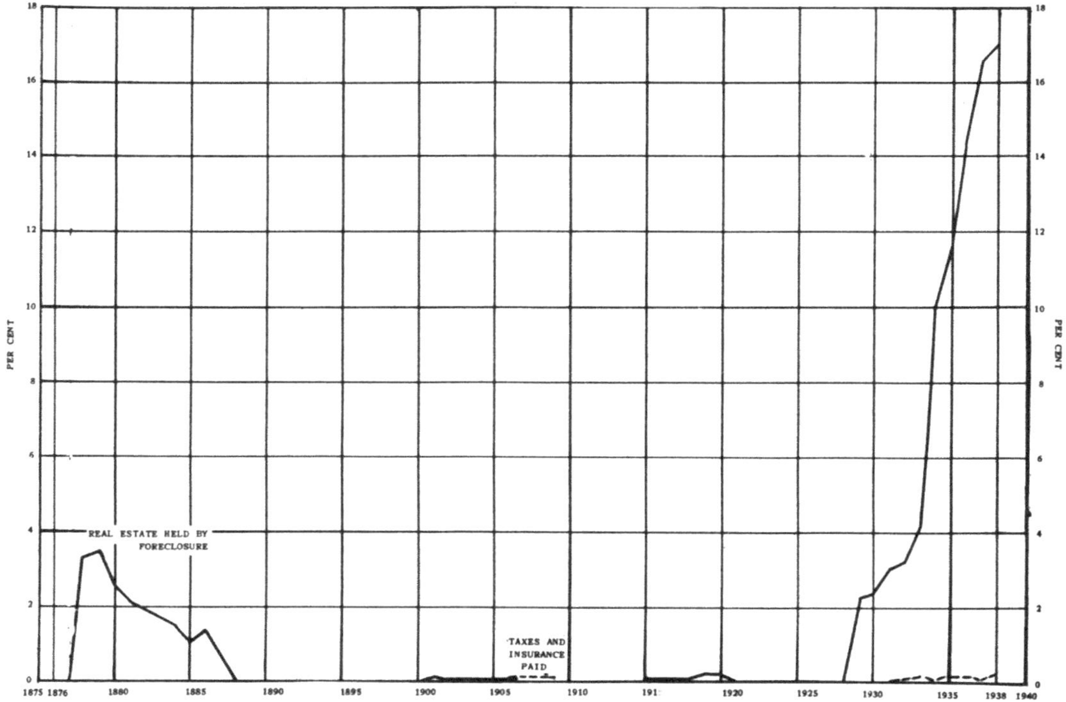

Source: Computed from data in the annual reports of the Commissioner of Banks.

Chart 17

REAL ESTATE HELD BY FORECLOSURE AND TAXES AND INSURANCE PAID ON MORTGAGED PROPERTY
in Per Cent of Real Estate Loans
Northampton Institution for Savings, October 31 of Each Year, 1876-1938

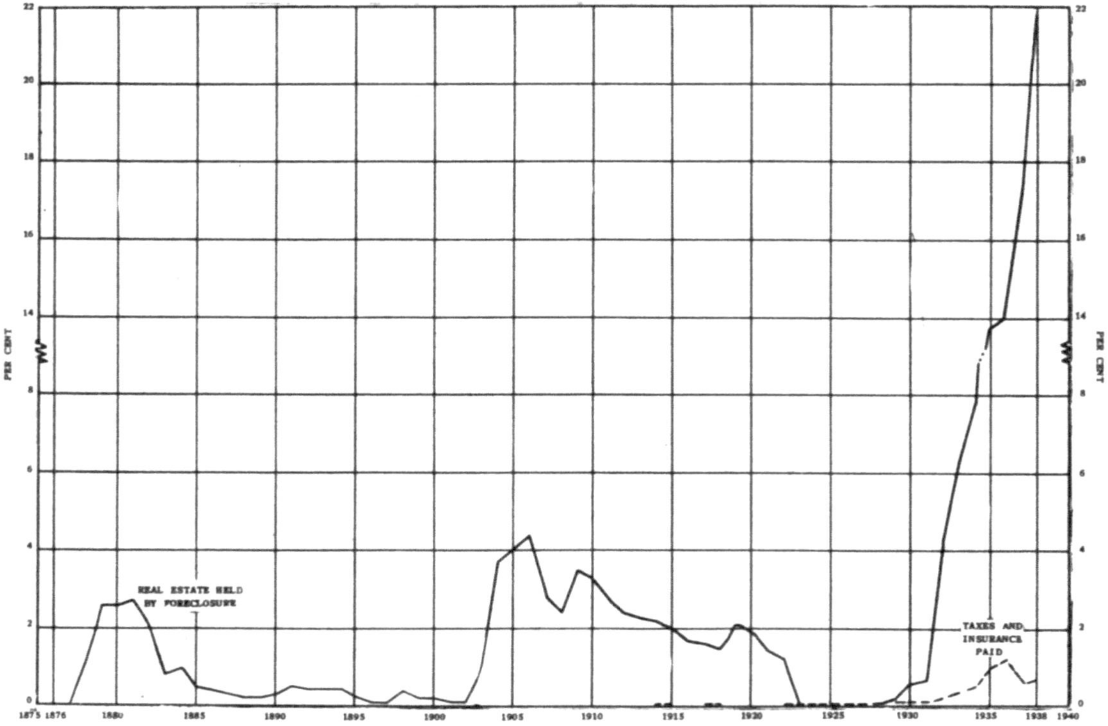

Source: Computed from data in the annual reports of the Commissioner of Banks.

foreclosure and the size of the guaranty fund indicates the security of position of a bank since the guaranty fund (which is more fully discussed in Section E of Chapter III) represents earned surplus accumulated, in accordance with legal requirements, for emergency use in the event of extraordinary losses. As indicated in Chart 18, the guaranty fund was more than adequate to cover possible losses from mortgage loans except in the earliest years of the period studied and in the depression of the 1930's. The high ratio of foreclosed real estate in the first ten years was a consequence of the fact that the banks did not begin to accumulate guaranty funds until 1876. Thus, when foreclosures were necessary in 1878 and 1879, the guaranty funds were still small. The high ratio in the Nonotuck Savings Bank in 1901 is likewise primarily a result of the fact that the bank had not been operating long enough to accumulate a large guaranty fund.

The relationship between foreclosures and the guaranty fund shows, as did the other comparisons, that the years around 1880 and the years of the depression of 1932 were the most difficult periods. The desirability of a required surplus is well indicated by the experience in the deflation of the late 1870's. During the early 1900's the real estate acquired through foreclosure was again large. The fact that from 1935 to 1938 the guaranty funds were smaller than the value of foreclosed property bore out the wisdom of the required increase in the size of the guaranty fund in the years after 1933.

Although the property acquired by the banks exceeded the guaranty fund after 1934, this did not necessarily mean that the banks were in a precarious position. The real estate could be sold eventually and at least part of the original loan value recaptured. Disposal of the real estate was slow, however, and the banks could not hope to sell over a million and a half dollars of real estate in the slow market existing in the 1930's.

Taxes and Insurance Paid on Mortgaged Property. The amount of taxes and insurance paid by the banks upon property mortgaged to them gives further indication of difficulty with loans. Such payments are made by the banks when the borrower himself is unable to meet his tax and insurance obligations, and thus the borrower may well be unable to make payments on his bank loan in the near future.

Chart 18

REAL ESTATE HELD THROUGH FORECLOSURE

in Per Cent of the Guaranty Fund, October 31 of Each Year, 1876-1938

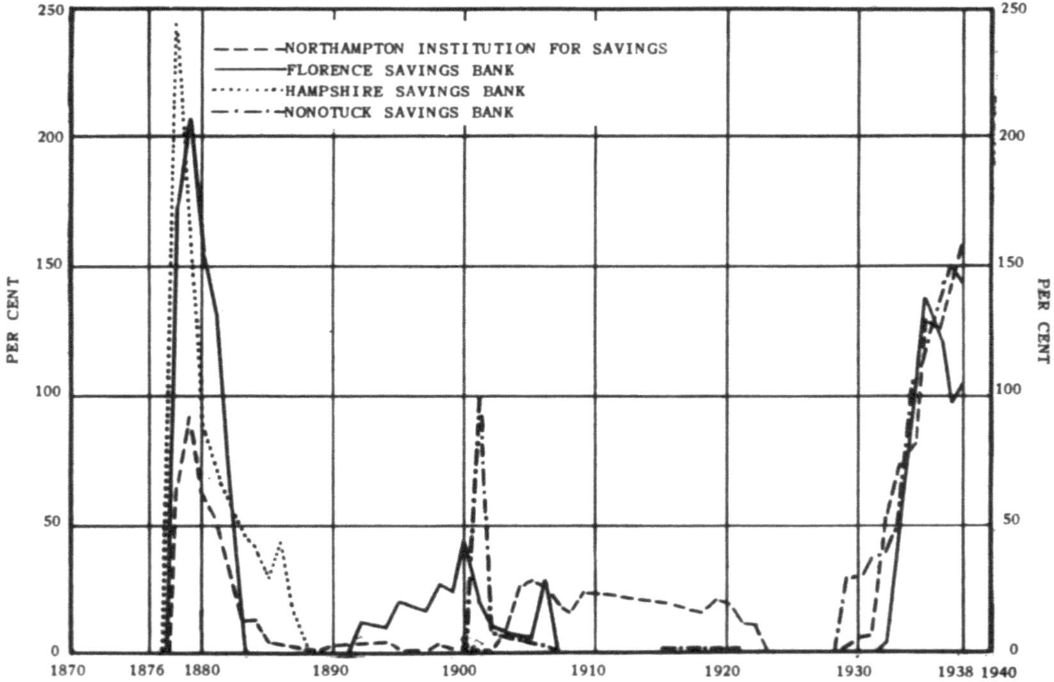

Source: Computed from data in the annual reports of the Commissioner of Banks.

In the past the banks often neglected to make sure that current tax and insurance payments were made by borrowers and therefore the banks sometimes found themselves holding a mortgage upon a building not covered by insurance or foreclosing a mortgage on property which was tax-delinquent. In recent years banks have consequently given careful attention to such items. If a borrower is unable to pay his property tax or insurance premium, the bank makes the payment and then seeks reimbursement through periodic payments by the property owner.

The tax and insurance items, as shown in Charts 15, 16, and 17, pages 38, 39, and 40, never reached significant proportions in the Northampton banks.

Loans at Reduced Rates of Interest. Further indication of distressed loan situations is found in the reduction of the rate of interest charged on loans. The asterisks on Charts 39, 40, and 41, pages 169, 170, and 171, show the prevailing, or modal, rates charged on loans at the Northampton banks. Although the banks set up prevailing rates of interest to which all savings banks in the community adhere, they may carry loans at rates sharply differing from the prevailing rate. The range of rates charged is indicated by vertical lines on the charts.

Although 5.5 per cent was the prevailing rate of interest in each of the banks throughout the 1930's, the actual interest rate charged on many loans dropped considerably below 5.5 per cent and some loans bore a rate as low as 1 or 3 per cent. The reduction of interest rates occurred in several situations. In the hope of eventual recovery on the part of the borrower who was having great difficulty in maintaining his loan, the banks made concessions in interest charges. The rate was also reduced in consideration for amortization payments. Occasionally loans at less than 5.5 per cent were granted to the purchasers of property which the bank had acquired by foreclosure.

Federal Assistance. The Northampton savings banks made little use of the Federal agencies established in the 1930's to assist distressed home owners and to strengthen the urban mortgage market. They made no use of the Federal Housing Administration or of the Federal Home Loan Bank, and in 1935 they held only about $80,000 of bonds of the Home Owners' Loan Corporation.

Summary. The amount of real estate acquired through foreclosure reflected depressed conditions, especially when the depression was severe or prolonged. Brief periods of slack business activity ordinarily brought little increase in foreclosures since such proceedings follow continued inability to pay. Foreclosures reached significant proportions from 1878 to 1881 because of the deflation of real estate values in the late 1870's. Although property acquired through foreclosure during these years involved only a small part of their total assets, the banks were not well protected by their guaranty funds, since these surplus accounts had not been set up until 1876 and they had not reached adequate proportions by 1878. Foreclosures increased again from 1900 to 1906, but the sums involved were small relative to the total assets, the outstanding loans, and the guaranty funds of the banks. After 1929 foreclosures reached a peak and they involved loan values large enough to place considerable strain upon the banks. Some slight assistance was given the banks by the operations of the Home Owners' Loan Corporation, which refinanced a few of the poorest loans. The banks themselves furthermore extended help to individual borrowers through the lowering of interest rates and the payment of taxes and insurance on mortgaged property.

The amount of real estate held through foreclosure was relatively highest in the largest bank. This may have resulted from the greater amount loaned upon business properties and multiple-dwelling houses and from the difficulty in finding a sufficient number of loans in which to invest its larger volume of funds.

With respect to foreclosures, the record of the savings banks is no more unsatisfactory than the experience of the Northampton Cooperative Bank, the chief competitor in home loans. Real estate acquired through foreclosure by the cooperative bank followed much the same pattern as that of the Northampton Institution for Savings.

B. OTHER LOANS

The Massachusetts savings banks have been permitted to make certain loans other than those based on real estate mortgages. All such loans were in 1938 classified in the annual reports as "loans on personal security," although certain collateral loans were formerly classified as separate items. This section deals with all loans that were in 1938 called loans on personal security whether or not they were so reported at the time they were outstanding.

1. Legal Regulation

In 1876 the banks were authorized to make loans to citizens of Massachusetts against collateral consisting of securities legal for investment by the banks themselves. The notes could thus be secured by certain public funds (United States Treasury bonds, obligations of certain governmental units of New England, and bonds of the State of New York), by first mortgage bonds of operating railroads incorporated in Massachusetts, which met specific dividend requirements, and by the stock of state banks of Massachusetts or national banks located within the state. The amounts that could be loaned on these types of collateral varied. On public funds banks could loan up to the par value of the securities, on bank stock not more than par or 80 per cent of the market value, and on railroad obligations not more than 80 per cent of the par value.[13]

Provision was further made for other loans if the depositors' funds could not be "conveniently invested" in prescribed modes, that is, if the funds could not be invested in real estate loans, in the above collateral loans, or in legal public funds, railroad securities, and bank stock. The banks could extend loans to citizens of Massachusetts secured by other collateral provided two citizens of Massachusetts served as security. The term in such a case was not to exceed one year. Not more than one-third of the funds held by a bank could be invested in this type of loan.[14]

Modifications of the legal requirements were made in subsequent years. In 1879 the banks were allowed to make loans to depositors provided they did not lend an amount greater than one-half of the amount credited to the depositor's account.[15] Loans made on three-name paper were limited in 1884 by the requirement that the amount loaned to any one person, partner-

[13] Mass. Acts 1876, c. 203, sec. 9, cls. 2d, 3d, and 4th.

[14] Mass. Acts 1876, c. 203, sec. 9, cl. 5th.

[15] Mass. Acts 1879, c. 57.

ship, or corporation was not to exceed 5 per cent of the deposits and income of a bank.[16] In 1887 banks were permitted to lend on the capital stock of railroads. The law provided that the railroad should be one incorporated under the authority of any of the New England states and located at least in part in New England, that it should have paid dividends of not less than 5 per cent annually for the preceding five years, and that it should be operating its own road. The amount of such loans was to be not more than 75 per cent of the market value of the stock pledged. The notes were to be payable on demand and to be renewed or paid within one year.[17] The law subsequently extended the provisions so that the stock of certain other railroads which served Massachusetts and whose bonds were legal investments could serve as collateral. In 1888 the limit placed upon notes secured by railroad bonds legal for investment was raised from 80 per cent to 100 per cent of par value.[18] Soon after street railway bonds became legal investments for the savings banks, it was provided that they might serve as collateral for loans to citizens of Massachusetts to an amount equal to their par value.[19]

In 1908 all of these various types of loans were treated together as one class.[20] All loans were to be made for not longer than one year. The total amount of such loans was not to be greater than one-third of the deposits and income of the bank, and the total liability of any person, corporation, or partnership was not to exceed 5 per cent of the deposits and income. By the act of 1908 this class of loans was divided into the following five groups.

First, the banks could accept a note which was the joint obligation of three or more citizens of Massachusetts. The total liability to the bank of any borrower under this provision was not to exceed 1 per cent of the deposits of the bank.

Second, the banks could make a loan upon the basis of a note of a corporation or association provided there were one or more

16 Mass. Acts 1884, c. 168.
17 Mass. Acts 1887, c. 196.
18 Mass. Acts 1888, c. 213.
19 Mass. Acts 1904, c. 210.
20 Mass. Acts 1908, c. 590, sec. 68, cl. 8th.

sureties or endorsers. These loans were largely restricted to concerns operating in Massachusetts or incorporated within the state.

Third, the banks could invest in a bond or note of a gas, electric, telephone, or street railway company incorporated in and doing business in Massachusetts if the net earnings during each of the three preceding years were not less than 4 per cent of the capital stock and if the principal was due within one year.

Fourth, the banks might purchase the bonds or notes of certain of the railroad companies whose bonds were legal investments, provided the principal was due within one year from the time of investment.

Fifth, the banks were permitted to extend loans based upon notes secured by any of the kinds of collateral in the following list, provided the amount of any such loan did not exceed the limits indicated below.

a) A first mortgage on real estate, similar to the mortgages upon which the banks might loan.

b) Bonds or notes legal for investment by the banks, up to 90 per cent of their market value.

c) Deposit accounts, up to 90 per cent of the balance.

d) Shares of certain railroad companies whose bonds were on the legal list, up to 80 per cent of their market value.

e) Other bonds, notes, and stocks satisfactory to the bank.

Modifications of the above requirements were made in subsequent years. In 1909 the fifth class of loan listed above was excluded from the general restrictions concerning the aggregate amount of such loans and the total liability of one person, corporation, or partnership, but the limitation of loans to a term of one year was retained. With respect to the bonds and notes of gas, electric light, telephone, and street railway companies, gross earnings of at least $100,000 in the year preceding investment were made a further prerequisite to purchase by the banks.[21] In 1924 the amount that could be loaned upon deposit books was increased from 90 per cent to 100 per cent of the account.[22] By an act of 1933, loans on any satisfactory

[21] Mass. Acts 1909, c. 491, sec. 8.
[22] Mass. Acts 1924, c. 68.

bonds, notes, or stocks were restricted to 80 per cent of the market value instead of leaving the amount to the discretion of the bank.[23]

After 1922 savings banks were required to extend pass-book loans when the loans were in reality withdrawals of deposits. The loans were not to extend beyond the next dividend date and they were limited to a maximum of 90 per cent of the amount of the deposit account.[24] Such loans are made in anticipation of withdrawal of the deposit and are, therefore, to be distinguished from the ordinary loans on pass-books referred to in the preceding paragraph. By the act of 1922, the rate of interest charged on the withdrawal loans was not to exceed the rate of the previous regular dividend by more than one-half of 1 per cent. In 1933 the law was changed to permit the banks to extend loans to the full amount of the deposit account.[25]

Other kinds of collateral were admitted from time to time. In 1910 the banks were authorized to grant loans secured by life insurance policies issued by insurance companies approved by the Bank Commissioner. These were not to be greater than 90 per cent of the cash surrender value, and not more than 1 per cent of the deposits were to be placed in such loans.[26] Shares of cooperative banks could serve as collateral for loans of not more than 90 per cent of the withdrawal value.[27]

Since 1918 bankers' acceptances and bills of exchange eligible for rediscount with the Federal Reserve Banks have been included among legal investments provided they were accepted by a bank whose principal place of business was in Massachusetts, whether the bank was a national bank or a trust company incorporated in the state. The amount that could be so invested was limited and there were certain restrictions concerning the banks whose acceptances could be purchased by the savings banks.[28] In this chapter "other loans" include bankers' acceptances unless otherwise stated.

23 Mass. Acts 1933, c. 334, sec. 26.
24 Mass. Acts 1922, c. 468, sec. 2.
25 Mass. Acts 1933, c. 334, sec. 20.
26 Mass. Acts 1910, c. 358.
27 Mass. Acts 1922, c. 159, sec. 3.
28 Mass. Acts 1918, c. 210.

2. Description of Loans

a) Kind of Collateral

Even though loans on personal security, like those based on mortgages, are demand loans, nevertheless, many of them have been relatively permanent.

From 1876 to 1908 most of the loans of the Northampton banks, other than mortgage loans, were secured by two sureties and by collateral not legal for investment by the savings banks. It was to be expected that loans based upon bonds eligible for investment by savings banks would be small in amount because a ready market existed for such securities. A small volume of loans was granted, however, upon the basis of bank stock which was legal for investment. Since the market for bank stock was narrow, investors in such stock were likely to borrow rather than to sell their stock when they were in need of funds. Loans based upon bank stock were especially large in the Hampshire Savings Bank and in the Northampton Institution for Savings.

In the years after 1908, loans secured by bonds and stocks continued to constitute an important part of the non-mortgage loans. Many of these were loans obtained for the purpose of the purchase of stocks and bonds and, therefore, reflected activity on the security markets. As a consequence, such loans declined during the 1930's, when few people were buying bonds and stocks.

The general decline in security loans was partially offset by the assistance rendered by the Northampton mutual banks to those buying stock in one of the local mills. A reorganization of the mill occurred in 1937 and at that time many local people bought its stock in order to keep the mill operating and to retain the mill in Northampton. The savings banks helped in the financing of these purchases by making small loans to the workers involved.

Until recent years corporate notes have constituted a part of the non-mortgage loans of the Northampton banks. These declined in importance, particularly after 1930, because lower activity reduced the borrowing needs of the Northampton mills and because of the fact that the firms had for the most part been consolidated with larger outside concerns which obtained funds elsewhere.

Tax anticipation notes of cities have also provided a satisfactory kind of temporary investment for savings bank funds. Cities and towns in the later years were reducing their use of such notes, and this type of loan was therefore largely eliminated from the savings bank portfolios. Furthermore, the low yield on these notes, in so far as they were available, discouraged investment.

Although they were unimportant in the early years, pass-book loans increased in importance and in the later period they, together with notes based upon bonds or stocks, constituted the major part of non-mortgage loans. The granting of loans secured by pass-books was authorized in 1879, but the amount was restricted to one-half of the deposit balance and consequently the volume of such loans was small. They became more important in all of the banks after 1908, when loans up to 90 per cent of the balance on deposit were legalized, and after 1924, when loans were allowed to the full amount of the account. Many pass-book loans matured on the next succeeding dividend day and were really of the nature of withdrawals rather than loans. These withdrawal loans increased after 1922 and after 1933, when loans of 100 per cent were allowed.

Several types of loans legally authorized were seldom extended by the Northampton banks. In the early years three-name paper was further secured by collateral, but after 1908 the banks were authorized to extend loans upon the basis of promissory notes without other security than two endorsers. This later type of loan has not been looked upon with favor, chiefly because the two signers are frequently members of the family of the borrower or people who lack financial standing and such loans are, therefore, inadequately secured. The banks rarely granted loans based upon life insurance policies. Although such loans are safe, troublesome procedure is involved and, furthermore, policy holders ordinarily borrow directly from their insurance companies.

The Northampton banks held bankers acceptances only in 1920 and in 1923, but in those years they amounted to a considerable part of the non-mortgage loans. Because of the relatively high interest rates growing out of the great activity on the security markets, a few brokers' loans were also made, but these were infrequent and of small volume, and none was made in the later years.

The non-mortgage loans of the Northampton savings banks were thus chiefly those secured by miscellaneous bonds and stocks. In the early years such loans were further protected by two sureties. Some financing of local business was undertaken by the banks, but, with the centralization of business control, business financing largely shifted to the financial centers. Pass-book loans came to occupy an important position after 1908 and especially after 1924.

Since the early years of the twentieth century, loans on personal security have occupied a relatively minor position in the asset structure of the banks. The emphasis upon safety of principal and the desire that savings banks serve primarily the local community suggest that these loans should not be large.

b) Average Size of Loans

Since 1909 the average size of loans on personal security[29] has varied widely not only from one bank to another but also from year to year in the same bank, as shown in Chart 19. The average size of loans on personal security fell rapidly from 1909 to 1920, most of the fall occurring before 1917. The loans of the Northampton Institution for Savings fell from an average of more than $6,300 in 1910 to $2,100 in 1918, while the average size of the loans of the Florence bank dropped from about $1,700 to $200. The size of the loans extended by the Nonotuck Savings Bank declined from $2,100 in 1910 to $900 in 1918.

The size of the loans of the Florence Savings Bank remained unchanged or decreased slowly from 1921 to 1938. Loans averaged around $300 or $400 from 1924 to 1930, were high in 1931 and 1932, and dropped to about $200 in 1938. The loans of the Nonotuck Savings Bank showed little change in size from 1920 until 1925, when a rapid rise began. This increase carried the average loan from $1,400 in 1925 to $2,600 in 1934. Then came a depression decline in size which lowered the average to $1,600 in

[29] Data concerning the average size of loans on personal security are available only since 1908, after the years when such loans were of greatest importance. Bankers' acceptances are not included in the data pertaining to the average size of loans.

Chart 19

AVERAGE SIZE OF NON-MORTGAGE LOANS OUTSTANDING
October 31 of Each Year, 1909-1938

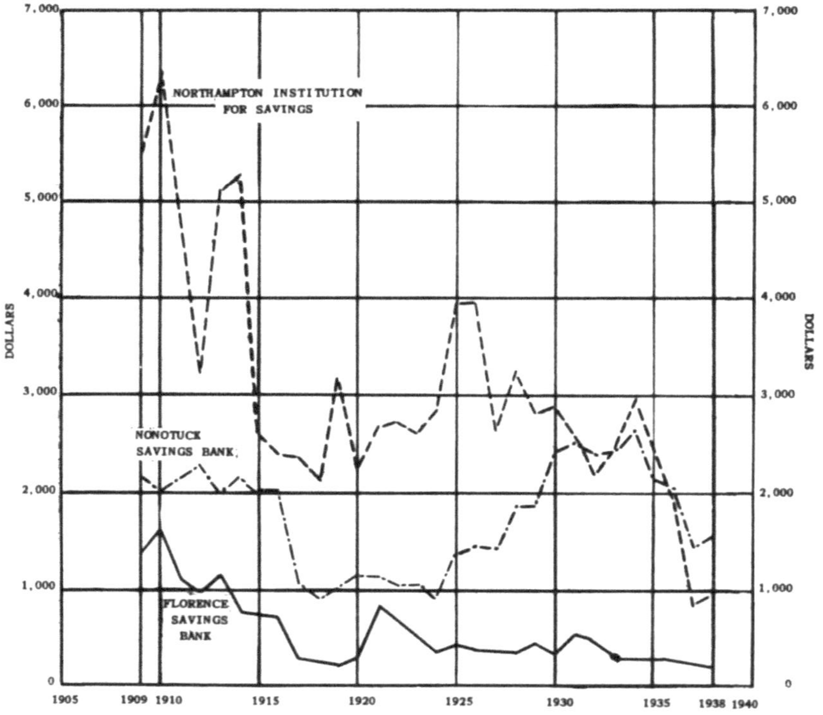

Source: Mass. Commissioner of Banks. *Annual Report*. 1909-1938. (Computed in part.)

1938. The Northampton Institution for Savings had by far the largest loans until 1932. The size of its loans increased from $2,200 in 1920 to almost $4,000 in 1925 and 1926. After 1926 the loans fluctuated in size but showed a general downward tendency which lowered the average to less than $1,000 in 1938.

The average size of loans varied directly with the volume of loans outstanding (see Charts 9, 10, and 11, pages 28, 29, and 30). When the volume fell, the drop occurred primarily in loans used to finance business needs or security dealings. This left the proportion of pass-book loans relatively high and since these were ordinarily small the average size of all loans on personal security consequently decreased.

The general decline in the average size of loans from 1909 to 1938 reflects the changing importance of different kinds of loans made under the general heading of loans on personal security. Pass-book loans were of greater importance in later years, less financing of local business was undertaken, and more of the loans partook of the nature of small consumer loans.

c) Number of Loans Outstanding

The number of loans outstanding in each of the banks expanded from 1909 to 1938, the growth being especially rapid during the war and in the late 1920's, as shown in Chart 20. The number of loans made by the Northampton Institution for Savings and by the Nonotuck bank were much the same, although loans extended by the Institution for Savings were slightly more numerous. From 1909 to 1916 the Florence bank made definitely fewer loans than the other two banks, but thereafter it showed a more rapid rate of increase and in 1927 it held a larger number than either of the other banks.

After a decrease from 1910 to 1914, the number of loans outstanding in the Northampton Institution for Savings began to increase and for ten years fluctuated around one hundred. In 1929 and the early years of the depression the number of loans on personal security was large, reaching 233 in 1932. The number then declined, except for a slight increase in 1937.

From 1908 to 1915 the number of loans made by the Nonotuck Savings Bank fluctuated between sixty and seventy. The number rose to 103 in 1918 and from then until 1927 the loans were

Chart 20

NUMBER OF NON-MORTGAGE LOANS OUTSTANDING

October 31 of Each Year, 1909-1938

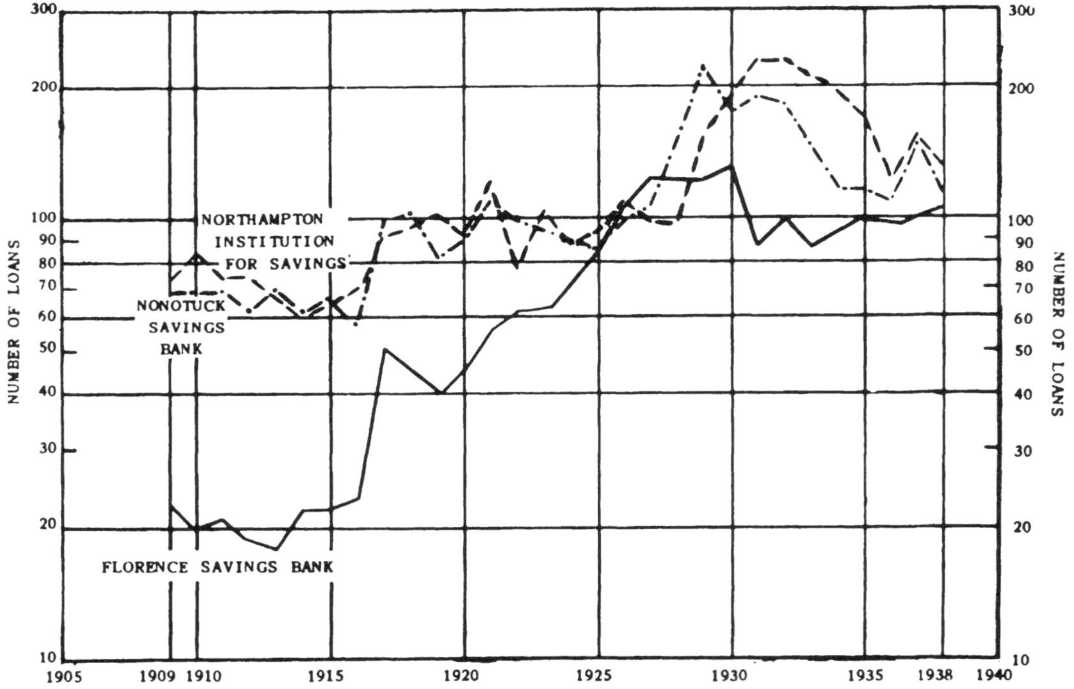

Source: Mass. Commissioner of Banks. *Annual Report*. 1909-1938.

maintained at a somewhat higher level than in the years preceding the war. A rapid increase took place from 1927 to 1929, when more than two hundred loans were outstanding. In the following years the number was generally declining and by 1938 the Nonotuck bank held only 116 loans.

The Florence Savings Bank had about twenty personal loans outstanding according to its annual reports for the years from 1909 to 1916. In 1917 there was a great increase in the number of loans, for in that year over fifty personal loans were outstanding. Except for a decline in 1918 and in 1919, the increase continued until 1927, when there were 126 loans outstanding. The number remained about the same until 1931, after which loans fluctuated around a somewhat lower level.

A comparison of the number of loans on personal security and the number of loans made on real estate during the year, as shown in Charts 5, 6, and 7, pages 21, 22, and 23, suggests an inverse relationship between the two series. When the number of real estate loans changed from one year to the next, the number of other loans tended to change in the opposite direction. Charts 12, 13, and 14, pages 32, 33, and 34, showing the amount of both loans on real estate and loans on personal security in relation to total assets, suggest a similar inverse relationship in the proportion of assets invested in real estate loans and in other loans.

In so far as loans on personal security are based upon stocks and bonds as collateral, they vary inversely with the market prices of stocks and bonds. If security prices are high a person in need of funds will likely sell his securities, but if prices are low he will probably prefer to borrow from the bank with the stocks or bonds as collateral and hold his securities until the market turns. This suggests that, in years of great prosperity and high prices on the stock market, loans on personal security will be few and, in periods when security prices seem abnormally low, loans on personal security will rise. This is opposite to the situation with mortgage loans, which rise in prosperous times and fall in periods of reduced business activity.

Loans on personal security, furthermore, provide a temporary investment for idle funds until the time when funds are needed for mortgage loans or until they can be profitably invested in bonds. Loans on personal security also serve as a temporary investment for funds which must be available for withdrawals. Since 1920 the expansion of Christmas club deposits with their concentrated withdrawals has placed the banks in greater need of funds available for withdrawals.

3. Investment in Other Loans

The volume of non-mortgage loans outstanding in the Northampton banks showed wide fluctuations from year to year and there was great variation in the relative importance of the loans in different banks (see Charts 9 to 14, pages 28 to 34). In each of the banks, however, the relative importance of these loans was less after 1910 than before that time.

Until 1908, non-mortgage loans were treated in law as a subordinate class of investment, for savings banks were authorized to make such loans only in case all bank funds could not be conveniently invested in other authorized uses. When both mortgage loans and other loans are expressed as percentages of the total assets of the banks, the inverse relationship between the two kinds of loans appears. In the preceding section it was suggested that this inverse relationship grew out of the use of non-mortgage loans as temporary investments when funds grew more rapidly than the demand for mortgage loans. The importance of stock loans also contributed to the inverse relationship.

Loans based upon security other than real estate were popular with the Massachusetts banks in the early years of this study because of the high rate of income which they yielded. In the Northampton Institution for Savings these loans amounted to as much as 31 per cent of the total assets in 1890, when the dollar volume was $825,000. Such loans increased to an all-time peak of $1,186,000 in 1906, but in this later year the loans amounted to only 23 per cent of the assets, since the total assets had increased rapidly after 1890. Almost one-half of the assets of the Florence Savings Bank were invested in non-mortgage loans in 1880. The loans never again reached this relative size, although their value increased from about $52,000 in 1880 to a peak of $91,000 in 1891. In the Hampshire Savings Bank, where non-mortgage loans were less important than in the other banks, the loans expanded to $160,000 in 1896 but they never amounted to more than 14 per cent of the assets.

After 1910, loans based upon personal security made up a smaller proportion of the assets of the banks than was the case in the earlier period. In the years after 1910 the Florence bank invested less than 5 per cent of its assets in non-mortgage loans, except for 1920, and the Northampton Institution for Savings invested only a slightly larger percentage in this manner. In the Nonotuck bank, however, non-mortgage loans constituted from 4 per cent to 17 per cent of assets.

The lower level of loans on personal security after 1910 resulted from the existence of other satisfactory types of investment. After 1910, increases in deposit funds were utilized in mortgage loans, the chief type of investment of the savings banks. Except for the interruption caused by the war, the demand for real estate loans was high until 1930. During the war years a large part of the deposit funds of the banks were placed in United States Treasury bonds and, as soon as the banks reduced their Treasury holdings, they expanded their investment in mortgage loans. These post-war years were, of course, a period of great activity in the real estate market. Moreover, additional outlets for funds had been provided the savings banks when many public utility bonds were made legal investments in 1926. Thus the availability of other forms of investment led to the low level of non-mortgage loans after 1910. As suggested earlier, the lessening of the demand for local financing of business in the years following the first World War was another factor contributing to the low level of loans on personal security after 1910.

PART II. BONDS AND STOCKS

Although loans were, for the most part, of greater importance among the earning assets of the Northampton savings banks, holdings of bonds and stocks were large and significant. On the whole, each of the banks invested about 30 or 40 per cent of its assets in bonds and bank stock.

Throughout the period there was a broadening of investment opportunities open to the savings banks, following the economic expansion and development of the country and the increase in deposit funds held by savings banks in Massachusetts. In addition to loans on real estate and loans on other security, the savings banks could, in 1876, invest their deposits in public funds, in railroad bonds, and in bank stock. These remained the only outlets for the banks until 1902, when investment in the then prosperous field of street railways was permitted. Soon investment in telephone company bonds was authorized. Gas, electric, and water company bonds were the last group admitted to the legal list of the Massachusetts mutual savings banks. The scope of investment has thus been widened both by expansion of the industrial groups whose bonds were legal for investment and by changes in the restrictions governing the bonds within each group.

The legal regulations concerning investment securities and the importance of each type in the balance sheets of the Northampton banks will be discussed in the following pages. It should be pointed out that the "amount invested" as reported by the banks, or the book value of securities, is usually par or the purchase price. If bonds were bought at a premium, the premium was generally charged to profit and loss immediately and the bonds entered at par. If securities were bought at a discount from the face value, they were entered at the purchase price. Apparently, the degree to which the book value of bonds was written down in the case of falling markets was left largely to the discretion of the banks. In 1932, however, the Bank Commissioner deemed it advisable to require the savings banks to write off their losses and to use part of their net earnings to offset the depreciation in market value of securities owned.[30] He advised that this might be accomplished by amortizing the loss over a period of five years.

A. PUBLIC FUNDS

1. Legal Regulation

According to the law in 1876, savings banks were permitted to invest in the public funds of any of the New England states, of New York State, and of the United States. They could, furthermore, invest in the bonds and notes of any city, county, or town in Massachusetts and in the bonds and notes of any city in

30 Mass., *Annual Report of the Commissioner of Banks*, Part I, 1932, p. ii.

one of the New England states.[31] In 1885 investment in public funds in Massachusetts was extended to bonds and notes of any incorporated district of Massachusetts whose net indebtedness was not more than 5 per cent of the preceding valuation of property for the assessment of taxes.[32]

It was provided in 1880 that banks could invest in the bonds and notes of only those counties or towns in other New England states whose net indebtedness did not exceed 3 per cent of the valuation of property for the assessment of taxes.[33] The same 3 per cent requirement was later placed on incorporated water districts of New England states.[34] Investment in bonds and notes of cities in New England states other than Massachusetts was limited in 1881 to the obligations of cities whose indebtedness was not more than 5 per cent of the preceding property valuation.[35]

In 1882 investment was permitted in the bonds of the District of Columbia and of the states of Pennsylvania, Ohio, Michigan, Indiana, Illinois, Wisconsin, and Iowa. Banks could also invest in the bonds of a city in these states or in the state of New York if the city had a population of more than fifty thousand and if its net indebtedness was not more than 5 per cent of the taxable property.[36] By an act of 1887, the above requirement concerning population was changed from fifty thousand to thirty thousand.[37]

Later legislation set up the further requirements that bonds of cities must have been issued for municipal purposes or for refunding and that interest on the bonds must have been fully paid.[38] In subsequent years other states were added to the approved list and varying requirements were established concerning the cities whose bonds or notes were eligible, varying as to the size of population and the ratio between net indebtedness and property valuation.

31 Mass. Acts 1876, c. 203, sec. 9, cl. 2d.
32 Mass. Acts 1885, c. 111.
33 Mass. Acts 1880, c. 177.
34 Mass. Acts 1904, c. 208.
35 Mass. Acts 1881, c. 214, sec. 2.
36 Mass. Acts 1882, c. 231.
37 Mass. Acts 1887, c. 423.
38 Mass. Acts 1888, c. 90; Acts 1890, c. 369.

In 1925 investment was permitted in the bonds of any state of the United States which had not defaulted in the payment of the principal or interest on its debt during the twenty years prior to investment by the bank.[39] Because of the financial difficulties of many state governments, it was further provided in 1933 that the full faith and credit of the state must be pledged against the bonds.[40]

The banks were permitted, by 1925, to invest in bonds issued by any city of any state, whether for refunding or for municipal purposes, provided the city had been incorporated for at least twenty-five years and provided its population was not less than thirty thousand. It was further required that interest on indebtedness must have been paid. When the population was between thirty thousand and one hundred thousand, the net indebtedness was required to be not greater than 5 per cent of the valuation of taxable property. If the population were over one hundred thousand, the net indebtedness must not exceed 7 per cent of the valuation of property.[41]

In 1933 a further provision was made that there should be no investment in the bonds or notes of any county, city, town, or district outside of Massachusetts which had been in default for more than 120 days in the payment of principal or interest within the last ten years prior to investment.[42] This provision was necessary to prevent investment in municipal obligations on which the interest was paid although the bonds themselves were in default.

"Public funds" here include not only the obligations of the various governmental units but also the obligations of agencies of the Federal Government whether or not these obligations are fully guaranteed by the United States. As early as 1918 the savings banks were permitted to invest in the Farm Loan bonds issued by the Federal Land Banks.[43] The banks could also accept the bonds of the Home Owners' Loan Corporation in connection with the refinancing of mortgage loans or of real estate acquired

39 Mass. Acts 1925, c. 209, sec. 1.
40 Mass. Acts 1933, c. 334, sec. 23.
41 Mass. Acts 1925, c. 209, secs. 2 and 3.
42 Mass. Acts 1933, c. 334, sec. 24.
43 Mass. Acts 1918, c. 67.

through foreclosure. These together with the obligations of the various governmental units have been treated as part of public funds.

2. Kinds of Public Funds Held

The public funds owned by the Northampton banks have taken the form of United States obligations, bonds and notes of cities and towns in Massachusetts, and bonds of cities outside of Massachusetts. There has been little investment in state bonds, although Massachusetts bonds have been held from time to time.

In the years before the entrance of the United States into the first World War, the public funds owned by the Northampton banks consisted primarily of bonds and notes of cities and towns, most of which were located in New England. Although the Northampton Institution for Savings held chiefly United States obligations from 1880 to 1889, its public funds in 1890 were entirely composed of bonds and notes of cities and towns. The decline in the Treasury obligations was caused by the retirement of the public debt and by the low yields on Treasury bonds. In 1894 and the next few years the Northampton Institution for Savings again held United States Treasury bonds but they were relatively small in amount. From the late 1890's until the participation of the United States in World War I, the public funds of the Northampton Institution for Savings consisted of the bonds and notes of cities and towns together with a few bonds of the state of Massachusetts. The other banks in Northampton held no United States obligations before the war, for they invested in the obligations of cities and towns.

The entry of the United States into the first World War altered the composition of the public funds owned by the banks. As a patriotic response to the war-time needs of the Federal Government and because of the large volume of Treasury bonds available at rising yields, the banks invested large sums in Treasury obligations. In 1918 United States bonds constituted from one-half to two-thirds of the amount invested in public funds and during the following years they made up almost all of the public funds held by the banks. Even in 1925 the holdings of public funds were still predominantly United States bonds. In the late twenties, Treasury bonds remained a large part of public funds but the total investment in governmental obligations had decreased greatly. With the retirement of the Federal debt and the relatively low yield on Treasury obligations, there was a gradual shift away from United States bonds. By 1930 the Northampton Institution for Savings owned no Treasury bonds and the holdings of the other banks were greatly reduced.

In the depression years the proportion of public funds invested in United States bonds became very large in all three banks. The rapid increase in the volume of Treasury bonds with their high credit rating and the deterioration of the credit of many state and local governmental units turned the investments of the banks toward Federal securities. In 1937 no state bonds and few municipal bonds were held.

The Northampton banks owned few bonds of Federal agencies. Federal Land Bank bonds were not allowed as deductions in calculating the tax on deposits, as were Treasury bonds and obligations of governmental units in Massachusetts, and investment in them by the savings banks was very small. The banks also acquired few bonds of the Home Owners' Loan Corporation.

3. Investment in Public Funds

Although the amount invested in public funds by the Northampton banks fluctuated widely, public funds were of great importance in the period as a whole, as indicated by Charts 21, 22, and 23. Investment in public funds was largest around 1895, during and after the first World War, and in the 1930's.

1876-1890. The Florence Savings Bank and the Hampshire Savings Bank held almost no public funds before 1890 (see Charts 24 and 25, pages 66 and 67). The Northampton Institution for Savings increased its investment in public funds, chiefly Treasury bonds, from $369,000 in 1876 to $564,000 in 1880, as shown in Chart 26, page 68. During these years there was a sharp demand for Treasury bonds because of distrust of other investments. As a result, primarily, of a decrease in investment in Treasury obligations, the public funds held by the Northampton Institution declined in volume after 1880, and by 1890 they had fallen to $141,000, or 5 per cent of the total assets. During this period the Federal debt incurred during the Civil War was being retired and refunded

Chart 21

SECURITY INVESTMENTS
in Per Cent of Total Assets
Florence Savings Bank, October 31 of Each Year, 1876-1938

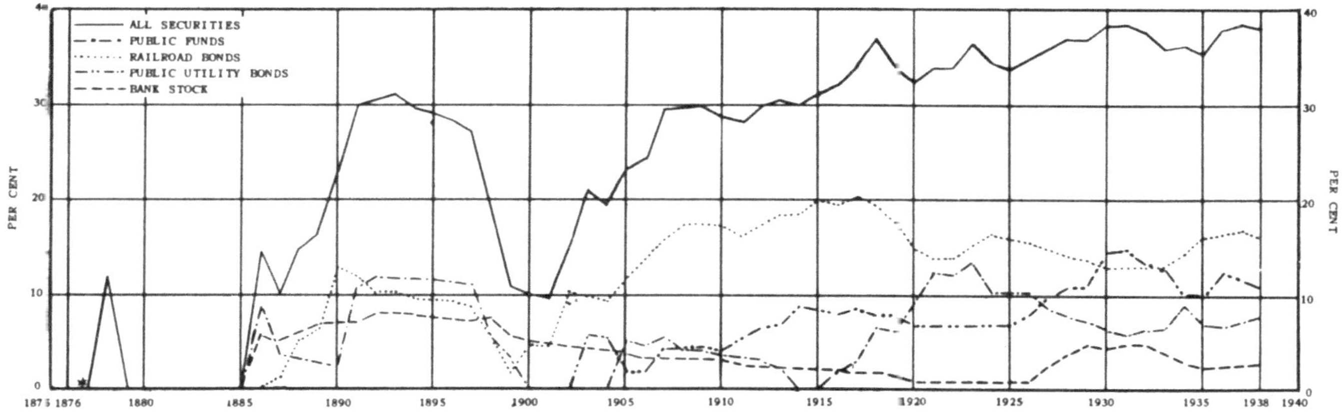

* Public funds constituted the entire security holdings in 1878.

Source: Computed from data in the annual reports of the Commissioner of Banks.

Chart 22

SECURITY INVESTMENTS
in Per Cent of Total Assets
Hampshire Savings Bank, 1876-1897
Nonotuck Savings Bank, 1899-1938
October 31 of Each Year

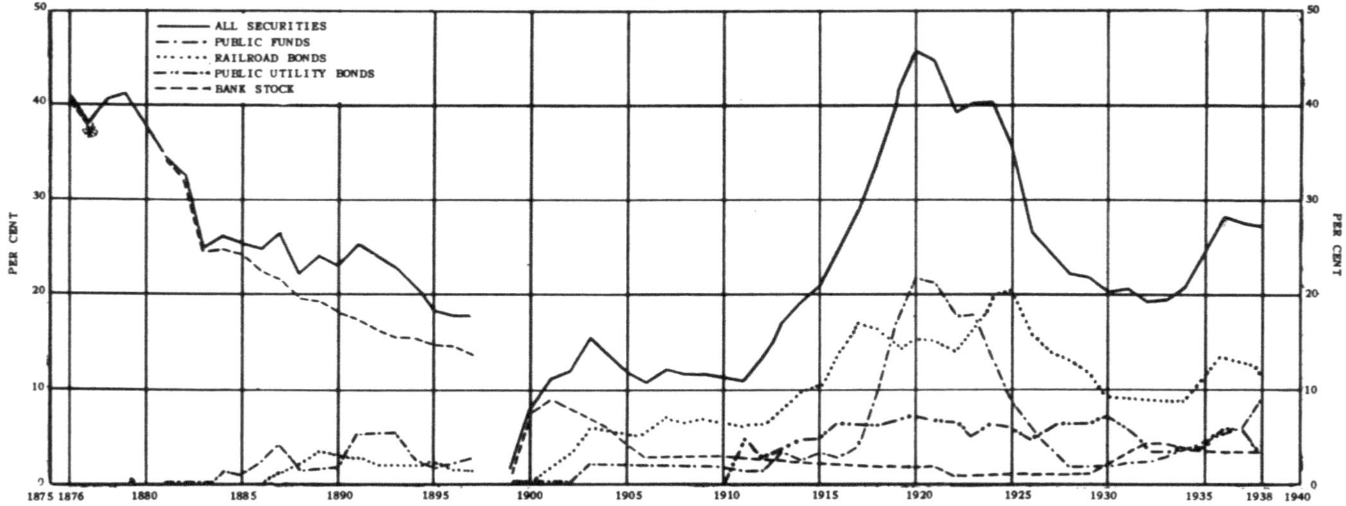

* Bank stock constituted the entire security holdings from 1877 to 1880.

Source: Computed from data in the annual reports of the Commissioner of Banks.

Chart 23

SECURITY INVESTMENTS
in Per Cent of Total Assets
Northampton Institution for Savings, October 31 of Each Year 1876-1938

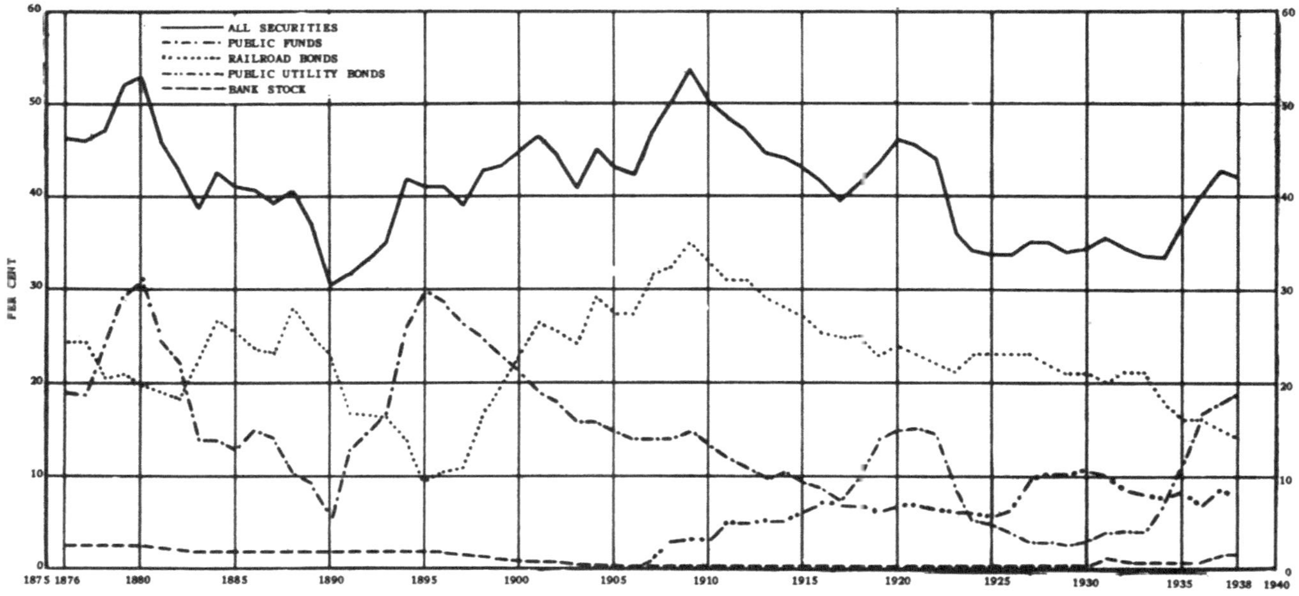

Source: Compu ed from data in the annual reports of the Commissioner of Banks.

Chart 24

SECURITY INVESTMENTS

Florence Savings Bank October 31 of Each Year, 1876-1938

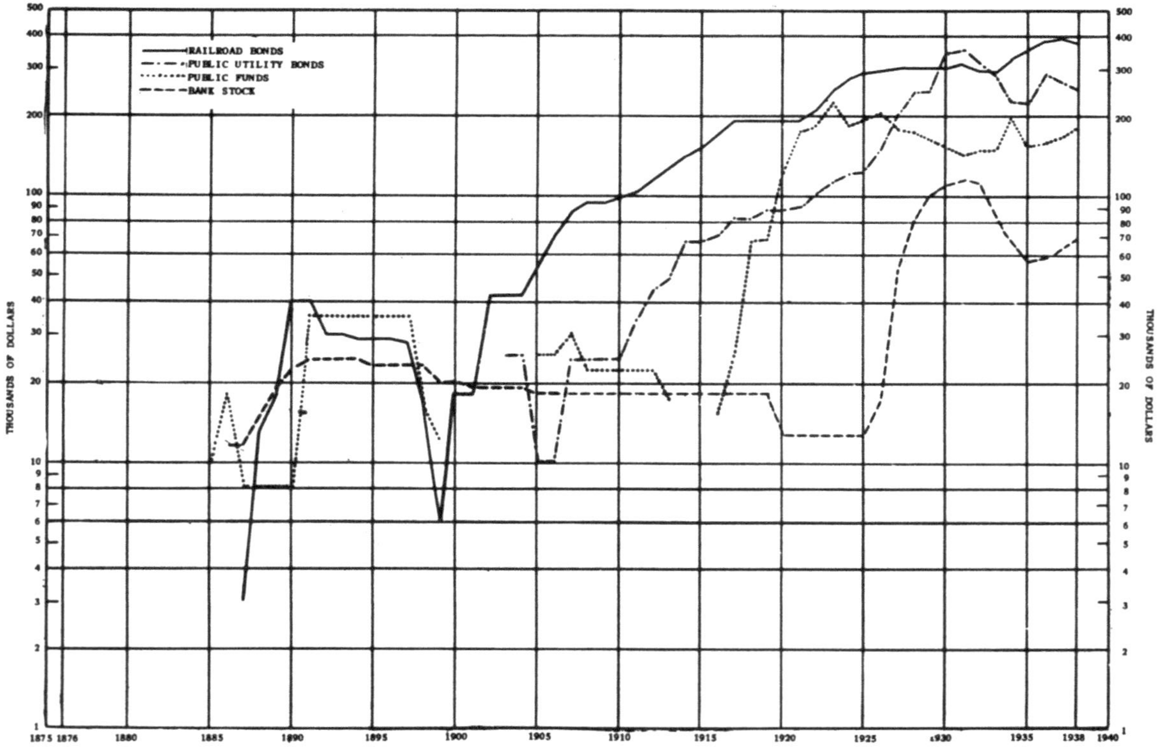

* Public Funds to the amount of $10,000 were held in 1878.

Source: Mass. Commissioner of Banks. *Annual Report*. 1876-1938.

Chart 25

SECURITY INVESTMENTS

Hampshire Savings Bank, 1876-1897

Nonotuck Savings Bank, 1899-1938

October 31 of Each Year

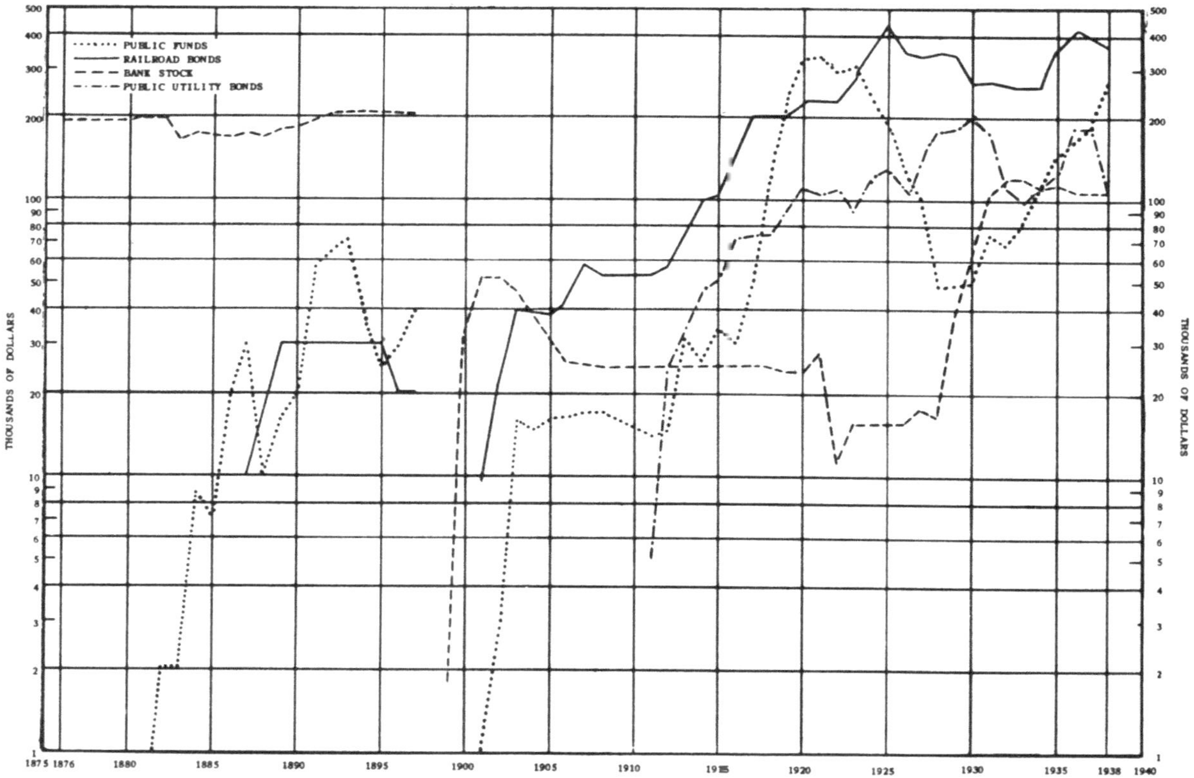

Source: Mass. Commissioner of Banks. *Annual Report*. 1876-1938.

Chart 26

SECURITY INVESTMENTS

Northampton Institution for Savings, October 31 of Each Year, 1876-1938

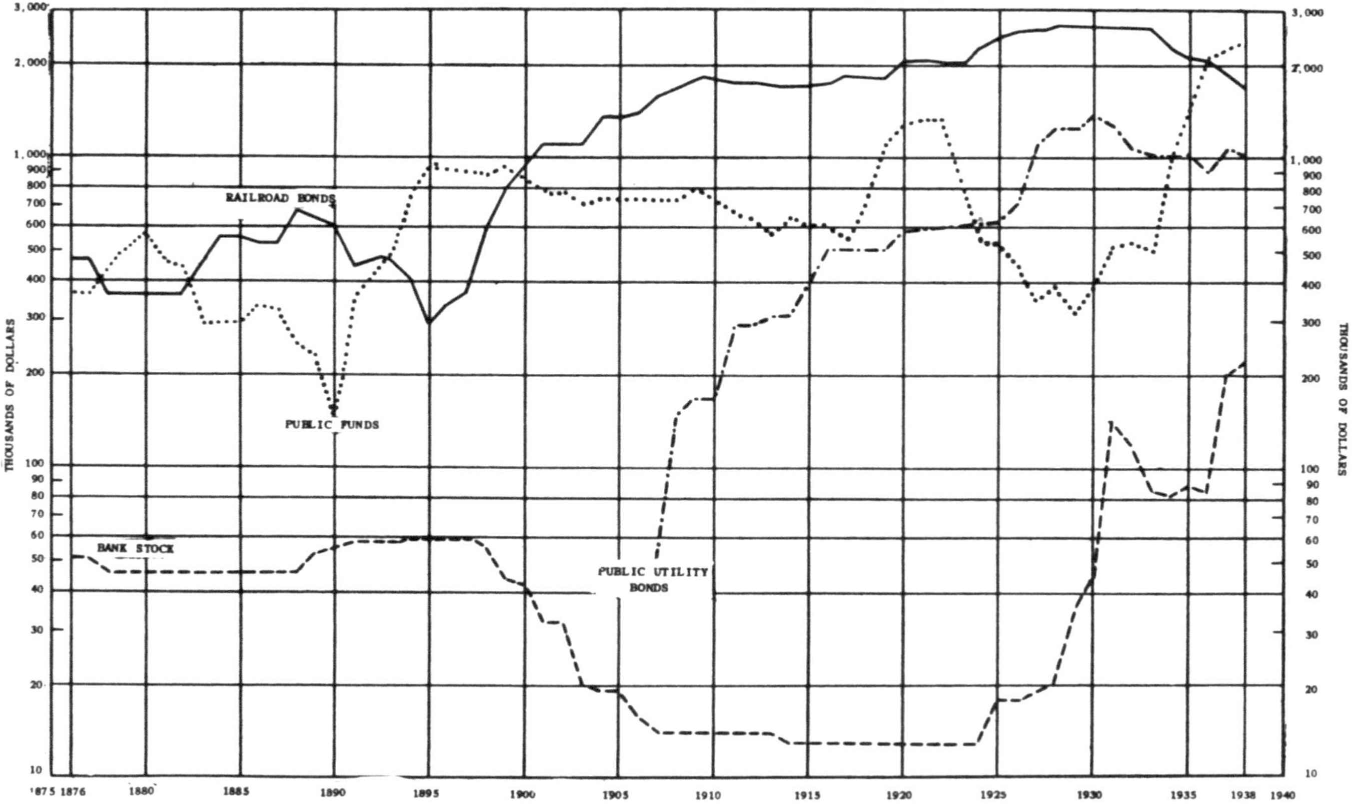

Source: Mass. Commissioner of Banks. *Annual Report*. 1876-1938.

into bonds bearing lower rates of interest. Yields on Treasury bonds continued to be so low that savings banks could not well invest in them and still maintain their dividend rates.

1890-1917. The public funds of each of the banks increased in 1890 and then remained high for several years. Since the Federal debt was relatively small from 1890 until World War I, investment by the banks was almost entirely confined to the obligations of cities and towns. The public funds of the Hampshire Savings Bank reached a peak of more than $70,000, or 4 per cent of the assets of the bank, in 1893. Thereafter the public funds declined until the time of the closing of the bank. The investment of the Florence Savings Bank in public funds amounted to $35,000, or slightly more than 10 per cent of its assets, from 1891 to 1897. The Florence bank held public funds only intermittently from 1897 to 1918 and they made up but a small part of the total assets of the bank. The public funds of the Northampton Institution increased sharply from 1890 to 1895, when they amounted to $916,000 and constituted 30 per cent of the total assets. They then declined very gradually until 1918 but their relative importance among the assets of the bank diminished rapidly because of the growth of total assets from 1895 to 1917. Slightly less than 8 per cent of the assets of the Northampton Institution for Savings were invested in public funds in 1917. Although the Nonotuck bank held public funds before 1918, they were comparatively unimportant. The relatively small volume of public funds held by each of the savings banks in 1900 and in the following years was primarily a consequence of the greater attractiveness of higher yielding railroad securities.

1918-1930. The heavy borrowing program undertaken by the Treasury when the United States entered the war in 1917 was reflected in the bond portfolios of the Northampton savings banks. Investment in Treasury obligations was largely achieved through the diversion of new funds to this type of security. In 1920, public funds owned by the Northampton Institution for Savings amounted to almost $1,272,000 and those of the Florence Savings Bank to $118,000. Such investment constituted 15 per cent of the assets of the Northampton Institution for Savings and 9 per cent of the assets of the Florence bank. The Nonotuck bank invested a larger share of its assets in public funds, for the $328,000 investment in 1920 made up 22 per cent of its assets.

The volume of public funds continued to be large in each of the banks for several years after 1920. Investment then declined until the depression years of the 1930's -- although the decrease in the case of the Florence bank was slight -- and the funds freed were placed in more profitable investments, such as mortgage loans.

1930-1938. As a result of depression conditions the banks increased their investment in public funds. Other uses for the sums deposited in the banks were scarce. The real estate and bond markets were dull, and yields on bonds legal for investment were low. Many railroads had encountered financial difficulties and their bonds had been removed from the legal lists. The supply of Treasury bonds was large and the market active. Moreover, Government bonds offered a safe type of investment at a time when there was a general lack of confidence. The banks, therefore, increased their investment in Treasury bonds, even though the yields were low.

The Nonotuck bank increased its holdings of public funds from $49,000 in 1930 to $275,000, or 9 per cent of assets, in 1938. The Northampton Institution for Savings likewise increased its investment in public funds. In 1930 it held less than $400,000 in various governmental obligations, but by 1938 these bonds and notes had increased to almost $2,380,000 and they amounted to 19 per cent of the assets of the bank. The public funds held by the Florence Savings Bank increased little during the 1930's, just as its public funds had decreased but slightly in the 1920's. By 1938 the Florence bank held $176,000, or 8 per cent of its assets, in public funds.

Conclusion. The history of the investment in public funds indicates that the yield on such bonds and notes is ordinarily too low to make them attractive to the savings banks, although in unusual circumstances, such as war or depression, the banks may resort to them. In the early years the Federal debt was too small for savings banks as a whole to invest heavily in Treasury bonds. Obligations of state and local governments presented other difficulties since the market for such bonds is often limited, the risks uncertain, and the yields low.

B. RAILROAD BONDS

1. Legal Regulation

In 1876 railroad bonds were the most recent type of security to have been added to the legal list for the mutual savings banks of Massachusetts. The banks were permitted to invest in the first mortgage bonds of any railroad company incorporated in Massachusetts if the company was in possession of and operating its own road and if it had earned and paid regular dividends for the two years preceding investment.[44]

In 1881 the law was but slightly changed. It allowed investment in bonds of companies in other parts of New England as well as Massachusetts. The banks could also invest in first mortgage bonds guaranteed by such companies. In addition, the banks could invest in bonds and notes which were not secured by a mortgage if the railroad company was incorporated in Massachusetts, if the road lay at least partly in Massachusetts and was unencumbered by mortgage, and provided the company had paid dividends of not less then 5 per cent annually for the two years preceding investment.[45] In subsequent years the bonds and notes of specific railroads serving Massachusetts, such as the Old Colony Railroad and the Fitchburg Railroad companies, were added to the legal list.

In the 1880's many railroad bonds were not legal for investment because of leases and consolidations. To provide for such cases, the requirement concerning the operation of the railroad was therefore dropped in 1889 and the banks were allowed to invest in the first mortgage bonds of roads which were leased to other companies.[46]

Because of the many roads which were forced to undergo reorganization after 1893 and 1894, requirements concerning dividends were raised in 1898. Thereafter bonds of companies incorporated in New England and located wholly or in part therein were not eligible for investment by savings banks unless they had earned and paid dividends of not less than 3 per cent a year during the two preceding years.[47]

44 Mass. Acts 1876, c. 203, sec. 9, cl. 3d.
45 Mass. Pub. Stat. (1882), c. 116, sec. 20, cl. 3d.
46 Mass. Acts 1889, c. 305.
47 Mass. Acts 1898, c. 184.

Funds of the savings banks were increasing rapidly and the banks were eager to expand their investments. By 1899 most of the railroad mileage of the country had been constructed and the roads to the West offered an enlarged field for investment. In 1899 the banks were authorized to invest in the bonds of many roads other than those incorporated in Massachusetts and serving Massachusetts directly. The banks could invest in the first mortgage bonds of certain specified railroads: New York Central and Hudson River; Michigan Central; Lake Shore and Michigan Southern Railway; Illinois Central; Pennsylvania; Delaware, Lackawanna and Western Railroad; Chicago, Burlington, and Quincy; Chicago and Northwestern; and the Delaware and Hudson Canal Company. However, it was required that the railroad should have earned and paid dividends of not less than 4 per cent on all of its capital stock for each fiscal year in the ten years preceding investment and the capital stock was to be at least one-third of the par value of all bonded indebtedness. The banks could also invest in the first mortgage bonds of railroads incorporated in New York, Pennsylvania, Ohio, Michigan, Indiana, Illinois, and Iowa if the roads had met the dividend requirements as stated above and if the bonds were guaranteed both as to principal and interest by the companies named above.[48]

In subsequent years the provisions were changed slightly but the same kinds of requirements were set up concerning dividends and giving special preference to Massachusetts and New England railroads. Provisions concerning the ratio of gross earnings to interest and rentals, the number of miles of track owned, the relationship between bonded indebtedness and capital stock, and the size of gross earnings were applied to railroads other than those in New England.[49] Requirements were altered in order that bonds of railroads throughout the entire country might be eligible for investment. In 1926, equipment securities were made legal under conditions similar to those required of first mortgage bonds.[50]

The savings banks have also been permitted to invest in bonds secured by mortgages on Boston Terminal property. In 1888, they

48 Mass. Acts 1899, c. 269.
49 Mass. Gen. Laws (1932), c. 168, sec. 54, cl. 3d.
50 Mass. Acts 1926, c. 283.

were granted authority to invest in bonds of the New York and New England Railroad Company secured by terminal lands in Boston,[51] and in 1896 they were permitted to invest in bonds of the Boston Terminal Company secured by first mortgage.[52]

From time to time the requirements were eased in order to permit the banks to invest in railroad bonds that would otherwise have become illegal. In 1913 it was provided that if a railroad company complied with the dividend requirements after a two-year failure to meet the dividend requirement, its bonds were not illegal for investment. This exception applied only to the bonds of railroad companies which had complied with all requirements for ten consecutive years preceding the two-year failure.[53] Special provisions were necessary when the Federal Government took over the operation of the railroads during World War I. The time during which the roads were so operated was excluded in determining the eligibility of bonds that had been legal investments when the roads were taken over by the Government.[54]

In the 1930's, decreasing revenues together with heavy fixed costs made it difficult for the railroads to maintain the dividends necessary for their remaining legal investments for the savings banks. To prevent heavy liquidation of the bonds and consequent losses to the banks, steps were again taken to preserve the legality of railroad bonds. In 1933 it was provided that wherever there were requirements for a certain number of fiscal years, the years 1931 and 1932 should be excluded if such exclusion would make the railroad securities legal investments. Thus railroad obligations that were eligible for investment on January 1, 1931, were to continue to be legal for investment until April 1, 1934, except that securities which had been in default on either principal or interest payments between 1931 and 1934 should not be eligible for investment.[55] This moratorium was continued by successive acts[56] so that the years from 1931 through 1937 were excluded from the count and bonds were to con-

51 Mass. Acts 1888, c. 301, sec. 6.
52 Mass. Acts 1896, c. 516, sec. 4.
53 Mass. Acts 1913, c. 291.
54 Mass. Acts 1919, c. 13.
55 Mass. Acts 1933, c. 111.
56 Mass. Acts 1934, c. 79; Acts 1935, c. 72; Acts 1936, c. 84; Acts 1937, c. 56.

tinue to be eligible until 1939 (instead of 1934 as provided in the act of 1933).

It therefore appears that, after setting up careful requirements, it proved necessary in times of stress to suspend the re quirements in order that bonds might continue to be legal. This may indicate not only a temporary situation but also a need to revise the requirements relating to the legality of railroad bonds. The extension of requirements such as those relating to the size of gross earnings, the ratio of earnings to fixed charges, and the relationship between bonded indebtedness and capital stock would possibly have provided more satisfactory standards. In connection with public utility bonds the state established a maximum term to maturity, and a similar provision might well have been applied to railroads. The requirement concerning the payment of dividends does not necessarily safeguard the bond holder since it stimulates the maintaining of dividends when earnings do not justify such payments.

2. Investment in Railroad Bonds

The Northampton savings banks invested a substantial part of their funds in railroad bonds, which were a favorite kind of security in the general investment market from the Civil War to World War I. In the late nineteenth century, railroad companies needed a great deal of capital and consequently railroad bonds and stocks constituted the largest single class of security. In addition, they were considered an essentially sound type of investment. Rapid expansion of mileage and of capitalization occurred in the last quarter of the nineteenth century and contributed to the financial difficulties of the railway companies in 1893 and 1894, when about one-fourth of the total railroad capitalization passed through bankruptcy courts.[57] Although in most cases holders of first mortgage bonds suffered no losses, the general standing of railroad securities was affected. Railroad obligations recovered however and again were considered prime investments until World War I and Government operation. The importance of railroad bonds in the period preceding the war resulted in part from the fact that there were few Treasury bonds,

[57] Alexander Dana Noyes, *Forty Years of American Finance*, p. 218.

and consequently railroad bonds were about the only type of security in which the banks could invest.

After the post-war return of the roads to private operation, railroad securities continued to be an important factor in the bond market, with a considerable volume of buying and selling and with relatively stable yields. Their pre-eminence was lost, however, and the securities of industrial and public utility companies and obligations of the Federal Government grew in importance.[58]

Aside from loans, railroad bonds were the largest class of investment held by the Northampton banks throughout most of the period included in this study. The book value of railroad bonds varied widely in the years prior to 1900, as shown in Charts 24, 25, and 26, pages 66, 67, and 68. Investment in railroad bonds increased from 1900 to 1925, but after 1925 expansion ceased for the most part, and railroad bonds either declined or remained unchanged in amount.

The relative importance of railroad securities among all the assets of the banks varied considerably during the period studied (see Charts 21, 22, and 23, pages 63, 64, and 65). Although the total amount invested in railroad bonds grew fairly steadily after 1900, the growth did not keep pace with the rise in total assets, and the proportion of assets invested in railroad bonds was not, therefore, generally increasing.

1876-1900. The Hampshire Savings Bank held few railroad bonds from 1876 to the time when it ceased operations. It owned no railroad bonds until 1887. From 1889 to 1895 it had $30,000 invested in railroad obligations but such investment amounted to only 3 per cent of the assets.

The Florence Savings Bank likewise held few railroad bonds prior to 1900. It first owned railroad securities in 1887 and by 1890, $40,000, or 13 per cent of the assets of the bank, was so invested. Holdings declined after 1891, however, and by 1899 they constituted less than 2 per cent of the assets of the Florence bank.

The Northampton Institution for Savings invested a substantial part of its assets in railroad bonds in the years preceding 1900.

58 Evans Clark, *The Internal Debt of the United States*, Table 1, p. 10.

In 1876, $472,000, or 25 per cent of assets, was invested in railroad bonds. Although a drop occurred in 1878 and little change took place for the next four years, investment in railroad bonds was higher from 1883 to 1890, reaching $675,000 in 1888 and amounting to 28 per cent of assets. Thereafter the volume of investment in railroad bonds was lower until 1896, when there began an increase that continued for many years.

In 1876 railroad securities were suffering from a depressed market, but improvement soon occurred and many bonds were offered because of consolidations and combinations. Because various securities exceeded an amount justified by immediate prospects of earning capacity, the banks were cautious in buying railroad bonds. Moreover, legal regulations of savings bank investments precluded the purchase of many issues. By the late 1880's various changes in regulations together with the high volume of traffic encouraged investment in railroad bonds. Thus, the Northampton Institution for Savings shifted funds from investment in United States obligations to the more profitable investment in railroad bonds. The Florence bank likewise bought railroad securities.

The railroad industry suffered so severely in the depression of 1893 and 1894 that its investment status was injured. In consequence the Northampton banks decreased their holdings of railroad bonds.

1900-1917. In the years before the World War, railroads were prosperous and their securities were favorite investments. Bond yields were generally rising. The list of railroad bonds legal for investment by the savings banks was again enlarged and the Massachusetts banks could invest in railroads operating throughout the country. These factors, together with the scarcity of other forms of security investment, led to increased holdings of railroad bonds by the Northampton banks.

The Northampton Institution for Savings increased its investment from $931,000 in 1900 to $1,834,000 in 1917. The greatest increase occurred before 1910, when railroad securities amounted to as much as one-third of the assets. Thereafter the volume of railroad investment was comparatively stable and the percentage of assets so invested declined.

The railroad investments of the Florence Savings Bank increased from $18,000 in 1900 to about $192,000 in 1917. This meant that an increasing percentage of assets consisted of railroad securities, for only 5 per cent was invested in railroad bonds in 1900 and about 20 per cent in 1917.

The Nonotuck bank likewise invested an increasing percentage of its assets in railroad bonds. The holdings increased from 2 per cent of assets in 1901 to 17 per cent in 1917, and the dollar value of railroad bonds rose from $10,000 to $197,000.

1917-1922. During and immediately after the war, investment in railroad bonds was retarded by Government operation and by uncertainty concerning the future status of the roads. New investment funds of the banks were largely diverted to Treasury bonds.

1922-1929. After 1922, railroad investment by the Northampton banks increased and remained high for several years. In the late 1920's, however, such investment either decreased or failed to increase. This resulted from the low yield on railroad securities and the opening of public utility investment to the savings banks. Furthermore, real estate loans were expanding rapidly and absorbing the increase in deposit funds which occurred during these years.

The railroad securities owned by the Nonotuck bank reached a peak of $424,000 in 1925, when they amounted to 20 per cent of assets. Holdings of railroad bonds by the Northampton Institution for Savings amounted to $2,661,000, or 22 per cent of assets, in 1928. The Florence Savings Bank had $301,000 so invested in 1928 and the bonds amounted to 14 per cent of its assets.

1930-1938. There was little change in the railroad investments of the Northampton banks from 1930 to 1933. After 1933 the holdings of both the Florence and the Nonotuck banks were slightly higher. On the other hand, a decline occurred in the Northampton Institution for Savings, which preferred to increase its public funds greatly rather than to invest further in railroad bonds.

Conclusion. The Northampton banks invested heavily in railroad bonds, especially after 1900. The bonds proved themselves to be generally a satisfactory non-speculative type of investment, bearing a yield higher than that of public funds. During World War I and in the years immediately following the war, their investment standing declined. The zenith of railroad securities had probably passed before the 1920's but considerable improvement occurred during those years. The depression of the 1930's drastically lowered their investment quality, many of the bonds fell into a somewhat speculative class, and defaults occurred in a number of issues held by the banks. On the whole, railroad bonds served the banks well in the past but experience in the later years was less satisfactory, and further great expansion of savings bank investment in this field seems unlikely.

C. BANK STOCK

1. Legal Regulation

In 1876, savings banks could invest in the stock of banks incorporated in Massachusetts or in the stock of national banks located within the state. Total investment in a single bank was limited by the requirement that bank stock owned and held as collateral for loans was not to exceed one-fourth of the capital stock of any one bank. In addition, not more than $100,000 nor more than 10 per cent of savings deposits was to be invested in a single bank.[59] By act of 1881, stock of national banks located in other New England states was also made eligible for investment.[60]

Further legislation altered the provisions restricting the amount of investment in bank stock. In 1882 savings banks were prohibited from holding, both by way of investment and as collateral, more than 3 per cent of their deposits in the stock of any one bank.[61] It was later determined that a savings bank should not hold more than 35 per cent of its deposits in bank stock (both as direct investment and as collateral).[62] In 1908, this maximum was reduced from 35 per cent to 20 per cent.[63]

In 1929 additional requirements were established concerning

59 Mass. Acts 1876, c. 203, sec. 9, cl. 4th.
60 Mass. Acts 1881, c. 214, sec. 3.
61 Mass. Acts 1882, c. 224.
62 Mass. Acts 1883, c. 202.
63 Mass. Acts 1908, c. 590, sec. 68, cl. 7th.

investment in bank stock. For stock to be eligible for purchase by a savings bank, cash dividends of at least 4 per cent must have been paid in the five years preceding investment. Furthermore, it was required that the surplus of the bank be at least 50 per cent of the capital. The initial cost of the stock of any one bank was to be not more than 1 per cent of the deposits of the savings bank, and the aggregate initial cost of all bank stock was limited to 15 per cent of the deposits of the savings bank.[64]

Thus, by successive acts after 1876, the restrictions placed upon investment in bank stock were gradually tightened, both by limitations on the total amount so invested and by requirements concerning the banks whose stock was legal for investment.

2. Investment in Bank Stock

Although the volume of bank stock available was relatively small as compared with other types of securities, it yielded such a good return and in consequence was so much desired until the late 1920's and the depression of 1932 that a ready market for it existed. The Bank Commissioner from time to time issued warnings against heavy investment in bank stock with its double liability feature, and legal restrictions concerning this type of investment were gradually tightened.

The actual amount invested in bank stock by the Northampton savings banks has never been great. From 1876, to 1897, the Northampton Institution for Savings held between $45,000 and $60,000 of bank stocks. The amount decreased in the following years and, from 1907 to 1924, less than $15,000 of bank stock was owned. From 1925 to 1931 holdings increased so that in 1931 the Institution for Savings held bank stock with a book value of $143,000. It fell to a lower figure from 1933 to 1936 but increased to $204,000 in 1937 and $220,000 in 1938. In the late 1930's bank stock was considered a good investment, for the double liability provision had been dropped and the commercial banks had already taken their losses. The national banks and trust companies were therefore in a good position and prospects for profits when business improved were excellent.

64 Mass. Acts 1929, c. 315, sec. 1.

The percentage of its assets invested in bank stock by the Northampton Institution for Savings was less than 1 per cent from 1901 to 1931. The percentage increased after 1931 but did not reach 2 per cent.

The Florence Savings Bank held no bank stock until 1886, and in that year it held only about $12,000 of stock. In the following years such investment increased and by 1891 the Florence bank held $24,000 of bank stock. The amount remained about the same for several years and then declined, reaching $18,000 in 1905 and dropping still lower in 1920. After 1925, investment in bank stock increased and by 1931 it amounted to $113,000. The book value of bank stock owned by the Florence Savings Bank declined from 1932 to 1935 and then increased slightly to $67,000 in 1938.

In 1886 the Florence bank held about 6 per cent of its assets in bank stock. The percentage rose slightly in the following years but did not reach 9 per cent. After 1896 the percentage of assets invested in bank stock showed a very slow decrease and by 1920 only 1 per cent of the assets were so invested. This drop in percentage was a result of both the increase in total assets and the slight decrease in dollar investment in bank stock. After 1925 the percentage increased and by 1930 about 5 per cent of assets were invested in bank stock. After 1932 the percentage dropped and in 1938 bank stock made up only 3 per cent of the assets of the Florence bank.

The Hampshire Savings Bank invested heavily in bank stock. From 1876 to 1897 about $200,000 was invested in this manner, the amount being slightly smaller from 1883 to 1890. Although in the early years the investment in bank stock was actually as great as the amount loaned on real estate, after 1880 real estate loans increased rapidly while investment in bank stock remained almost unchanged. About 40 per cent of the assets of the Hampshire bank were invested in bank stock from 1876 to 1879. From 1879 until the time when the bank was closed, the percentage decreased because of the failure of investment in bank stock to keep pace with the growth of total assets. By 1897 only about 14 per cent of the assets were so invested.

In its first years, the Nonotuck Savings Bank invested more heavily in bank stock than in any other type of security. Its investment in bank stock amounted to $32,000 in 1900 and rose above $50,000 in 1901 and 1902. The holdings then decreased to about $25,000 in 1906 and remained at that level until 1922, when a further drop occurred. From 1923 to 1928 the amount invested was about $16,000 or $17,000. Thereafter, investment in bank stock rose rapidly and, in 1932, $121,000 was so invested. Thus, at this time, the Nonotuck bank held a larger sum invested in bank stock than in either public funds or public utilities. The amount of bank stock remained almost unchanged after 1932.

The Nonotuck bank invested the largest percentage of its funds in bank stock in 1901, when stock constituted 9 per cent of its assets. The percentage decreased thereafter and in the period of the twenties was only about 1 per cent. From 1932 to 1935, 4 per cent was so invested and in 1938, 3 per cent.

In their buying of bank stock, the savings banks were limited to the stock of banks located in New England, but actually the Northampton banks rarely held the stock of institutions located outside of the commonwealth. The Northampton savings banks have held the stock of banks in Boston, Springfield, Worcester, and Northampton, as well as the stock of banks in smaller communities in Massachusetts. Investment was made in both trust companies and national banks.

D. PUBLIC UTILITY BONDS

Public utility holdings of the mutual savings banks in Massachusetts are composed of the following three groups, in the order of their admission to the list of legal investments: street railway company bonds, telephone company bonds, and bonds of gas, electric, and water companies.

1. Legal Regulation

a) Street Railway Bonds

In the early years of the twentieth century there was a great deal of interest in street railway companies and they were considered a promising field of investment. In 1902 the list of legal investments for savings banks was consequently expanded to include certain street railway bonds approved by the Board of Commissioners of Savings Banks. Investment was limited to issues of companies incorporated in Massachusetts and situated at least in part within the state. Furthermore, it was required that the companies must have earned and paid annual dividends of not less than 5 per cent on outstanding capital stock for the five years preceding investment.[65]

In 1913, a provision was made similar to that pertaining to railroads, namely, that bonds which had been legal investments for ten years should not become illegal because of the failure of the company to pay dividends for two years. The two-year failure was to be overlooked only in the case of a company which had not failed to comply for any other period within the preceding ten years and which had fulfilled the legal requirements in the year following the period of failure.[66] By a later act, street railways were treated somewhat differently from railroads. It was provided that during the two years of non-compliance the company must have earned interest on its indebtedness and fixed charges, and the period of compliance required of street railway companies was reduced from ten years to five years.[67]

In 1922 it was recognized that the provisions concerning street railway bonds encouraged the payment of dividends when they should not be paid and when such dividends impaired the security of the bonds. A special commission on banking therefore recommended that the requirements be restated in terms of the ratio of assets to indebtedness and the ratio of net earnings to bond interest.[68] However, the recommendations were not adopted.

In 1932 savings banks were granted special permission to invest in bonds of the Boston Elevated Railway Company if the bonds matured during public management, even though the company should not otherwise meet the requirements for investment.[69]

b) Telephone Company Bonds

The bonds of telephone companies were added to the legal list shortly after investment in street railways was authorized. In 1908, savings banks were given authority to invest in the bonds

65 Mass. Acts 1902, c. 483.
66 Mass. Acts 1913, c. 291.
67 Mass. Acts 1915, c. 273, sec. 1.
68 Mass. House Doc. No. 1275 (1923), pp. 62-63.
69 Mass. Acts 1932, c. 112.

of telephone companies doing business in Massachusetts, if the majority of the directors were Massachusetts residents. It was further provided that, during the five years preceding investment, the company must have had an annual gross income of not less than ten million dollars, all matured principal and interest must have been paid, cash dividends of not less than 6 per cent a year must have been paid, and the dividends paid must have amounted to at least as much as the sum of all interest payable on the entire indebtedness of the company. For bonds of such companies to be eligible they were to be secured by a first mortgage on 75 per cent of the property or by the deposit of bonds and shares of other telephone companies. The amount of bonds secured by collateral was limited to 75 per cent of the value of securities deposited, and the yearly interest and dividends on the deposited securities were required to be at least 50 per cent in excess of the annual interest on the bonds secured by this collateral. Investment in telephone company bonds was limited to 2 per cent of the deposits of the bank.[70]

In 1913 telephone companies were granted the same privilege granted railroads concerning failure to meet requirements for two years.[71]

Various modifications of the restrictions placed upon the purchase of telephone company bonds were made in later years in order to permit greater investment by the savings banks. The restriction that the telephone company conduct business in Massachusetts was removed in 1925,[72] and thereafter the banks could invest in the bonds of companies organized in any state. In 1928 the total amount that could be invested in telephone companies was raised from the former 2 per cent of deposits to 5 per cent. It was further provided that not more than 2 per cent of the deposits of a savings bank were to be invested in the bonds of any one telephone company.[73]

70 Mass. Acts 1908, c. 590, sec. 68, cl. 8th.
71 Mass. Acts 1913, c. 291.
72 Mass. Acts 1925, c. 208.
73 Mass. Acts 1928, c. 42.

c) Bonds of Gas, Electric, and Water Companies

Bonds of gas, electric, and water companies were added to the legal list by an act of 1919. Such bonds were eligible for investment if the net earnings of the issuing company amounted to not less than 4 per cent of the capital stock in the three years preceding investment and if the gross earnings were not less than $100,000 in the last year preceding investment. The bonds were to be secured by a first mortgage on the franchise and property of the company.[74]

In 1926 came the general law making possible wider investment in bonds of public service companies.[75] In addition to bonds made legal by the act of 1919, the banks were authorized to buy bonds if they would mature within 30 years (later changed to 40 years[76]) and if the bonds were issued or assumed by a gas, electric, or other public service company incorporated anywhere in the United States and operating under the supervision of the public service commission of the United States or of a state and doing at least 80 per cent of its business within the United States. A minimum gross operating revenue of one million dollars was established and not less than 75 per cent of this revenue must have come from the sale and distribution of electricity or gas. The banks were thus allowed to invest in operating utilities but not in holding companies. Seventy-five per cent of the gross revenue must have come from operation under a franchise extending at least three years beyond the maturity of the bond. The capital stock was required to be at least two-thirds of the funded debt. In the five years preceding investment, the net earnings available for interest charges must have been at least twice the interest on the total funded debt. It was further required that the funded debt and underlying bonds were not to exceed 60 per cent of the value of the fixed property securing the bonds. The obligations were to be first mortgage bonds or other carefully protected mortgage issues. Such investment was limited to not more than 15 per cent of the deposits of the savings banks and not more than 2 per cent of the deposits was to be invested in the bonds of any one corporation.

[74] Mass. Acts 1919, c. 104, sec. 2.
[75] Mass. Acts 1926, c. 351.
[76] Mass. Acts 1937, c. 96.

This change in regulations in 1926 was made in order to increase the investment opportunities of the savings banks and to allow them to enter the public utility field which had grown to great importance by 1926. According to the Bank Commissioner, more than $500,000,000 of bonds became available for investment through the 1926 law.[77]

2. Investment in Public Utility Bonds

The Northampton Institution for Savings first invested in public utility securities in 1907, when it owned $50,000 of street railway bonds. In 1910, it held $168,000 of public utility bonds and, by 1916, it had invested over $500,000 in utilities (street railway and telephone company bonds). From 1916 until 1926, the holdings increased gradually. After 1926 there was a considerable increase in utility bonds because of the change in legal restrictions and the wider admission of gas and electric companies. The Northampton Institution for Savings held $1,370,000 of public utility bonds in 1930, but after 1930 the amount was somewhat smaller, fluctuating around one million dollars.

The percentage of its assets invested in public utility bonds by the Northampton Institution for Savings increased to 7 per cent in 1916. The proportion remained about the same until 1927, when it rose to 10 per cent. The highest percentage investment in utilities was reached in 1930, when 11 per cent of the assets were so invested. After 1932 about 8 per cent of assets were invested in utility bonds.

The Florence bank likewise showed a great increase in utility holdings during the period studied. In 1903 it had invested $25,000 of its assets in street railway bonds, and the amount dropped to $10,000 in 1905 and 1906. From then until 1932 the public utility investments of the Florence bank increased almost continuously, growth being especially rapid after 1925. In 1931 the Florence bank had placed about $348,000 in utility bonds. The investment decreased to $217,000 in 1935 and increased slightly in the following years.

By 1914 the Florence bank had invested 9 per cent of its assets in public utilities. Between 1915 and 1925 the percentage

77 Mass., *Annual Report of the Commissioner of Banks*, Part I, 1926, p. ii.

dropped to 7 per cent, but thereafter it rose to 14 per cent, where it remained from 1930 to 1932. In the latter years more public utility bonds were held than any other class of security -- even more than railroad bonds. From 1934 to 1938 approximately 10 per cent of assets were invested in public utilities.

The Nonotuck Savings Bank first invested in public service company bonds in 1911. Its investment increased rapidly to $109,000 in 1920. The holdings of public utility bonds remained much the same from 1920 to 1926 but they increased after 1926 and reached $202,000 in 1930. Successive decreases occurred from 1930 to 1933, when the bank held $99,000 of utility bonds. The holdings then increased and in 1936 and 1937 public utility investment was almost twice that of 1933. In 1938, investment in utility companies had dropped back to $102,000.

The Nonotuck bank did not invest quite as large a proportion of its assets in utility bonds as did the other two banks. In 1920 it held 7 per cent of its assets in public utilities and by 1926 the proportion had dropped to 5 per cent. From 1928 to 1930, utility bonds constituted 7 per cent of the assets, but they declined to 3 per cent in 1933. The percentage rose to 6 per cent in 1936 and 1937 and fell to 3 per cent again in 1938.

Throughout most of the period, the Northampton banks invested more heavily in street railway than in telephone bonds. After 1927, however, the investment in gas, electric, and water company bonds was larger than that in either street railway or telephone company bonds and, in fact, was larger than the other two combined. In the early years of the twentieth century, street railway bonds were generally considered a highly satisfactory kind of security, but their investment standing was soon impaired. Telephone company bonds were considered high grade investments but in the later years their yield was so low that they were not attractive to the banks. After 1920 electric utility companies were perhaps the favorite kind of investment in the market and during the depression years of the 1930's the bonds of electric utility companies constituted a large part of the new issues. The Northampton banks reflected these general conditions in that, after 1926, their utility bonds consisted almost exclusively of securities issued by electric power and light companies. During the years following 1929 the public utility company bonds showed perhaps the most satisfactory record of any type of investment made by the savings banks.

E. INVESTMENT RATING OF BOND HOLDINGS

In order to obtain some test of the goodness of the bond portfolios of the Northampton banks and to observe the way in which changing economic conditions affected the quality of portfolios, the ratings placed by Moody's Investors Service on the bonds owned by the banks were examined for seven years: 1911, 1914, 1919, 1922, 1929, 1932, and 1938. Since changes in the ratings of bonds occur slowly, yearly ratings were not recorded.

The rating given by Moody's Investors Service is based upon several factors. Chief among them are the legal standing of the issue, the past earnings of the enterprise, and the marketability of the bonds. The general nature of the industry and the position of the particular company within the industry are also taken into consideration. Since the "seasoning" of the issue is also considered, new bonds are often given no rating even though their potentialities seem good.

The meaning of the symbols used in rating bonds is widely understood. The Aaa bonds are those of the very highest investment quality, and bonds rated Aa and A are also of high grade and essentially sound. The Baa securities are considered good investments but likely to be "substantially" affected by changes in earning power, that is, they have some speculative element. The Ba and B bonds are increasingly less certain or less well secured, and the B bonds are in a speculative position. The three grades of C bonds are definitely speculative rather than investment securities. Caa bonds are highly speculative securities of uncertain value or junior bonds which are inadequately protected by earnings.

Although bond ratings must be used with great caution and careful judgment and must be supplemented by additional information, such ratings, whether those of Moody's or those of other rating agencies, are widely used by banks and by private investors. They have been employed, furthermore, by both Federal and state agencies in setting up standards by which to judge the quality of the bond portfolios of banks and insurance companies.

Both the Comptroller of the Currency and the Federal Reserve System have used bond ratings as standards. In 1931 the Comptroller made use of ratings in distinguishing between those bonds which could be carried at cost and those which had to be written off. The regulations issued by the Comptroller on February 15, 1936, prohibited national banks from purchasing securities in which the investment characteristics were predominantly and distinctively speculative or securities lower than these. The terms were to be interpreted as they were used in the rating manuals. Thus it seems that Federal supervisory agencies have recognized the usefulness of investment ratings.

An investigation[78] of the bond ratings made by various agencies during the years from 1929 to 1935 showed that ratings were good guides to investment, although they were by no means infallible. During the years from 1930 to 1935 the market behavior of those bonds which had been rated high by the agencies in 1929 was better on the whole than the market behavior shown by bonds rated lower by the agencies in 1929. The analysis was made in terms of bond prices and yields. Bonds which had been rated progressively higher in 1929 showed progressively lower rates of default in subsequent years.

It would seem legitimate, therefore, to use ratings as an indication of quality. It is possible that the rating agencies tended to become more cautious in their estimate of "investment" quality after the 1936 ruling of the Comptroller of the Currency. In so far as this is true, the ratings of some of the bonds were lower in 1938 than they would have been had the Comptroller not issued his ruling.

The ratings of bonds held by each of the three banks are shown in Table 1 for each of the seven selected years. There it is apparent that great changes occurred in the quality of the bond portfolios, especially from 1929 to 1938.

1911. In 1911 Moody's Investors Service published ratings upon railroad bonds only. Since railroad bonds then constituted the largest class of security investment of the Northampton savings banks, the ratings give a fairly adequate picture of the bond portfolios at that time.

78 Gilbert Harold, *Bond Ratings as an Investment Guide.*

Table 1

Moody Ratings of Bond Holdings for Selected Years*

Northampton Institution for Savings

All Bonds

Rating	Par Value (thousands of dollars)				
	1919	1922	1929	1932	1938
Aaa	1,884	2,522	2,448	981	2,454
Aa	380	456	791	1,131	565
A	351	240	655	989	548
Total	2,615	3,218	3,894	3,101	3,567
Baa	390	715	375	685	611
Ba	315	--	194	290	631
B	--	207	--	238	345
Total	705	922	569	1,213	1,587
Caa	--	--	--	--	315
No rating	229	29	2	246	46
Total	3,549	4,169	4,465	4,560	5,515

Rating	Percentage of Par Value				
	1919	1922	1929	1932	1938
Aaa	53.1	60.5	54.8	21.5	44.5
Aa	10.7	10.9	17.7	24.8	10.3
A	9.9	5.8	14.7	21.7	9.9
Total	73.7	77.2	87.2	68.0	64.7
Baa	11.0	17.1	8.4	15.0	11.1
Ba	8.9	--	4.3	6.4	11.4
B	--	5.0	--	5.2	6.3
Total	19.9	22.1	12.7	26.6	28.8
Caa	--	--	--	--	5.7
No rating	6.4	0.7	0.1	5.4	0.8
Total	100.0	100.0	100.0	100.0	100.0

* Data, which refer to holdings as of October 31, were compiled from information furnished by the banks and from Moody's manuals of investment. No ratings were placed by Moody's Service upon the bonds of public utility companies in 1911 or upon municipal, state, and Treasury bonds in 1911 and 1914.

Table 1 (Cont'd)

Moody Ratings of Bond Holdings for Selected Years

Nonotuck Savings Bank

All Bonds

Rating	Par Value (thousands of dollars)				
	1919	1922	1929	1932	1938
Aaa	351	449	309	98	266
Aa	34	59	142	97	85
A	11	58	73	86	49
Total	396	566	524	281	400
Baa	83	80	46	91	157
Ba	25	--	25	30	157
B	3	30	--	40	25
Total	111	110	71	161	339
Caa	--	--	--	--	47
No rating	36	3	--	25	12
Total	543	679	595	467	798

Rating	Percentage of Par Value				
	1919	1922	1929	1932	1938
Aaa	64.6	66.1	51.9	21.0	33.3
Aa	6.3	8.7	23.9	20.8	10.7
A	2.0	8.6	12.3	18.4	6.1
Total	72.9	83.4	88.1	60.2	50.1
Baa	15.3	11.8	7.7	19.5	19.7
Ba	4.6	--	4.2	6.4	19.7
B	0.5	4.4	--	8.6	3.1
Total	20.4	16.2	11.9	34.5	42.5
Caa	--	--	--	--	5.9
No rating	6.7	0.4	--	5.3	1.5
Total	100.0	100.0	100.0	100.0	100.0

Table 1 (Cont'd)

Moody Ratings of Bond Holdings for Selected Years

Florence Savings Bank

All Bonds

Rating	Par Value (thousands of dollars)				
	1919	1922	1929	1932	1938
Aaa	133	245	386	215	214
Aa	38	45	105	155	93
A	15	40	150	168	127
Total	186	330	641	538	434
Baa	70	137	40	105	208
Ba	45	--	40	50	150
B	10	35	--	50	44
Total	125	172	80	205	402
Caa	--	--	--	--	55
No rating	50	5	5	35	--
Total	361	507	726	778	891

Rating	Percentage of Par Value				
	1919	1922	1929	1932	1938
Aaa	36.8	48.3	53.2	27.7	24.0
Aa	10.5	8.9	14.5	19.9	10.4
A	4.2	7.9	20.6	21.6	14.3
Total	51.5	65.1	88.3	69.2	48.7
Baa	19.4	27.0	5.5	13.5	23.4
Ba	12.4	--	5.5	6.4	16.8
B	2.8	6.9	--	6.4	4.9
Total	34.6	33.9	11.0	26.3	45.1
Caa	--	--	--	--	6.2
No rating	13.9	1.0	0.7	4.5	--
Total	100.0	100.0	100.0	100.0	100.0

Table 1 (Cont'd)

Moody Ratings of Bond Holdings for Selected Years

Northampton Institution for Savings

Railroad Bonds

Rating	Par Value (thousands of dollars)						
	1911	1914	1919	1922	1929	1932	1938
Aaa	744	863	600	970	1,729	734	25
Aa	425	200	380	456	501	406	50
A	180	330	351	--	215	629	338
Total	1,349	1,393	1,331	1,426	2,445	1,769	413
Baa	165	165	150	715	375	685	437
Ba	--	100	315	--	--	290	631
B	--	--	--	--	--	100	345
Total	165	265	465	715	375	1,075	1,413
Caa	--	--	--	--	--	--	315
No rating	50	76	75	--	--	--	20
Total	1,564	1,734	1,871	2,141	2,820	2,844	2,161

Rating	Percentage of Par Value						
	1911	1914	1919	1922	1929	1932	1938
Aaa	47.6	49.8	32.1	45.3	61.3	25.8	1.2
Aa	27.2	11.5	20.3	21.3	17.8	14.3	2.3
A	11.5	19.0	18.7	--	7.6	22.1	15.6
Total	86.3	80.3	71.1	66.6	86.7	62.2	19.1
Baa	10.5	9.5	8.0	33.4	13.3	24.1	20.2
Ba	--	5.8	16.9	--	--	10.2	29.2
B	--	--	--	--	--	3.5	16.0
Total	10.5	15.3	24.9	33.4	13.3	37.8	65.4
Caa	--	--	--	--	--	--	14.6
No rating	3.2	4.4	4.0	--	--	--	0.9
Total	100.0	100.0	100.0	100.0	100.0	100.0	100.0

Table 1 (Cont'd)

Moody Ratings of Bond Holdings for Selected Years

Nonotuck Savings Bank

Railroad Bonds

Rating	Par Value (thousands of dollars)						
	1911	1914	1919	1922	1929	1932	1938
Aaa	35	35	92	112	201	60	--
Aa	5	21	34	54	82	17	10
A	--	17	11	--	20	61	49
Total	40	73	137	166	303	138	59
Baa	5	10	35	80	46	91	142
Ba	--	--	25	--	5	30	137
B	--	--	3	10	--	20	25
Total	5	10	63	90	51	141	304
Caa	--	--	--	--	--	--	47
No rating	10	20	6	--	--	--	--
Total	55	103	206	256	354	279	410

Rating	Percentage of Par Value						
	1911	1914	1919	1922	1929	1932	1938
Aaa	63.6	34.0	44.7	43.7	56.8	21.5	--
Aa	9.1	20.4	16.5	21.1	23.2	6.1	2.4
A	--	16.5	5.3	--	5.6	21.9	12.0
Total	72.7	70.9	66.5	64.8	85.6	49.5	14.4
Baa	9.1	9.7	17.0	31.3	13.0	32.6	34.6
Ba	--	--	12.1	--	1.4	10.7	33.4
B	--	--	1.5	3.9	--	7.2	6.1
Total	9.1	9.7	30.6	35.2	14.4	50.5	74.1
Caa	--	--	--	--	--	--	11.5
No rating	18.2	19.4	2.9	--	--	--	--
Total	100.0	100.0	100.0	100.0	100.0	100.0	100.0

Table 1 (Cont'd)

Moody Ratings of Bond Holdings for Selected Years

Florence Savings Bank

Railroad Bonds

Rating	Par Value (thousands of dollars)						
	1911	1914	1919	1922	1929	1932	1938
Aaa	42	52	47	38	164	40	11
Aa	18	10	38	40	40	50	20
A	--	25	15	--	65	69	52
Total	60	87	100	78	269	159	83
Baa	45	45	35	137	40	100	137
Ba	--	--	45	--	5	35	140
B	--	--	10	--	--	15	44
Total	45	45	90	137	45	150	321
Caa	--	--	--	--	--	--	55
No rating	--	10	10	--	--	--	--
Total	105	142	200	215	314	309	459

Rating	Percentage of Par Value						
	1911	1914	1919	1922	1929	1932	1938
Aaa	40.0	36.6	23.5	17.7	52.2	12.9	2.4
Aa	17.1	7.1	19.0	18.6	12.8	16.2	4.4
A	--	17.6	7.5	--	20.7	22.3	11.3
Total	57.1	61.3	50.0	36.3	85.7	51.5	18.1
Baa	42.9	31.7	17.5	63.7	12.7	32.4	29.8
Ba	--	--	22.5	--	1.6	11.3	30.5
B	--	--	5.0	--	--	4.8	9.6
Total	42.9	31.7	45.0	63.7	14.3	48.5	69.9
Caa	--	--	--	--	--	--	12.0
No rating	--	7.0	5.0	--	--	--	--
Total	100.0	100.0	100.0	100.0	100.0	100.0	100.0

Table 1 (Cont'd)

Moody Ratings of Bond Holdings for Selected Years

Northampton Institution for Savings

Public Utility Bonds

Rating		Par Value (thousands of dollars)					
		1914	1919	1922	1929	1932	1938
Aaa		110	146	186	395	160	125
Aa		--	--	--	290	565	515
A		125	--	240	440	310	205
	Total	235	146	426	1,125	1,035	845
Baa		100	240	--	--	--	150
Ba		--	--	--	194		
B		--	--	207	--	138	--
	Total	100	240	207	194	138	150
Caa		--	--	--	--	--	--
No rating		--	150	--	--	--	--
Total		335	536	633	1,319	1,173	995

Rating		Percentage of Par Value					
		1914	1919	1922	1929	1932	1938
Aaa		32.8	27.2	29.4	29.9	13.6	12.6
Aa		--	--	--	22.0	48.2	51.7
A		37.3	--	37.9	33.4	26.4	20.6
	Total	70.1	27.2	67.3	85.3	88.2	84.9
Baa		29.9	44.8	--	--	--	15.1
Ba		--	--	--	14.7	--	--
B		--	--	32.7	--	11.8	--
	Total	29.9	44.8	32.7	14.7	11.8	15.1
Caa		--	--	--	--	--	--
No rating		--	28.0	--	--	--	--
Total		100.0	100.0	100.0	100.0	100.0	100.0

Table 1 (Cont'd)

Moody Ratings of Bond Holdings for Selected Years

Nonotuck Savings Bank

Public Utility Bonds

Rating	Par Value (thousands of dollars)					
	1914	1919	1922	1929	1932	1938
Aaa	20	28	33	59	--	15
Aa	--	--	5	60	75	65
A	16	--	58	53	25	--
Total	36	28	96	172	100	80
Baa	15	48	--	--	--	10
Ba	--	--	--	20	--	20
B	--	--	20	--	20	--
Total	15	48	20	20	20	30
Caa	--	--	--	--	--	--
No rating	--	25	--	--	--	2
Total	51	101	116	192	120	112

Rating	Percentage of Par Value					
	1914	1919	1922	1929	1932	1938
Aaa	39.2	27.7	28.5	30.7	--	13.4
Aa	--	--	4.3	31.3	62.5	58.0
A	31.4	--	50.0	27.6	20.8	--
Total	70.6	27.7	82.8	89.6	83.3	71.4
Baa	29.4	47.5	--	--	--	8.9
Ba	--	--	--	10.4	--	17.9
B	--	--	17.2	--	16.7	--
Total	29.4	47.5	17.2	10.4	16.7	26.8
Caa	--	--	--	--	--	--
No rating	--	24.8	--	--	--	1.8
Total	100.0	100.0	100.0	100.0	100.0	100.0

Table 1 (Cont'd)

Moody Ratings of Bond Holdings for Selected Years

Florence Savings Bank

Public Utility Bonds

Rating	Par Value (thousands of dollars)					
	1914	1919	1922	1929	1932	1938
Aaa	11	18	27	77	52	22
Aa	--	--	5	55	105	73
A	25	--	40	85	99	75
Total	36	18	72	217	256	170
Baa	35	35	--	--	5	71
Ba	--	--	--	35	15	10
B	--	--	35	--	35	--
Total	35	35	35	35	55	81
Caa	--	--	--	--	--	--
No rating	--	40	--	--	10	--
Total	71	93	107	252	321	251

Rating	Percentage of Par Value					
	1914	1919	1922	1929	1932	1938
Aaa	15.5	19.4	25.2	30.6	16.2	8.7
Aa	--	--	4.7	21.8	32.7	29.1
A	35.2	--	37.4	33.7	30.9	29.9
Total	50.7	19.4	67.3	86.1	79.8	67.7
Baa	49.3	37.6	--	--	1.5	28.3
Ba	--	--	--	13.9	4.7	4.0
B	--	--	32.7	--	10.9	--
Total	49.3	37.6	32.7	13.9	17.1	32.3
Caa	--	--	--	--	--	--
No rating	--	43.0	--	--	3.1	--
Total	100.0	100.0	100.0	100.0	100.0	100.0

Table 1 (Cont'd)

Moody Ratings of Bond Holdings for Selected Years

Northampton Institution for Savings

Public Funds

	Par Value (thousands of dollars)				
Rating	1919	1922	1929	1932	1938
Aaa	1,138	1,366	324	87	2,304
Aa	--	--	--	160	--
A	--	--	--	50	5
Total	1,138	1,366	324	297	2,309
Baa	--	--	--	--	24
Ba	--	--	--	--	--
B	--	--	--	--	--
Total	--	--	--	--	24
Caa	--	--	--	--	--
No rating	4	29	2	246	26
Total	1,142	1,395	326	543	2,359

	Percentage of Par Value				
Rating	1919	1922	1929	1932	1938
Aaa	99.6	97.9	99.4	16.0	97.7
Aa	--	--	--	29.5	--
A	--	--	--	9.2	0.2
Total	99.6	97.9	99.4	54.7	97.9
Baa	--	--	--	--	1.0
Ba	--	--	--	--	--
B	--	--	--	--	--
Total	--	--	--	--	1.0
Caa	--	--	--	--	--
No rating	0.4	2.1	0.6	45.3	1.1
Total	100.0	100.0	100.0	100.0	100.0

Table 1 (Cont'd)

Moody Ratings of Bond Holdings for Selected Years

Nonotuck Savings Bank

Public Funds

Rating	Par Value (thousands of dollars) 1919	1922	1929	1932	1938
Aaa	231	304	49	38	251
Aa	--	--	--	5	10
A	--	--	--	--	--
Total	231	304	49	43	261
Baa	--	--	--	--	5
Ba	--		--	--	--
B	--	--	--	--	--
Total	--	--	--	--	5
Caa	--	--	--	--	--
No Rating	5	3	--	25	10
Total	236	307	49	68	276

Rating	Percentage of Par Value 1919	1922	1929	1932	1938
Aaa	97.9	99.0	100.0	55.9	91.0
Aa	--	--	--	7.3	3.6
A	--	--	--	--	--
Total	97.9	99.0	100.0	63.2	94.6
Baa	--	--	--	--	1.8
Ba	--	--	--	--	--
B	--	--	--	--	--
Total	--	--	--	--	1.8
Caa	--	--	--	--	--
No rating	2.1	1.0	--	36.8	3.6
Total	100.0	100.0	100.0	100.0	100.0

Table 1 (Cont'd)

Moody Ratings of Bond Holdings for Selected Years

Florence Savings Bank

Public Funds

Rating	Par Value (thousands of dollars)				
	1919	1922	1929	1932	1938
Aaa	68	185	145	123	181
Aa	--	--	10	--	--
A	--	--	--	--	--
Total	68	185	155	123	181
Baa	--	--	--	--	--
Ba	--	--	--	--	--
B	--	--	--	--	--
Total	--	--	--	--	--
Caa	--	--	--	--	--
No rating	--	--	5	25	--
Total	68	185	160	148	181

Rating	Percentage of Par Value				
	1919	1922	1929	1932	1938
Aaa	100.0	100.0	90.6	83.1	100.0
Aa	--	--	6.3	--	--
A	--	--	--	--	--
Total	100.0	100.0	96.9	83.1	100.0
Baa	--	--	--	--	--
Ba	--	--	--	--	--
B	--	--	--	--	--
Total	--	--	--	--	--
Caa	--	--	--	--	--
No rating	--	--	3.1	16.9	--
Total	100.0	100.0	100.0	100.0	100.0

In the Northampton Institution for Savings, which had the largest investment in railroad securities, 86.3 per cent of the par value of its railroad bonds were rated A or better by the Moody agency, indicating high investment quality. Some of its railroad bonds, however, fell in the more speculative Baa class, and 3.2 per cent were given no rating.

The railroad obligations owned by the Nonotuck Savings Bank were extremely small in amount, and their ratings were not as high as those placed on the securities held by the Northampton Institution for Savings. Bonds rated A or better amounted to 72.7 per cent of the total railroad holdings of the Nonotuck bank, and about 18.2 per cent received no rating. All others were classed in the Baa group.

The Florence bank likewise owned relatively few railroad bonds. All these were rated Baa or better, with 40.0 per cent given the highest rating of Aaa, 17.1 per cent rated Aa, and 42.9 per cent rated Baa.

1914. In 1914 there were few changes made by Moody's in the investment rating of railroad securities held by the Northampton banks. In both the Northampton Institution for Savings and the Nonotuck bank there was some shift to lower ratings, although the changes were slight. In the Florence bank a larger proportion of railroad bonds was rated A or better in 1914 than in 1911, but in the later year some of the bonds received no rating.

In 1914, ratings were placed by Moody's upon the bonds of public utility companies as well as upon railroad bonds. The public utility holdings of the Northampton banks were smaller in amount than the railroad bonds and the investment standing of the utility bonds was lower on the whole than that of the railroad securities, except in the case of the Nonotuck Savings Bank. However, none of the public utility bonds was rated below Baa by Moody's Service.

1919. In 1919 and subsequent years, Moody ratings were published for public funds and comparisons may therefore be made of the entire bond portfolios of the Northampton banks for 1919 and the years following.

About 73 per cent of the bonds owned by both the Northampton

Institution for Savings and the Nonotuck Savings Bank in 1919 were rated A or better, about 20 per cent were in the three B classes, and about 6 per cent received no rating. The bonds of the Florence bank received somewhat lower ratings on the whole than did the securities of the other two banks. Of its bonds, 51.5 per cent were rated A or better, 34.6 per cent were placed in B classes, and 13.9 per cent were given no rating. The somewhat lower rating of the bonds of the Florence bank can be explained in part by the smaller importance of United States Treasury bonds in that bank than in the other two banks, since Treasury bonds received the highest possible rating.

In each of the banks the distribution of railroad bonds among the different rating classes shifted slightly downward from 1914 to 1919. This would be expected as a result of the intervening war years. Two-thirds of the railroad bonds of the Nonotuck bank were still rated A or better, however, and a somewhat larger percentage of the bonds of the Northampton Institution for Savings. In the Florence bank only one-half of the railroad bonds were considered above Baa grade.

The public utility securities owned by each of the banks underwent a definite downward movement from 1914 to 1919. This resulted from the ownership of bonds of street railway companies, which suffered a decline during these years, in part because of the abnormal war period and in part because of the increasing competition of motor vehicles. Those utility bonds which did maintain their rating in the Aaa group were American Telephone and Telegraph Company bonds.

1922. From 1919 to 1922 the Northampton banks increased their investment in bonds and their bond portfolios showed a general improvement in quality, as indicated by the Moody ratings. The higher standing resulted from the post-war expansion and from the continued heavy investment in Aaa Treasury bonds.

In 1922 there was still great uncertainty about the future earning capacity and investment status of railroads, and consequently no great improvement occurred in the rating distribution of the railroad securities owned by the banks. However, bonds formerly rated B or Ba largely disappeared, chiefly through rises in their ratings. In 1922 none of the Northampton banks owned bonds upon which Moody's Service had placed no rating.

The quality of the public utility bonds owned by the Northampton banks improved to a marked degree from 1919 to 1922. This resulted from the further purchase of telephone company bonds of high standing and from the improved rating of the bonds of certain of the street railway companies which had undergone reorganization.

1929. From 1922 to 1929, when conditions were moving from the brief post-war decline through a period of prosperity and of tremendous activity in the security markets, there was great improvement in the ratings of the bonds held by the Northampton banks. Although the banks largely withdrew from ownership of Treasury bonds, they purchased high grade railroad securities and public utility company bonds, chiefly those of telephone and electric power companies. Furthermore, the investment status of many railroad bonds improved.

Upon the basis of the ratings of securities held by the banks, the portfolios reached a peak of investment quality in 1929. Between 87 and 89 per cent of the bonds owned by the banks were rated A or better, and more than one-half received the highest rating of Aaa. Almost all of the remainder of the bonds were rated Baa or Ba. Improvement in quality occurred in both railroad and public utility bonds. In 1929 most of the public utility group consisted of power company bonds which had become legal investments by the act of 1926.

1932. The collapse of the security markets in 1929 and the continued depression of the following years are reflected sharply in the downward changes in bond ratings from 1929 to 1932. Almost 90 per cent of the bonds owned by the banks had been classed as A or better in 1929 but three years later only 68.0 per cent of the bonds of the Northampton Institution for Savings and 69.2 per cent of those of the Florence bank were so classed. The bonds of the Nonotuck Savings Bank suffered a greater decline to 60.2 per cent. The remainder of the bonds of the banks were either distributed among the three B classes or given no rating.

The apparent deterioration in the quality of the bond portfolios reflected the general pessimism, the low level of business activity, and the depression in the bond market. The decline in ratings occurred chiefly as a consequence of changes in the rating of railroad bonds held by the banks from 1929 to 1932. Many railroad bonds dropped one or two rating classes and some fell even further. Public utility holdings of the banks suffered few changes in standing, although the distribution of ratings was altered slightly by the almost complete turnover which took place in this group.

1938. The bond market continued to reflect a pessimistic outlook in 1938 and business had not recovered the buoyancy of the prosperous twenties. Consequently, the rating of securities owned by the Northampton banks showed no improvement over 1932. Although bonds in the Aaa group continued to be the largest single class of investment, the proportion of bonds considered A or better declined further and the B, Ba, and Baa groups increased. Moreover, the banks held certain bonds which received a rating of Caa, that is, Moody's Investors Service considered them of highly uncertain value. The quality of the bond portfolios as a whole was upheld by United States Treasury bonds, with their high investment standing.

The rating of railroad bonds owned by each of the banks showed a sharp decline from 1932 to 1938 and the ratings in 1932 had been lower than in the previous years shown. Baa and Ba bonds were the largest classes, with few bonds rated Aaa or Aa. The rating of Caa was placed upon a considerable portion of the bonds.

The status of utility bonds was much higher in 1938 than that of rails. The utility holdings were rated slightly lower in 1938 than in 1932, but a substantial part were considered high grade and sound investments. Few were rated lower than Baa. Although the total volume decreased slightly from 1932 to 1938, the public utility holdings of the banks were perhaps the most active in the portfolios. This activity was caused, at least in part, by the calling and refunding of bonds by public utility companies.

Conclusion. The bond portfolios of the Northampton banks improved in quality, as measured by Moody ratings, when conditions lapsed back toward normal from 1919 to 1922. Improvement continued over the years of prosperity from 1922 to 1929. After 1929, however, a drastic decline occurred and the distribution of bonds among the ratings was much lower in 1932 than in 1929. In 1938 the distribution remained low.

As rated by Moody's Service, railroad bonds held by the banks represented sound investments in the early years. Their quality was adversely affected in the war years and they did not recover their standing until after 1922. By 1929, however, they again ranked high. They suffered especially severely in the years after 1929 and this decline was particularly serious because of the great volume of investment in them.

The nature of the public utility company bonds underwent great changes from 1914 to 1938 and the ratings reflected these changes. In the early years this class of investment consisted chiefly of street railway company bonds. These fell in investment quality before and during the first World War and in general remained somewhat lower in quality in the 1920's than did other bonds of the utility group. The banks also invested in telephone company bonds before the war and they continued to hold such bonds through 1938, for telephone company bonds consistently received the highest possible rating. After 1926 the banks could invest widely in electric power companies and such investments constituted the majority of the public utility holdings in 1929, 1932, and 1938. On the whole, the experience of the banks with power and light companies was more satisfactory than with street railway or railroad bonds.

United States Treasury bonds greatly improved the quality of the bond portfolios in 1919, 1922, and 1938, when investment in Government obligations was high and when other bonds owned by the banks had declined in quality.

In each of the banks, individual issues of street railway company bonds and of railroad obligations were held for relatively long periods, as compared with public funds and bonds of electric power companies. Although the banks would have improved their positions by disposing of certain of their street railway and railroad bonds, such disposal would have involved very considerable losses and the banks were unwilling and unable fully to realize these losses. Furthermore, their need for liquidity was not sufficiently pressing to necessitate their sacrificing bonds which were falling in price.

F. DATE OF MATURITY OF BONDS

It has been many times suggested that banks should follow a policy of staggering the maturity dates of their loans and investments in order to insure that they will continually have funds becoming available for withdrawals and in order to spread the risk of changes in the yield on investments. In order to determine what had been the practice of the Northampton banks the maturity distribution of the bond portfolios was calculated for seven years, as shown in Table 2.

Definite change occurred from the preponderance of long-term bonds in the first two years shown in the table to the dispersion of maturities which existed in the later years. In 1911 (1908 for the Northampton Institution for Savings) and in 1914, more than half of the bonds owned by each of the banks were to mature after an interval of more than twenty years. Almost three-fourths of the bonds of the Florence bank were of this length. In 1919 and subsequent years, the bonds spread themselves over time rather than congregating in the eleven to fifty year groups as they had done in 1911 and 1914.

The long maturities, especially those exceeding twenty years, resulted from the relatively long terms for which railroad bonds were issued. Gas and electric company bonds, which were legally limited to forty years (thirty years during part of the period studied), contributed heavily to the twenty-one to fifty year group. The spreading of maturities was brought about chiefly through public funds, since these bonds varied greatly in currency and their maturity rarely extended beyond twenty years. The shift to less than twenty year bonds in 1932 and 1938 was brought about largely through the purchase of United States Treasury bonds. In addition, some bonds were held throughout all these years after 1911 and, in so far as this was true, merely the passing of time meant a shortening of the remaining currency of the bonds.

Low yields, such as those prevailing in the later years, together with the possibility of higher rates in the future, encouraged banks to invest in relatively short-term obligations, in so far as these were available. A slight rise in the interest rate on the bond market causes a greater drop in the value of long-term bonds already issued than in the value of short-

Table 2

Maturity Distribution of Bond Holdings for Selected Years*

Florence Savings Bank

Years to Maturity	Percentage of the Par Value of All Bonds Owned 1911	1914	1919	1922	1929	1932	1938
0- 2	--	--	0.6	3.5	4.8	0.6	1.7
3- 5	--	--	6.1	8.9	4.8	3.2	6.8
6-10	4.3	--	14.1	4.5	16.5	13.4	12.0
11-20	23.9	23.9	18.0	15.2	22.7	27.6	26.5
21-50	71.8	71.4	51.5	58.0	38.9	43.1	35.6
over 50	--	4.7	9.7	9.9	12.3	12.1	17.4
	100.0	100.0	100.0	100.0	100.0	100.0	100.0

Nonotuck Savings Bank

Years to Maturity	Percentage of the Par Value of All Bonds Owned 1911	1914	1919	1922	1929	1932	1938
0- 2	2.0	1.1	7.6	3.3	--	3.2	1.5
3- 5	--	0.8	13.7	2.6	5.4	9.0	0.8
6-10	--	7.5	16.0	18.3	8.2	9.4	24.2
11-20	40.3	36.5	30.5	50.5	17.3	13.5	17.5
21-50	57.7	54.1	27.6	18.7	42.2	38.1	34.8
over 50	--	--	4.6	6.6	26.9	26.8	21.2
	100.0	100.0	100.0	100.0	100.0	100.0	100.0

Northampton Institution for Savings

Years to Maturity	Percentage of the Par Value of All Bonds Owned 1908	1914	1919	1922	1929	1932	1938
0- 2	2.0	3.6	0.6	0.1	0.3	1.9	2.8
3- 5	8.0	2.1	6.5	7.4	1.5	6.0	6.7
6-10	7.5	1.9	14.2	14.8	11.4	16.1	25.6
11-20	21.6	28.9	32.7	38.1	28.6	21.9	24.7
21-50	54.6	56.1	34.7	27.0	35.2	30.7	26.3
over 50	6.3	7.4	11.3	12.6	23.0	23.4	13.9
	100.0	100.0	100.0	100.0	100.0	100.0	100.0

* Percentages, which refer to holdings as of October 31 of each year, were computed from information furnished by the banks. It was assumed that the maturity of serial issues was spread evenly over the years during which the bonds were maturing and that Treasury bonds would be paid at maturity.

term bonds. Furthermore, if bonds are of short maturity, it is possible to reinvest at higher rates when and if these occur in the near future. If bonds are of longer maturity, however, reinvestment at the higher rate is impossible without the sale of securities, and such sale would involve a loss because of the increase in current yields on the market, that is, the drop in bond prices. On the other hand, in times of low yields it is to the advantage of the corporation to issue bonds for as long a term as possible.

Although the banks recognize the desirability of spreading the maturity of bonds through the coming years, such a distribution is difficult to achieve in actual practice. Market offerings and the divergence in yields on bonds of different terms may lead to a lack of scattering of maturities. In the later years the calling and the refunding of many issues disrupted any schedule of maturities which the banks set up. This is to be expected in periods of low interest rates, when it is profitable for a corporation to refund its debt into bonds bearing the current low rate of interest.

G. CREDIT SERVICE TO NEW ENGLAND

Legal regulations pertaining to investments of Massachusetts savings banks indicate the belief that these banks should serve Massachusetts first of all. Investments elsewhere have been permitted, but preference has been shown first to Massachusetts citizens, corporations, and governmental units, then to corporations and units of government in New England, and last to corporations and governments in other regions of the United States. Because real estate loans have been limited to property situated in Massachusetts, a large proportion of the funds placed on deposit in the banks has been invested within the state. Loans on personal security were also extended primarily to Massachusetts citizens and corporations. Although investment was permitted in the stock of banks located anywhere in New England, the Northampton savings banks invested only in banks located within Massachusetts. Thus, with respect to loans and bank stock, which together made up a very considerable part of the assets, the Northampton banks served Massachusetts exclusively in the extension of credit.

In the case of securities other than bank stock, the banks invested heavily in companies operating chiefly in New England. The bonds held by the banks have been classified at five-year intervals into two groups: bonds issued by companies serving primarily the New England states, and those issued by companies operating outside of New England. In Table 3 the par value of the bonds of companies serving primarily the New England area is shown as a percentage of the par value of all bonds. This reflects not only the investment opportunities in various regions and the need of the banks for investment outlets but also changes in legal requirements.

Table 3

Investment in Bonds of New England Issuers in Per Cent of All Bonds Owned by the Banks at Five Year Intervals from 1880 to 1935*

Year	Percentage of the Par Value of All Bonds Owned: Northampton Institution for Savings	Florence Savings Bank	Hampshire Savings Bank	Nonotuck Savings Bank
1880	49	**	**	
1885	67	**	**	
1890	94	100	100	
1895	59	100	100	
1900	70	6		**
1905	71	11		27
1910	69	56		36
1915	72	64		59
1920	39	44		26
1925	41	43		22
1930	40	38		33
1935	32	26		28

* Percentages, which refer to holdings as of October 31 of each year, were computed from information obtained from the annual reports of the Commissioner of Banks and from Moody's manuals of investment.

** No bonds were owned.

Before 1900 the railroads in whose bonds the banks invested were roads incorporated in or serving New England; this resulted from legal limitations. After 1900 there was a gradual easing of the restrictions and investment in certain railroads outside of New England was authorized. The banks took advantage of this broadening of the investment field, as indicated by the decreasing percentages shown in the table.

Public funds reflected to a considerable degree the amount of financing being undertaken by the Federal Government. When the United States Treasury issued many bonds, the banks invested in them, but in the intervals when the volume of Federal financing was small the banks invested more heavily in municipal bonds and, during the later years, in state bonds. With the flotation of large issues after the United States entered the War of 1914, the savings banks' investment in United States bonds increased and it did not decrease until the middle of the twenties. When the depression of 1932 brought continued heavy borrowing by the Treasury and lack of private investment opportunities, the banks increased and maintained their holdings of Treasury obligations.

Public utility investment was at first restricted to New England companies. Street railway bonds, which were only a small proportion of the bond portfolios, were exclusively those issued by Massachusetts companies. Telephone company bonds, which were small in amount, were for the most part those issued by companies not serving New England exclusively; they were chiefly American Telephone and Telegraph Company bonds. Investment in bonds of gas, water, and electric companies became important only in the later years after the revision of the law in 1926, and few of the issues were those of New England companies.

In the years preceding the War of 1914, the bonds of New England companies constituted the major part of the entire bond portfolios of the Northampton banks, but after the war the New England bonds were of less importance, ranging between 20 per cent and 45 per cent of all bonds held. Two important elements entered into this change: the increased investment in Treasury obligations during and immediately after the war and during the depression, and the increase in public utility holdings following the 1926 change in the legal list. In addition there was a gradual easing of the geographical restrictions placed upon all kinds of bonds eligible for investment by the savings banks. In the later years the banks did not invest primarily in bonds of companies serving New England; nevertheless, from the viewpoint of total investments, including loans (which were granted exclusively to Massachusetts citizens and corporations), stocks, and bonds, the banks served primarily the New England area in which they are located and thus they were fulfilling one of the fundamental purposes of the mutual savings banks.

Chapter III

THE DEPOSITS OF THE SAVINGS BANKS

A. AMOUNT DUE DEPOSITORS

1. Growth of Amount Due Depositors

The balance on deposit in each of the banks grew almost continuously from 1876 until 1938, as shown in Charts 27, 28, and 29. The increase in the amount due depositors is about equivalent, however, to the dividends [interest] paid on the deposit balances. In a sense, therefore, the savings banks simply maintained themselves.

Through the period covered by the charts, the Northampton Institution for Savings has had the largest total deposits of any of the Northampton mutual savings banks. Its deposits rose from somewhat less than two million dollars in 1876 to twelve million dollars in 1931 and remained between eleven and twelve million dollars in the 1930's. With the exception of a few years, deposits grew steadily. In 1877, 1878, and 1879, in 1908, in 1918, and in certain of the years following 1931, total deposit liabilities decreased but in every other year they showed an increase.

The years in which deposits failed to rise were years in which business was dull. The late 1870's were years of depression, following the Civil War inflation and the panic of 1873. Thus deposits declined in 1877, 1878, and 1879. The fall in deposit liabilities in 1908 was a reflection of the lull in manufacturing activity in Northampton in 1907 and in the early part of 1908. As shown in Chart 2, page 7, the drop in manufacturing activity was apparent in the value of product, in the number employed, and in the sum of all wages paid in manufacturing. Again in 1918 there was a temporary lessening of business activity by reason of the tapering off of war contracts. The resulting decline in business activity, together with the competition of war bonds, led to a decrease in deposit balances in the Northampton Institution for Savings.

Chart 27

AMOUNT OF DEPOSITS AND WITHDRAWALS

Florence Savings Bank, 1876-1938

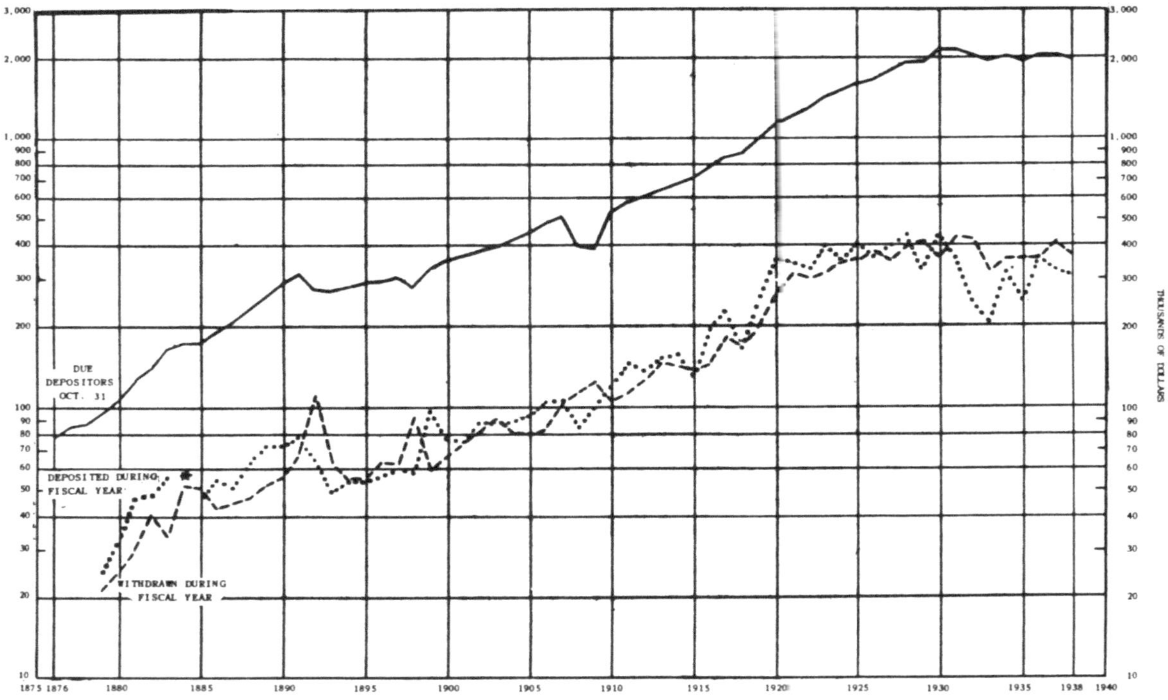

* Data are not available for amount deposited in 1884.

Source: Mass. Commissioner of Banks. *Annual Report*. 1876-1938.

c-38

Chart 28

AMOUNT OF DEPOSITS AND WITHDRAWALS

Hampshire Savings Bank, 1876-1897

Nonotuck Savings Bank, 1899-1938

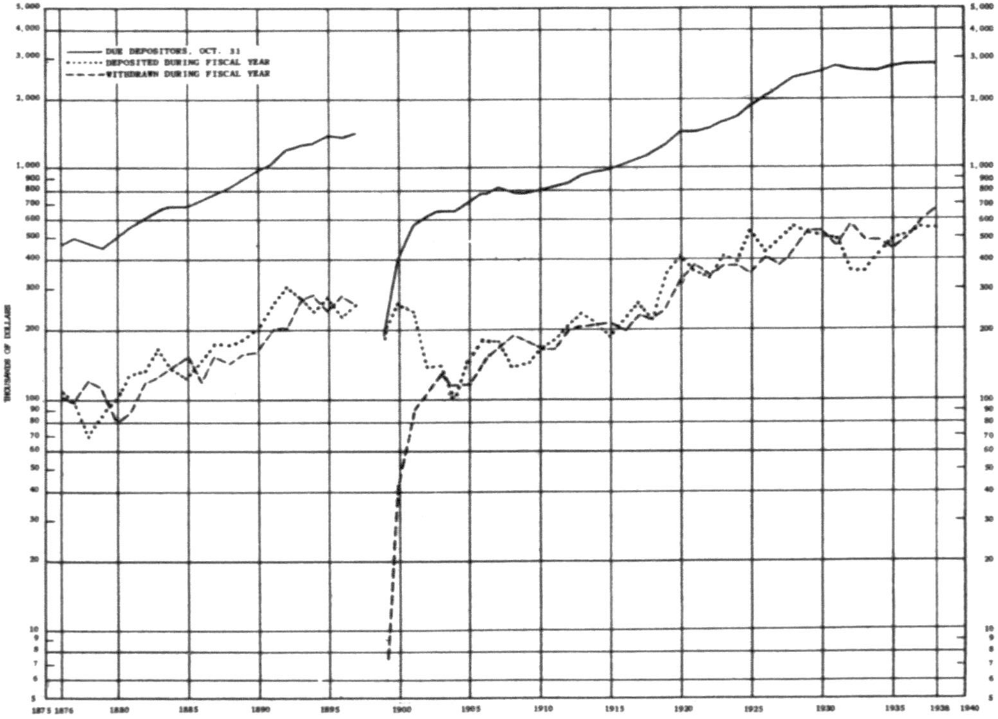

Source: Mass. Commissioner of Banks. *Annual Report.* 1876-1938.

Chart 29

AMOUNT OF DEPOSITS AND WITHDRAWALS

Northampton Institution for Savings, 1876-1938

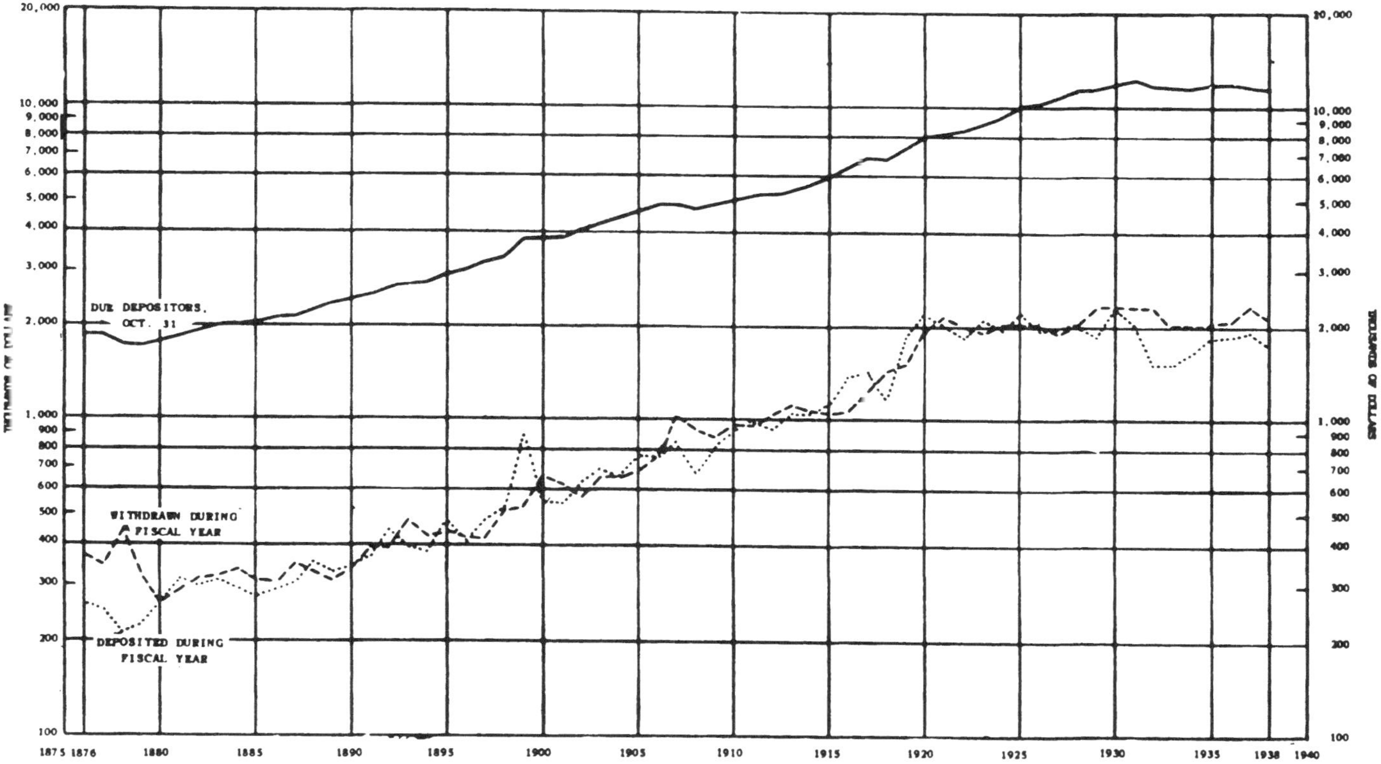

Source: Mass. Commissioner of Banks. *Annual Report*. 1876-1938.

The decline in deposit liabilities after 1931 resulted from the country-wide depression. In the early years of the depression the Northampton factories either were not operating or were operating with a reduced staff, and many wage earners, therefore, found it necessary to draw heavily upon their savings. Inasmuch as the incomes of other groups were also reduced, there were no compensating increases in savings deposits.

Growth of the amount due depositors in the Northampton Institution for Savings may well be compared with the amount of dividends paid by the bank. For the period as a whole, the amount due depositors increased at a rate about equivalent to the semi-annual dividend. From 1879 to 1899 and from 1912 to 1918, deposits grew at about the rate at which dividends were paid. From 1899 to 1906 and from 1918 to 1920 the deposit liabilities increased more rapidly than the semi-annual dividend would have indicated, but from 1907 to 1912 and from 1920 to 1931, dividends exceeded the growth of deposit balances.

In contrast to the Northampton Institution for Savings, the Florence Savings Bank shows a somewhat greater percentage growth in its total deposit liabilities from 1876 to 1938, a growth from $79,000 to $1,991,000. Deposits in the Florence Savings Bank grew continuously with the exception of the following years: 1892 and 1893, 1898, 1908 and 1909, and the years after 1931. Growth was especially rapid during the 1880's, from 1900 to 1907, and from 1910 to 1925.

The deposit liabilities of the Florence Savings Bank grew at rates higher than the semi-annual dividends from 1876 until 1929, except in the years from 1892 to 1898 and in 1908 and 1909.

Balance due depositors in the Hampshire Savings Bank was lower in 1879 than in 1876 (which was also true in the case of the Northampton Institution for Savings) but it increased from about one-half million dollars in 1879 to almost one and one-half million dollars in 1897. The most rapid increase occurred in the years from 1887 to 1892, which were also years of rapid growth in the deposit liabilities of the other two banks.

The Nonotuck Savings Bank grew rapidly after its organization and the balance due its depositors soon exceeded the deposits in the Florence Savings Bank. Throughout the entire period the deposit liabilities of the Nonotuck bank showed a strong upward trend and reached almost three million dollars in 1937. Decreases occurred in only a few years: in 1908 and 1909, when deposits in the Florence Savings Bank and the Northampton Institution for Savings were also low, and in the 1930's. The peak in the deposit liabilities of the Nonotuck bank came in 1937, although deposits were only slightly larger then than in 1931.

Except for the period from 1912 to 1917, the amount due depositors in the Nonotuck bank grew at a rate equal to or higher than the rate of semi-annual dividend payments. Deposits showed a particularly rapid growth in the earliest years of the bank. After 1901 the expansion was less rapid and was similar to the rate of increase in the deposits at the other banks.

Balances on deposit in the Nonotuck bank continued to rise slightly in the 1930's and reached a new high level in 1937. This is contrary to the experience of the other banks, whose deposit liabilities reached a peak in 1931. The reason for this divergent trend is that the Nonotuck bank received deposits from people who for a number of years had maintained accounts in the older banks, especially the Northampton Institution for Savings, and who either wished to place their additional savings in another bank or were forced to do so because of the legal maximum prevailing on deposits. Another factor in the continued growth of the Nonotuck bank as compared with the Florence bank was that several establishments moved out of the Florence manufacturing area, while activity was better maintained in the trading center, where the Nonotuck bank is located. The greater convenience of location enjoyed by the Nonotuck bank may also have contributed to its rapid and continued growth.

In all four banks, deposits maintained a strong upward trend throughout the years. The occasional declines in the amount due depositors or decreases in the rate of growth reflected changes in general business conditions in Northampton.

2. Seasonal Variation in Deposit Liability

Information is not available for showing in detail the typical monthly variations in deposit liabilities. However, the pattern of seasonal variation seems fairly well defined. During the year there are two peaks in deposit balances, which occur at the time of dividend payments.

In the case of the Northampton Institution for Savings and the Florence Savings Bank, withdrawals rise immediately after the payment of dividends in April and October. It is to avoid the loss of interest income that withdrawals are frequently deferred until the dividend date. Some of the withdrawals are not of the deferred-withdrawal kind, however, but are the result of the need for money with which to pay October taxes, to buy coal, and to meet other expenses recurring each year. From May to October deposit liabilities are usually relatively stable. In the case of the Nonotuck bank, withdrawals are high in October, when taxes are payable, and again at the end of December after the December dividend payment.

Cash for meeting the fairly highly concentrated withdrawal demand is provided by synchronizing the due date of interest payments on the loans extended by the banks. In earlier years tax anticipation notes were often purchased by the banks in order to provide cash for withdrawal.

3. Christmas Club Deposits

Since 1919 the savings banks of Massachusetts have been permitted to accept Christmas club deposits. Both the size of such deposits and the interest to be paid are regulated by statute.[1]

The Florence bank, which was the first of the Northampton banks to report Christmas club deposits, showed about $22,000 of such deposits in October, 1920, the first year after club deposits had been authorized. The amount doubled in the next three years and remained high throughout the 1920's. In the 1930's, club deposits were smaller, reaching a low point in 1933, but by 1938 they were somewhat larger and amounted to $26,000.

The Northampton Institution for Savings first reported Christmas club deposits in 1921. The club deposits were generally at a higher level in the 1930's than in the 1920's, and in 1938 they reached a peak of $33,000. Not until 1936 was the amount

[1] According to Chapter 37, Acts of 1919, Christmas club deposits were not to exceed the statutory limit upon the size of deposits in savings banks and the maximum rate of interest was established at 1 per cent less than the rate of the last regular dividend.

of club deposits in the Northampton Institution for Savings as large as the deposits of the Florence bank.

The Nonotuck bank reported no Christmas club deposits until 1923 and in each year until 1936 such deposits were less than $10,000, even though the total deposit liabilities of the Nonotuck bank were larger than those of the Florence bank. In 1936 and in the following years the Christmas club deposits of the Nonotuck bank were larger than was formerly the case but even so they were decidedly smaller than those of the other two banks.

Christmas club deposits have varied considerably from bank to bank. They were larger in the Florence bank during the 1920's than in either of the other two institutions; in the 1930's, the other two banks experienced an increasing volume of club deposits. Relative to size, Christmas club deposits have been largest in the case of the Florence bank. Variations between the banks are to be accounted for in part by the extent to which such deposits were solicited and in part by the difference in the economic communities served by the banks. The Florence bank, originally known as the "Workingmen's Savings Bank," is located in an industrial area of the city and its depositors have represented a somewhat lower income level than the depositors of the downtown banks. Such groups are more interested in plans for the regular setting aside of funds for Christmas expenditures than are other income groups.

B. SIZE OF DEPOSIT ACCOUNTS

1. Legal Regulation

From their earliest years, Massachusetts mutual savings banks have been looked upon as institutions to encourage thrift and to provide for the safety of the savings of the less well-to-do. The petition to the General Court relating to the organization of the Provident Institution for Savings, the first mutual savings bank chartered in Massachusetts, states that the bank was to be organized in order that "all classes of the community may be exercised to the practice of frugality and especially industrial mechanics, either journeymen or masters, seamen, laborers, and men of small capital, widows, and others, may receive from their savings of wages or profits, regularly deposited and systematically invested in public stocks or otherwise, a profit proportional to the success of the institution and prosperity of the country."[2]

To insure that the banks are used primarily by small savers, the state of Massachusetts has limited the size of the balance which an individual may hold on deposit in any one savings bank. In 1876, Massachusetts savings banks were permitted to receive deposits from any one person until they amounted to $1,000. The banks were allowed to pay interest on the sum of the balance deposited and the accumulated interest until the sum amounted to $1,600.[3] After 1876 the maximum deposit which the banks could accept was gradually increased so that after 1927 the banks could receive deposits from one person until the deposit balance amounted to $4,000. The banks were allowed to pay interest on the principal and on the accumulated interest until the sum amounted to $8,000, after which no interest could be paid.[4] The changes in the limits are shown below.

Table 4

Legal Limits upon the Size of Deposit Balances*

Year	Deposits may be received until they amount to	Interest may be paid until the sum of principal and accrued interest amounts to
1876	$1,000	$1,600
1908	1,000	2,000
1919	2,000	4,000
1924	3,000	6,000
1927	4,000	8,000

* Mass. Acts 1876, c. 203, sec. 8; Acts 1908, c. 590, sec. 46; Acts 1919, c. 11; Acts 1924, c. 67, sec. 1; Acts 1927, c. 109, sec. 1.

These limits have not applied to certain deposits, such as those of religious, charitable, and labor organizations and

2 As quoted in Mass. House Doc. No. 1262 (1922), p. 12.
3 Mass. Acts 1876, c. 203, sec. 8.
4 Mass. Acts 1927, c. 109, sec. 1.

those of credit unions. In addition, provision was made for doubling the maximum in the case of joint accounts.

Restriction of the size of deposits safeguards the banks in that the danger of large concentrated withdrawals is thereby reduced. Northampton savings banks have further protected themselves in this regard by their reluctance to accept either deposits originating outside of Hampshire County or large initial deposits which seem to constitute funds awaiting investment opportunity. When the maximum size of the deposit is kept low, money that is temporarily idle and awaiting permanent investment opportunities is not likely to be placed in savings banks.

2. Average Size of Deposit Account

In each bank a long-time upward movement in the average size of the balance on deposit has taken place. This has resulted from the crediting of dividends to the deposit accounts, increases in the legal maxima, and the decline in the purchasing power of the dollar. For identical years the average size of deposit accounts was approximately the same in the Northampton Institution for Savings and in the Hampshire Savings Bank or in the Nonotuck bank, but average deposits in the Florence Savings Bank were considerably smaller throughout the entire period. These facts are brought out in Chart 30.

From 1876 to 1905 the average size of deposit accounts in the Northampton Institution for Savings fluctuated around $400. While there was variability in the average, it tended to increase slightly during these years. In the years before 1905 the average size of deposits in the Florence bank showed a more definite increase, for the average grew from about $160 to $270. The average in each bank remained at about the same level from 1905 to 1915, but a marked increase occurred from 1915 to 1931. Only part of the increase represented an expansion in the purchasing power of the average deposit, by reason of the rapid rise in prices during the war and the high level of prices in the 1920's. After 1931, average deposits showed further increases in size and consequently by 1938 the average balance in the Northampton Institution for Savings was more than $700 and in the Florence bank slightly less than $600.

Chart 30

AVERAGE SIZE OF DEPOSIT ACCOUNTS
October 31 of Each Year, 1876-1938

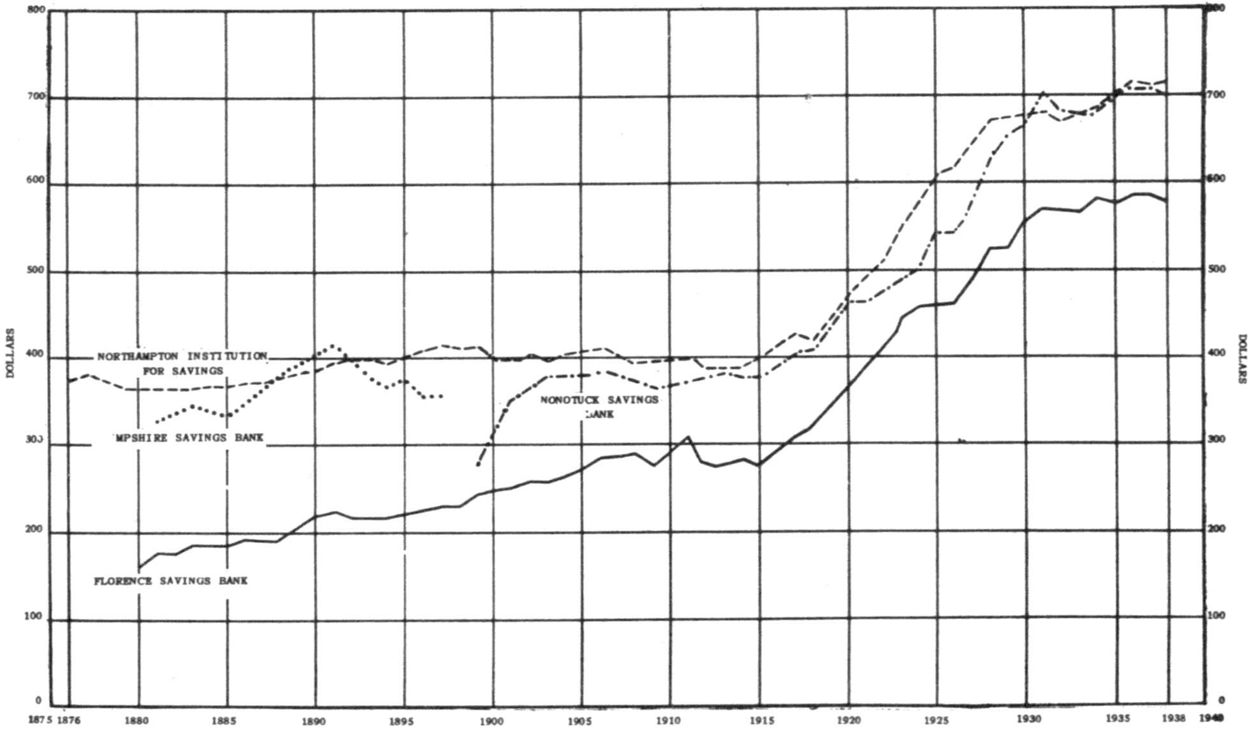

The average size of accounts in the Nonotuck Savings Bank increased rapidly in the first three or four years during which it was operating. Thereafter the average size followed a pattern similar to that of the Northampton Institution for Savings.

In general the average size of deposits varied with the total amount due depositors, as indicated by a comparison of Chart 30, page 122, with Charts 27, 28, and 29, pages 113, 114, and 115. In the years when total deposit liabilities were increasing rapidly, the average size of deposit accounts was usually high and, conversely, when the total deposit liabilities were increasing slowly or falling, the average size of deposits was usually low.

3. Size of Deposits Received during the Year, 1889-1914

In the early years of this period the Bank Commissioner published a classification of deposit receipts for each bank at five year intervals. Each deposit received during the year was classified according to size and according to depositor. The classification for each Northampton bank is presented in Table 5, on the following page. From 1889 to 1914 approximately 15 per cent of the deposits received during the year by each bank consisted of amounts varying between $51 and $100, and deposits of amounts between $101 and $200 made up about the same percentage. The size of the remaining 70 per cent of deposits varied greatly among the different banks.

In the Florence Savings Bank more funds were deposited in amounts of $50 or less than in any other size category. The percentage varied from about 25 per cent to 45 per cent of all deposits made during the year. In 1894 and in 1904, deposits of this size reached their greatest relative importance. Deposits ranging in size from $201 to $500 were the next most important class.

In the Northampton Institution for Savings the deposits of less than $50 were slightly more important than any other size class in 1889 and much more important in 1894. In 1899 and thereafter, however, individual deposits of $201 to $500 became the largest class.

In both the Hampshire Savings Bank and the Nonotuck bank, deposits whose size ranged between $201 and $500 consistently

Table 5

Classification of Amounts Deposited during the Year 1889 to 1914, at Five Year Intervals*

Item	Percentage of the Amount Deposited					
	1889	1894	1899	1904	1909	1914
Size of Deposits						
Florence Savings Bank						
0-$ 50	31.4	33.9	25.4	44.5	32.2	23.7
$ 51- 100	13.6	17.3	14.4	14.3	13.0	14.3
101- 200	12.6	15.2	15.2	11.5	11.0	15.6
201- 500	22.9	17.3	26.5	11.8	23.0	22.0
501-1,000	16.5	8.8	9.3	7.6	11.7	14.7
Over 1,000	3.0	7.5	9.3	10.3	9.1	9.7
Hampshire Savings Bank						
0-$ 50	15.7	13.2				
$ 51- 100	14.7	11.7				
101- 200	12.0	10.3				
201- 500	27.0	27.7				
501-1,000	13.5	35.8				
Over 1,000	17.0	1.2				
Nonotuck Savings Bank						
0-$ 50			4.8	18.6	19.9	18.1
$ 51- 100			6.7	15.4	15.1	14.1
101- 200			12.5	13.5	15.2	13.3
201- 500			37.7	25.7	21.4	25.4
501-1,000			17.7	12.0	11.5	16.4
Over 1,000			20.6	14.7	16.9	12.8
Northampton Institution for Savings						
0-$ 50	22.4	37.6	15.3	21.4	21.0	19.7
$ 51- 100	14.8	12.5	12.9	14.9	15.7	15.3
101- 200	14.1	9.6	15.6	13.5	13.5	12.7
201- 500	21.4	13.1	27.8	23.0	23.0	22.7
501-1,000	13.6	9.3	14.1	13.3	14.1	13.2
Over 1,000	13.8	17.9	14.3	13.9	12.7	16.4
Deposits Made by Women						
Florence Savings Bank	43.7	46.4	45.5	40.3	36.7	36.3
Hampshire Savings Bank	41.0	40.0				
Nonotuck Savings Bank			40.6	42.2	45.2	38.3
Northampton Institution for Savings	37.4	48.3	50.1	45.4	49.0	41.8

* Percentages were computed from data published in the annual reports of the Bank Commissioner, referring to the fiscal year.

exceeded the smaller sized deposits. The data for the Nonotuck bank in 1899 indicate that the size of the first deposits received after the bank was organized was much larger than that of deposits in the other banks in that year and larger than that of deposits in later years.

If account is taken of the number of deposits of various sizes rather than the total amount of such deposits, it is apparent that small deposits predominate (see Table 6). Except for the Nonotuck bank in 1899, deposits of $50 or less always amounted to more than 65 per cent of the total number of deposits received. In five of the six years for which data are available, such deposits were 75 per cent or more of the number of deposits received by the Northampton Institution for Savings. For the three years, 1904, 1909, and 1914, deposits of less than $50 were almost 75 per cent of all deposits made in the Nonotuck bank. Small deposits were of the greatest importance, however, in the Florence Savings Bank, where those of $50 or less ranged from 81 to 86 per cent of the number of deposits received.

Thus, if it can be assumed that the six years for which the classifications are given were typical, the funds held by the Northampton banks were chiefly accumulations of relatively small sums. This is in accordance with the general policy that mutual savings banks should serve primarily the small savers.

4. Deposits Made by Women, 1889-1914

From the beginning it was believed that savings banks should be organized in such a way as to satisfy the needs of the low income groups and of widows and minors. A large proportion of the deposits made during selected years actually were made by women, both adult and minor.

The classification made by the Bank Commissioner at five year intervals treated deposits made by women as a separate item. This classification is shown in Tables 5 and 6. In the six years for which there are reports, the amount deposited by women varied from 36.3 per cent to 50.1 per cent of all the funds deposited during the year in any one of the banks. The number of deposits made by women during the year was between

Table 6

Classification of the Number of Deposits Made during the Year 1889 to 1914, at Five Year Intervals*

Item	Percentage of the Number of Deposits					
	1889	1894	1899	1904	1909	1914
Size of Deposits						
Florence Savings Bank						
0-$ 50	86.2	84.8	80.9	84.3	85.3	85.6
$ 51- 100	6.9	8.7	9.0	8.5	7.2	6.8
101- 200	3.3	3.8	4.9	3.5	3.3	3.9
201- 500	2.6	1.9	4.0	3.0	3.0	2.4
501-1,000	0.9	.0.5	0.7	0.3	0.8	0.8
Over 1,000	**	0.3	0.5	0.4	0.4	0.4
Hampshire Savings Bank						
0-$ 50	66.1	67.4				
$ 51- 100	16.4	13.2				
101- 200	7.2	7.0				
201- 500	6.9	8.2				
501-1,000	1.8	4.1				
Over 1,000	1.6	**				
Nonotuck Savings Bank						
0-$ 50			39.0	74.4	73.9	72.5
$ 51- 100			14.9	12.5	12.8	12.9
101- 200			15.1	5.9	6.8	6.3
201- 500			21.8	5.0	4.3	5.4
501-1,000			5.3	1.2	1.1	1.8
Over 1,000			3.9	1.0	1.2	1.0
Northampton Institution for Savings						
0-$ 50	76.0	81.0	67.3	75.1	74.8	77.0
$ 51- 100	11.7	10.4	13.8	12.3	12.8	11.7
101- 200	6.0	4.1	8.9	6.0	5.7	5.1
201- 500	4.1	2.5	7.2	4.4	4.5	4.0
501-1,000	1.4	0.9	1.7	1.3	1.4	1.2
Over 1,000	0.9	1.2	1.1	0.9	0.8	1.0
Deposits Made by Women						
Florence Savings Bank	46.7	46.8	41.9	41.2	38.2	42.9
Hampshire Savings Bank	45.0	43.2				
Nonotuck Savings Bank			43.3	40.2	40.5	37.9
Northampton Institution for Savings	35.3	41.9	52.1	49.3	46.2	46.3

* Percentages were computed from data published in the annual reports of the Bank Commissioner, referring to the fiscal year.

** Less than one-tenth of one per cent.

37.9 and 46.8 per cent of the total number of deposits made in the Florence, Hampshire, and Nonotuck banks. In the Northampton Institution for Savings, deposits made by women ranged from 35.3 to 52.1 per cent of the total number of deposits. The savings banks were thus serving this group whose needs have been given special recognition.

C. NUMBER OF OPEN ACCOUNTS

The number of open accounts in the banks showed almost continuous growth until the later years of the period considered in this study. The growth is apparent in Chart 31, which shows the total number of deposit accounts on the books of the banks on the thirty-first of October of each year. The accounts in the Northampton Institution for Savings leveled off after 1920, but in the Nonotuck and Florence banks they continued to rise until 1926 or 1927, after which there was little or no increase. Over the entire period the number of accounts in each of the banks showed relatively little variability from one year to the next.

Long-continued growth and lack of fluctuation from year to year are characteristic of the number of open accounts in the Nonotuck Savings Bank. There the number of accounts grew from 1,600 in 1901 to nearly 4,000 in 1930 and to slightly more than 4,000 after 1935. In only a few years did the number of accounts decrease. In 1908, when local business conditions were poor, the number declined; in 1929 and in the 1930's, decreases again took place.

From 1901 to 1931 the number of open accounts in the Florence Savings Bank was almost the same as that in the case of the Nonotuck bank, although the number of accounts in the Florence bank fluctuated more widely from year to year. From 1880 to 1930 there was a definite upward trend which carried the number of accounts from less than 700 to 3,800. In 1938 the number of accounts had fallen to slightly more than 3,400.

The accounts in the Northampton Institution for Savings increased in number from 5,000 in 1876 to 17,000 in 1920. In the 1920's and the 1930's the number was relatively stable.

Changes in the population of Northampton at five year intervals are shown in Chart 1, page 2, to which changes in the

Chart 31

NUMBER OF DEPOSIT ACCOUNTS

October 31 of Each Year, 1876-1938

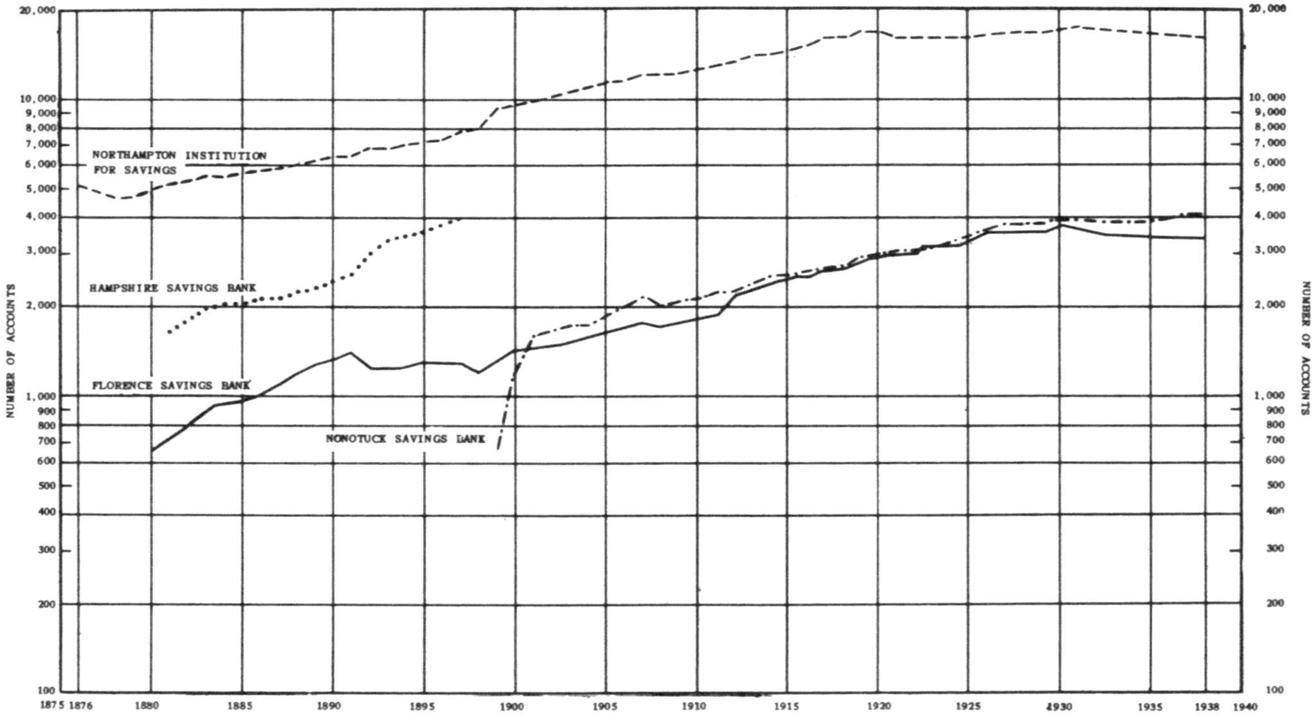

Source: Mass. Commissioner of Banks. *Annual Report*. 1876-1938.

number of accounts shown in Chart 31 may be compared. Both expanded gradually through the period studied. Except for the interval from 1905 to 1910 the population grew slowly but steadily. After 1910, however, the rate of growth was low. Until about 1920 the number of accounts grew more rapidly than population, indicative of the fact that an increasing proportion of the people were making use of the savings banks. In 1920 the number of depositors was approximately the same as the number of people living in Northampton and this relationship continued through 1935. Since some depositors maintained several accounts the total number of accounts overstates the number of depositors.

Table 7

The Number of Open Accounts in Relation to the Total Population*

Year	Accounts as a Percentage of the Population	Year	Accounts as a Percentage of the Population
1885	67	1915	93
1890	68	1920	106
1895	73	1925	98
1900	66	1930	104
1905	75	1935	99
1910	86		

* Computed from data relative to the number of accounts on October 31 as reported in the annual reports of the Bank Commissioner and from data of the decennial census compilation by the Secretary of the Commonwealth of Massachusetts.

D. ACTIVITY OF ACCOUNTS

The activity of deposits in the mutual savings banks of Northampton was studied in much the same manner in which Professor Steiner analyzed the activity of deposits in the mutual savings banks of Massachusetts, Connecticut, New Jersey, and New York from 1900 to 1935.[5] The number of accounts opened and the number

[5] W. H. Steiner, "Activity of Mutual-Savings-Bank Deposits," *Journal of Political Economy*, XLV (1937), 789-803.

closed each year were expressed as percentages of the number of open accounts in order to indicate the yearly turnover. The percentage relationship between the amount deposited and withdrawn during the year and the total amount due depositors was also calculated to show the rate at which dollars were received and paid out.

1. Opening and Closing of Accounts

a) Trends in the Opening and Closing of Accounts

In the Northampton Institution for Savings (Chart 32), the number of accounts opened each year increased on the whole from 1876 to 1916, after which there was a general decline. The closing of accounts followed much the same pattern, although trends were not as sharp as in the number of accounts opened.

Similar long-time movements occurred in the opening and closing of accounts in the other banks (Charts 33 and 34, pages 132 and 133), although fluctuations were not as wide as in the case of the Northampton Institution for Savings. In both the Nonotuck bank and the Florence bank the opening of accounts leveled off from 1915 to 1925 and the downturn in the long-time trend came after 1925, somewhat later than was true for the Northampton Institution for Savings. The decline in the closing of accounts likewise took place somewhat later than in the Institution for Savings.

b) Opening and Closing of Accounts in Relation to the Number of Accounts

As shown in Chart 35, the number of accounts opened each year in the Northampton Institution for Savings and in the Florence Savings Bank was a slightly decreasing proportion of the total number of open accounts taken as of October 31 each year. From 1881 to 1897 an average of about 15 to 17 per cent of the accounts on the books of the two banks represented new accounts opened during the year. The average declined in later years and in the period from 1926 to 1938 only about 8 or 9 per cent of the accounts were new ones. These facts are shown in Table 8 on page 136.

The number of accounts closed was likewise a decreasing per-

Chart 32

OPENING AND CLOSING OF ACCOUNTS
During Each Fiscal Year, 1876–1938
Northampton Institution for Savings

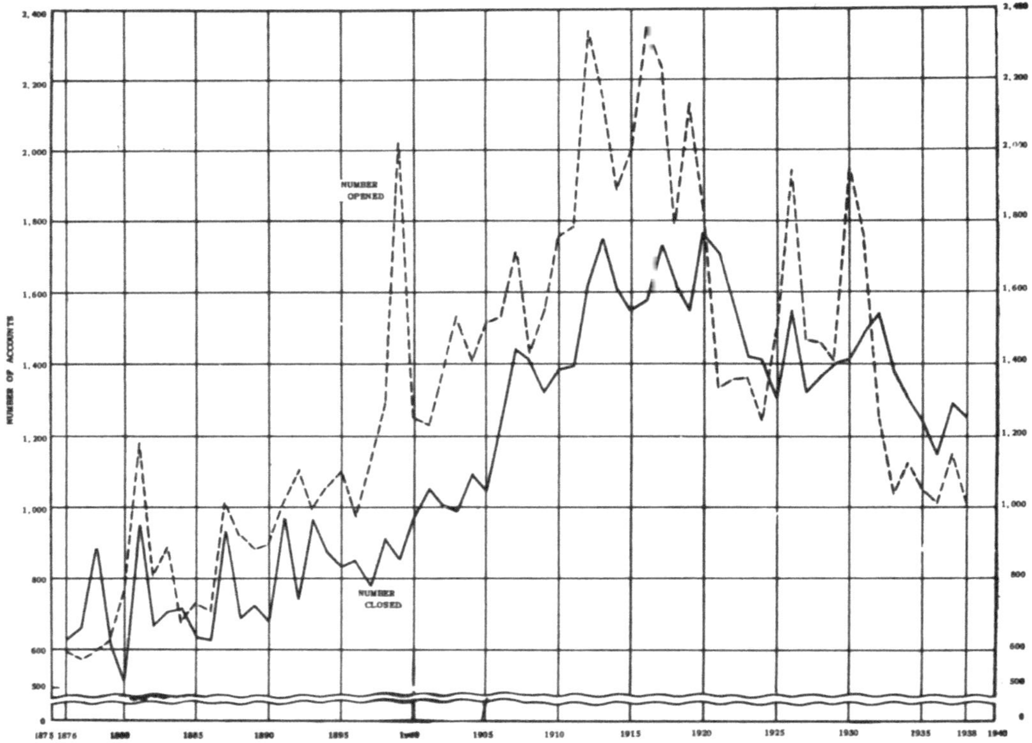

Source: Mass. Commissioner of Banks. *Annual Report*. 1876–1938.

Chart 33

OPENING AND CLOSING OF ACCOUNTS
During Each Fiscal Year, 1880–1938
Florence Savings Bank

Source: Mass. Commissioner of Banks. *Annual Report*. 1880-1938.

Chart 34

OPENING AND CLOSING OF ACCOUNTS

During Each Fiscal Year

Hampshire Savings Bank, 1881-1897

Nonotuck Savings Bank, 1899-1938

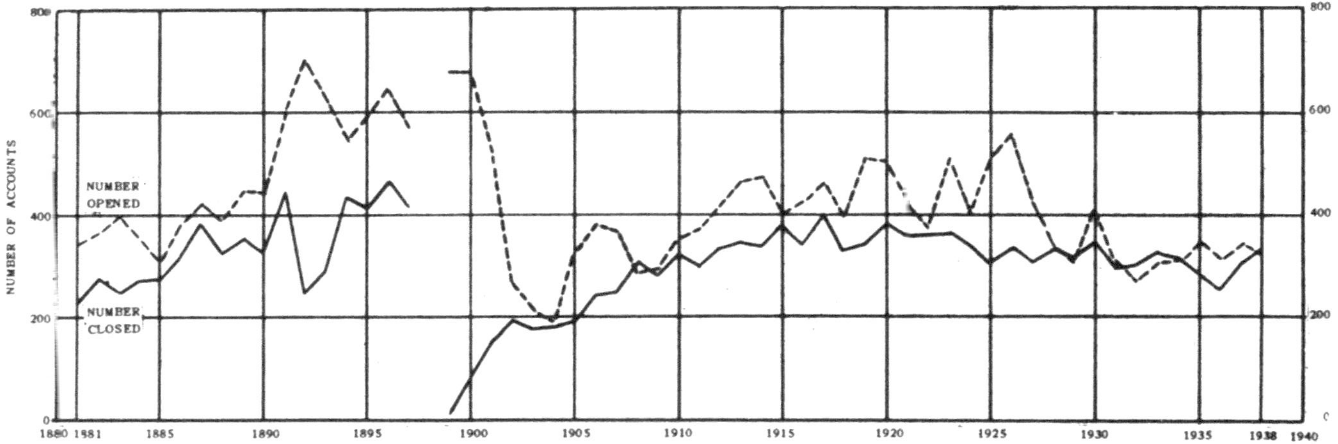

Source: Mass. Commissioner of Banks. *Annual Report*. 1881-1938.

Chart 35

NUMBER OF ACCOUNTS OPENED AND NUMBER CLOSED DURING FISCAL YEAR
in Per Cent of Total Number of Accounts on October 31, 1876-1938

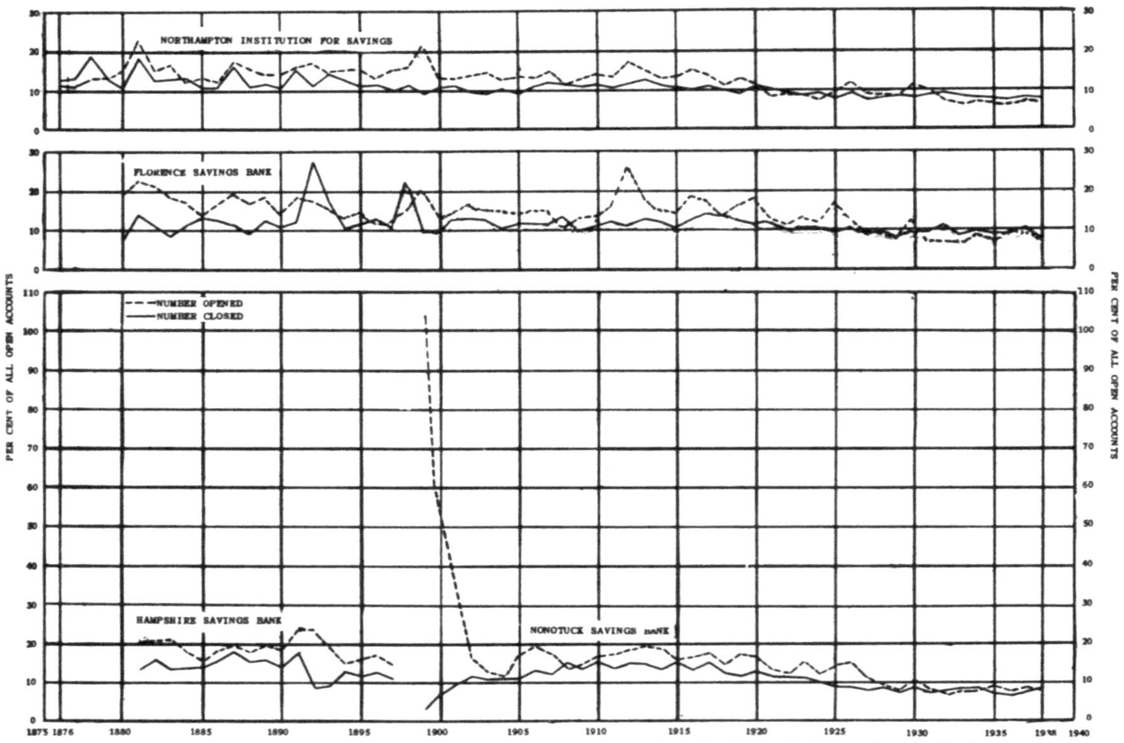

Source: Computed from data in the annual reports of the Commissioner of Banks.

centage of the number of open accounts in the Northampton Institution for Savings and the Florence Savings Bank, but the decrease was smaller and more irregular than that in the case of accounts opened. About 13 per cent of the number of accounts in the banks were closed each year between 1881 and 1897. The average fell in the following years to 10 or 12 per cent from 1910 to 1925 and 8 or 9 per cent from 1926 to 1938.

In the first few years of the operation of the Nonotuck bank the number of accounts opened each year was a relatively large percentage of the number of open accounts and the number of accounts closed was a small percentage. This would be expected in a newly organized bank. The percentages moved toward the same levels that were apparent in the other banks, however, and they showed the same tendency to be somewhat lower in the later years, especially after 1925.

Table 8

Activity of Deposit Accounts as Shown by the Number of Accounts Opened and Closed during the Year Expressed as Percentages of the Number of Accounts Open on October 31 for Five Periods from 1881 to 1938*

Item	Average Percentage				
	1881-1897	1898-1909	1910-1925	1926-1938	1901-1935
Florence Savings Bank					
Number closed	13.2	12.5	11.6	9.2	11.0
Number opened	17.0	14.8	15.8	8.9	13.4
Hampshire Savings Bank					
Number closed	13.3				
Number opened	18.6				
Nonotuck Savings Bank					
Number closed			12.8	8.0	
Number opened			16.0	9.0	
Northampton Institution for Savings					
Number closed	12.5	10.3	10.1	8.0	9.6
Number opened	15.1	14.0	11.9	7.9	11.2

* Computed from information published in the annual reports of the Commissioner of Banks.

Prior to 1900 the relationship between the number of new accounts and the total number of accounts in the Northampton banks showed no definite tendency to change. The data for the later years, however, agree with the more general conclusion of Professor Steiner that the proportion of new accounts to the number of open accounts in all savings banks in Massachusetts was declining from 1900 to 1935, although in the case of the Northampton banks the decline was slow and irregular. From 1900 to 1910, the number of accounts opened in Northampton fluctuated around about 14 per cent of the number of open accounts but declined in percentage from 1910 to 1925 and reached a new low level of about 8 or 9 per cent of the open accounts from 1926 to 1938.

In the Northampton banks throughout the whole period, the proportion of accounts closed each year tended to decrease. In his study Professor Steiner, however, found no clear trend in the proportion of accounts closed, except that the percentage was low in the 1920's. For the banks of Northampton, the proportion was only slightly lower in the 1920's than in the years immediately preceding, but the percentage fell further in the 1930's.

The magnitude of the average activity of accounts in Northampton from 1901 to 1935 was similar to that of accounts in all mutual savings banks within the state, the opening and closing of accounts being slightly higher than the state average in the case of the Florence Savings Bank and somewhat lower in the Northampton Institution for Savings. The average activity of accounts in Northampton was slightly lower than that of accounts in the mutual savings banks in Connecticut and considerably lower than that experienced in the banks of New York and New Jersey.[6]

Much of the significance of the variation in the activity of accounts may, of course, be lost through the use of averages. One recent investigation of mutual savings banks of New York shows that there is great variation in the life of deposit accounts.[7] Although one metropolitan bank reported that in April, 1938, one-fourth of its accounts were two years or less in age and one-fifth were between three and six years of age, a large

6 *Ibid.*, p. 795.

7 Weldon Welfling, "Some Characteristics of Savings Deposits," *American Economic Review*, XXX (1940), 753-54.

number of the accounts had been on the books of the banks for many years. About one-tenth of the accounts had existed from nineteen to forty-three years and another one-tenth had been held from fifteen to eighteen years. Of the accounts closed, about 43 per cent were less than one year in age and almost 75 per cent of the accounts closed were of less than five years' standing. These figures may not be representative of the banks of Northampton, for the average activity of accounts in New York as found by Professor Steiner was definitely higher than the activity in Northampton, and the figures may not even be representative of all mutual savings banks of New York. Nevertheless, the data suggest that the average activity of accounts reflects two quite different groups: a fringe of temporary accounts opening and closing in rapid succession and a stable group of more or less permanent accounts.

c) Timing of Changes in the Number of Accounts Opened and the Number Closed

Since it is to be expected that the opening and closing of accounts is related to economic conditions in the Northampton area, consideration was given to the manner in which the opening and closing reacted to business fluctuations. Comparison of Chart 2, page 7, and Charts 32 to 34, pages 131 to 133, indicates that until 1929 the year to year changes in the opening of accounts did reflect economic conditions in Northampton. When business was active many accounts were opened, and the peaks and low points of business activity and of the opening of accounts frequently coincided. There were occasional divergences and sometimes a lag, for example, in the Northampton Institution for Savings in 1888, 1889, and 1901 and in the Florence Savings Bank in 1888. In these cases the low point in the opening of accounts was reached after the low point in manufacturing activity, which indicated that the effect of the lowered incomes carried over into the year when incomes had begun to rise. In all of the banks the effects of the depression of 1921 were reflected in the number of accounts opened during both 1921 and 1922.

In spite of the continued decline in manufacturing, the number of accounts opened in each of the three banks rose in 1930 above the level of 1929. The reduction in the number of accounts during 1929 was not so much a consequence of lower incomes as it was a result of spending and investing elsewhere. The increase in the number of accounts opened in the banks during 1930 probably resulted from a feeling of uncertainty about most forms of investment, especially investment in securities, and a greater confidence in savings banks. Funds withdrawn from the security markets were therefore transferred to the banks, and some funds which were left idle by the lack of investment outlets accumulated in the savings banks.

Data relative to the closing of accounts did not fluctuate directly with changes in manufacturing activity, although in a few years a lag of one year occurred. It is possible, of course, that the relationship between the series may not have been revealed because of the use of yearly data rather than statistics referring to shorter time intervals.

For all of the savings banks of Massachusetts, the opening of new accounts quickly reflected alterations in business activity, and the closing of accounts tended to lag one year behind the opening of accounts. When business activity falls, the peak of new accounts has already been reached since the opening of accounts decreases promptly when business activity drops.[8] Many people do not start drawing on their savings immediately upon the downturn of business, however, but hold out as long as possible until necessity forces them to close their accounts or to make heavy withdrawals. As business depression continues, people become very reluctant to touch their savings and consequently closings and withdrawals decline. Therefore a lag is observed in the closing of accounts. This same lag occurs at the upturn of business. Openings are likely to increase promptly as soon as business revives, employment expands, and incomes rise. In the early part of revival, people remain cautious and are reluctant to withdraw their savings, and closings therefore do not begin to increase until after openings have risen.

Consideration of lines on Charts 32 to 34 (pages 131 to 133) shows that the lag of one year is not apparent in the Northampton banks for the whole period, although there is some indication of a lag in the data for the Northampton Institution for Savings. For the years following 1900, however, some tendency

[8] Steiner, *op. cit.*, pp. 792-94.

toward a lag of one year appears, which gives some slight confirmation of Professor Steiner's conclusion for the banks of the state as a whole for the period after 1900.

2. Deposits and Withdrawals Made during the Year

a) Trends in Deposits and Withdrawals

Throughout most of the years included in this study, as shown in Charts 27, 28, and 29, pages 113, 114, and 115, a strong upward trend is apparent in both withdrawals and deposits in each of the banks. In the Northampton Institution for Savings and the Florence bank the upward trend leveled off after 1920 and turned into a decline after 1930. New deposits in the Nonotuck bank and withdrawals from it continued to rise until 1929; the reasons for this difference have already been suggested. Changes in withdrawals followed a pattern similar to, but not identical with, that observed in new deposits.

In a majority of the years, the amount deposited with the Northampton banks exceeded the amount withdrawn during any particular year, although the reverse was true in the Northampton Institution for Savings for slightly more than half of the years. However, this did not mean that the total deposit liabilities in the Northampton Institution for Savings were decreasing, since dividends are included in the report of withdrawals but not in the record of amounts deposited during the year.

b) Deposits and Withdrawals in Relation to the Total Amount Due Depositors

There was no clear tendency throughout the period for deposits and withdrawals made during the year to become a larger or smaller percentage of the total amount on deposit (see Chart 36, page 140). From 1876 to 1910 the deposits and withdrawals of the Northampton Institution for Savings fluctuated around the same percentage of the amount due depositors. As shown in Table 9, page 141, about 15 or 16 per cent of the balances in accounts was deposited during the year and 16 per cent withdrawn. The percentages in the Hampshire Savings Bank likewise showed no long-run tendency to increase or decrease. About 20 per cent of the total amount on deposit was received annually and a like

Chart 36

AMOUNTS DEPOSITED AND AMOUNTS WITHDRAWN DURING FISCAL YEAR
in Per Cent of Total Amount on Deposit on October 31, 1876-1938

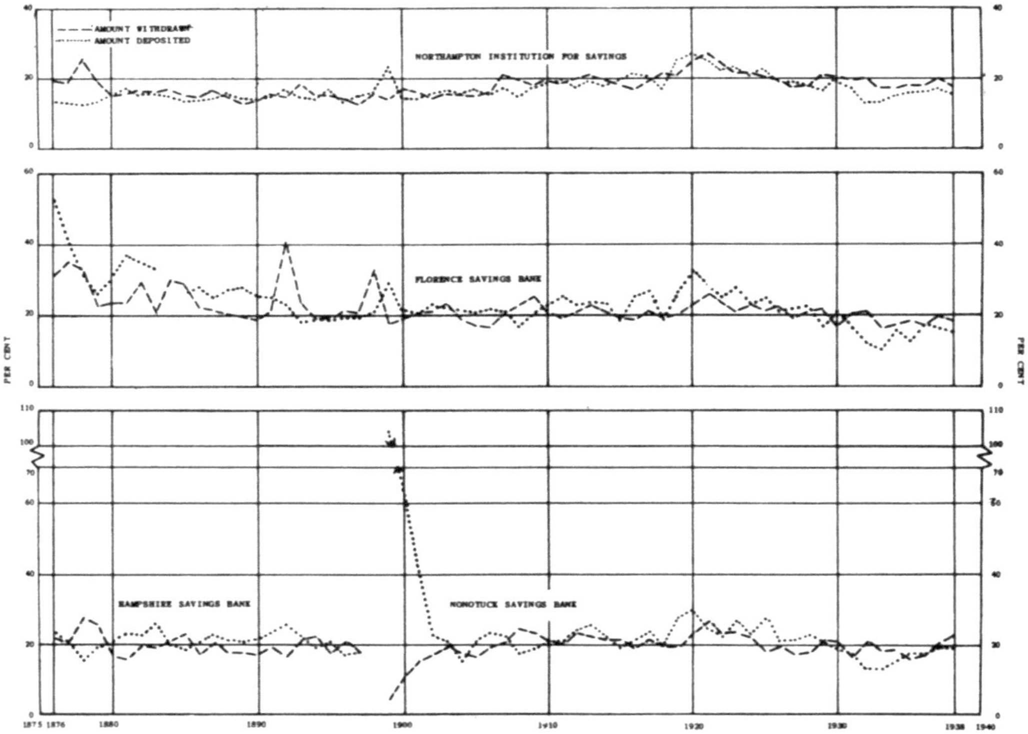

Source: Computed from data in the annual reports of the Commissioner of Banks.

proportion was paid out each year. In the Florence bank, however, the amounts deposited and withdrawn were declining percentages of the total balance on deposit from 1876 to 1895. From 1895 until 1910 the percentage remained at about the same level, with deposits and withdrawals each amounting to one-fifth of the total due depositors.

Table 9

Activity of Deposit Accounts as Shown by Amounts Deposited and Withdrawn during the Year Expressed as Percentages of the Amount Due Depositors on October 31 for Five Periods from 1876 to 1938*

Item	Average Percentage				
	1876-1897	1898-1909	1910-1925	1926-1938	1901-1935
Florence Savings Bank					
Withdrawals	24.9	21.4	21.4	19.3	20.7
New Deposits	27.9**	21.7	24.7	17.1	21.6
Hampshire Savings Bank					
Withdrawals	19.7				
New Deposits	20.8				
Nonotuck Savings Bank					
Withdrawals			21.7	19.0	
New Deposits			23.6	18.3	
Northampton Institution for Savings					
Withdrawals	16.3	16.5	20.7	18.7	19.1
New Deposits	14.6	16.4	21.1	16.2	18.4

* Computed from data published in annual reports of the Commissioner of Banks.

** Average of years 1876-87, omitting 1884.

From 1910 to 1925 the amount deposited and the amount withdrawn comprised slightly higher proportions of the total deposit liabilities of the Northampton Institution for Savings and of the Florence bank than in the other years. The percentages for each of the three banks dropped after 1925. This drop in activity is contrary to the movement for all mutual savings banks of New York.[9] Activity in New York was relatively stable from 1913 to 1918 and then rose to a new level in 1920, fluctuating around the new level until 1929, when a great increase occurred. In 1930 activity was at the pre-1929 level and by 1934 it was back at the 1913-1918 level. The higher level of activity in the New York banks between 1925 and 1933 may be explained by the greater impact upon their depositors of the speculative fever, the "silk-shirt" psychology, investment opportunities, and later the stock market crash.

From 1926 to 1938 the amount deposited annually in the Northampton Institution for Savings averaged about 16 per cent of the amount due depositors and the amount withdrawn was slightly greater than 18 per cent. Somewhat larger proportions were deposited in and withdrawn from the Florence and Nonotuck banks. Thus in each of the banks between one-fifth and one-sixth of all balances on deposit were withdrawn during each year, to be replaced by new funds.

The turnover in the deposits of the Northampton banks seems rather high for genuine savings of small amounts; yet the turnover is no higher than that of accounts in all savings banks of Massachusetts for the years 1901 to 1935. The average for the state falls between that for the Florence Savings Bank and that for the Northampton Institution for Savings. In the mutual savings banks of Connecticut and New York the turnover was considerably higher and in New Jersey banks the activity of accounts, as indicated by the relationship between the amounts deposited and withdrawn each year to total deposit balances, was about twice that of the Northampton banks.[10]

c) Timing of Changes in Deposits and Withdrawals

Changes in the amount of deposits made during the year reflected to a considerable degree the fluctuations in the economic prosperity of the Northampton community. Whenever manufacturing activity was declining or low the amount of new deposits was likewise low, except in 1930. In each of the banks, new deposits declined or leveled off during the following years:

9 Weldon Welfling, *Savings Banking in New York State*, pp. 155-57.
10 Steiner, *op. cit.*, p. 800.

1893-94, 1900-01, 1904, 1908, 1914 or 1915, 1918, 1921-22, 1924, 1926, 1929, and 1931-33. In 1893 and 1894 wages paid and value of product in manufacturing industries were low, and again in 1900 and early in 1901 there was a slowing down of industrial activity. The decline in new deposits in 1904 reflected the slight drop in activity in that year. The decrease in 1908 was a reflection of the disturbed conditions in 1907 and 1908, and the decline in 1918 was a result of both the decrease in number employed during the year and the Treasury drive for war savings. The drop in new deposits in 1922 may have resulted in part from the depression which occurred in 1921 and in part from the exuberant spending which characterized the post-war years. The decline in 1924 and after 1929 reflected again a decrease in manufacturing employment and payrolls. It was suggested in the discussion of the opening of accounts that the decreases which occurred in deposits in 1929 and the increases in 1930 resulted from a shift in the use of funds.

Changes in the amount withdrawn during the year do not directly reflect fluctuations in business conditions as do variations in the amount deposited.

As with the opening and closing of accounts, there is no uniformity in the relative timing of changes in the volume of withdrawals and of deposits made. Both deposits and withdrawals often reached a peak or a low point in the same year; there seems to be some evidence, however, of a lag of one year between deposits and withdrawals. The reasons for this have been suggested in an earlier discussion.

The effect of changes in business activity upon deposits and withdrawals in the mutual savings banks of Philadelphia has been noted in a study made by Dr. Carson.[11] There it was found that changes in economic conditions directly influenced the volume of savings deposits during the period from 1919 to 1930. Variations in business activity were reflected quickly in the amount of the deposits made during the year and much more slowly in the withdrawals. There, too, it was concluded that the withdrawal of savings is a last resort during depression and that expenditures are curtailed to fit income rather than maintained

[11] William J. Carson, *Savings and Employee Savings Plans in Philadelphia*, pp. 77-82.

by the reduction of savings. Similar observations concerning the behavior of withdrawals in depression years were made in a study of mutual savings banks in the state of New York.[12]

3. Summary

For genuine savings, the deposit accounts of the Northampton banks have thus shown a considerable degree of activity. Accounts were no more active, however, than the accounts of all savings banks in Massachusetts and they were considerably less active than accounts in the mutual savings banks of Connecticut, New Jersey, and New York from 1901 to 1935.

In the later years about one-eleventh or one-twelfth of the accounts were closed each year and a similar number was opened. During the period from 1876 to 1938, new accounts and accounts closed were a decreasing percentage of the number of open accounts, indicating increasing stability. On the average, between one-sixth and one-fifth of all funds on deposit in the banks were withdrawn during each year from 1926 to 1938 and a similar amount was deposited. In none of the Northampton banks was there a well defined tendency for these proportions to vary, although the deposits made during the year were slightly more than one-fifth in the 1920's and somewhat lower than one-fifth in the 1930's.

The activity of deposit accounts reflects year to year changes in business activity. When business is good the activity of accounts is usually high and, conversely, when business is poor the activity is likely to be low. The opening of new accounts and the making of deposits are especially responsive to general business conditions, but the closing of accounts and the making of withdrawals are not as responsive.

E. PROTECTION OF DEPOSITORS

For the protection of depositors in mutual savings banks the state has carefully regulated the investment of deposit funds and of earnings from these funds. In addition, the state has required each mutual savings bank to provide its deposit accounts

12 Weldon Welfling, "Some Characteristics of Savings Deposits," *American Economic Review*, XXX (1940), pp. 751-52.

with a cushion in the form of a surplus account, or guaranty fund. The state has, also, established a central reservoir of credit for its mutual savings banks and it has set up a deposit insurance fund.

1. Guaranty Fund

In 1876 the banks were required to set aside a reserve at the time of their semi-annual dividends. The additions to the reserve, or guaranty fund, were to be made from the net profits accumulated during the preceding six months. The amount added to the reserve was to be not more than one-fourth of 1 per cent of the total deposits and not less than one-eighth of 1 per cent. Contributions were required until the fund reached 5 per cent of deposits. The guaranty fund was to be maintained thereafter and held to meet losses which might occur from the depreciation of securities or otherwise.[13] If the fund was less than 5 per cent of deposits, no losses were to be met from the fund except by permission of the Bank Commissioner. No additions were to be made to the fund when it amounted to 5 per cent or more of deposits.[14] After 1912 transfers to the guaranty fund from profit and loss were permitted at any time and in any amount deemed advisable by the trustees, provided the guaranty fund did not exceed 5 per cent, and subject to the approval of the commissioner.[15]

Banking experience, especially after 1929, indicated that a guaranty fund of 5 per cent of the balance on deposit was not sufficiently large to give the best protection to depositors. The limit was, therefore, raised to 7.5 per cent in 1933.[16]

The guaranty funds, which the banks were just beginning to accumulate at the opening of the period under study, increased slowly and steadily throughout the years. The Bank Commissioner had early taken the attitude that ordinary losses should be absorbed by the profit and loss account of the bank and that the guaranty fund was to be called upon only in the case of extraordinary emergencies. The banks consequently seldom charged off

13 Mass. Acts 1876, c. 203, sec. 13.
14 Mass. Acts 1908, c. 590, sec. 59.
15 Mass. Acts 1912, c. 122.
16 Mass. Acts 1933, c. 334, sec. 16.

losses to the guaranty fund. This is borne out by the fact that the fund in each of the Northampton banks increased in almost every year from 1876 to 1938.

The Northampton Institution for Savings had already established a guaranty fund at the time of its report to the Bank Commissioners in 1876. The fund was then only a fraction of 1 per cent of the deposit liabilities, but it grew steadily until it reached 5 per cent in 1891. The fund remained at about 5 per cent from that time until it was increased to meet the new requirement of 7.5 per cent after 1933. The reserve increased in each year except 1894, 1908, 1909, 1910, 1932, and 1933. During each of these years the guaranty fund remained unchanged from the preceding year, but in each case the reserve was about 5 per cent of deposits. Although the Bank Commissioner had, in 1932, asked all banks to write off their losses from depreciated securities, this did not necessitate a reduction in the guaranty fund of the Northampton Institution for Savings. By 1938 the reserve had reached more than 6 per cent of the deposit liabilities.

The guaranty fund of the Florence bank was first reported in 1877 and it grew continuously from then until 1938, except for 1895, 1932, and 1933. In 1895 and in 1932 the fund was reduced, indicating the absorption of losses, and from 1932 to 1933 the fund remained unchanged. Although the guaranty fund of the Florence bank increased almost continuously, it did not remain at the 5 per cent maximum throughout the period. It reached 5 per cent in 1894 and then dropped below 5 per cent until 1913. After 1913 it was again slightly below the maximum, but after 1926 it was approximately 5 per cent of deposits, increasing to more than 6 per cent as a result of the change in requirements in 1933.

The guaranty fund of the Hampshire Savings Bank increased regularly each year from 1877 to 1897, reaching slightly more than 3 per cent of deposits in 1897.

The Nonotuck Savings Bank established a guaranty fund in 1900 and added to it each year through 1938, with the exception of 1933, when no change occurred. Although additions were made to the reserve in almost every year, deposits were increasing rapidly and the fund did not amount to as much as 5 per cent of the deposits until 1932. The guaranty fund had increased to more than 6 per cent of the deposits by 1938.

Thus the guaranty fund, which was required of all banks in order to protect depositors from losses, increased annually almost without exception. The fund provided a margin of safety for depositors which was seldom required by Northampton banks since their losses were such that with few exceptions they could be absorbed in the profit and loss account.

2. Mutual Savings Central Fund, Incorporated

Following the market collapse of 1929, steps were taken to provide the mutual savings banks of Massachusetts with some kind of central agency which would be able to assist banks in time of stress by making funds readily available and by preventing the forced disposal of assets on the market, possibly at great sacrifice. The Mutual Savings Central Fund, Incorporated, was established in 1932[17] and later the Deposit Insurance Fund was established as a part of the Central Fund.[18]

All savings banks in Massachusetts are members of the Central Fund. The purpose of the corporation, as stated in the originating act, is to assist member banks which are temporarily in need of cash or banks which hold investments that cannot readily be liquidated. Assistance is to be extended by making loans secured by mortgages or other securities legally held by member banks. The directors are elected by the members. The corporation may assess members in proportion to their deposits, exclusive of club deposits, and the total amount of the assessments is not to exceed 3 per cent of deposits. It was required that at the first meeting of the directors an assessment of at least three-twentieths of 1 per cent of deposits was to be made.[19] The corporation may also obtain funds by borrowing.

The establishment of the Central Fund corporation thus provided a means by which the liquidity of the mutual savings

17 Mass. Acts 1932, c. 44.

18 Mass. Acts 1934, c. 43.

19 During 1932, two assessments of three-twentieths of 1 per cent each were levied. After the establishment of the Deposit Insurance Fund, one-half of the above assessments was returned to the savings banks, and assessments amounting to three-twentieths of 1 per cent remained in the Central Fund thereafter.

banks could be preserved. The corporation could make advances to members upon the security of mortgages, characteristically the largest type of investment of the savings bank and one of the most non-liquid of assets. This was perhaps the most important power granted the Central Fund corporation since the mutual banks could ordinarily obtain funds elsewhere through use of their bonds.

Loans to members amounted to more than one million dollars on October 31, 1932, and October 31, 1938, but in the intervening years they were not so large. Thus, loans were not required to any considerable degree but only to an amount less than one-twentieth of 1 per cent of the deposits of all members.

3. Deposit Insurance

Although mutual savings banks were permitted to become members of the Federal Deposit Insurance Corporation, the record of loss in the mutual savings banks of Massachusetts was so low that it was deemed advisable to set up a separate deposit insurance corporation rather than to have the mutual banks join the Federal insurance plan.

In 115 years of operation of the savings banks, from February, 1817, to February, 1932, the actual losses following liquidation of banks amounted to only $2,549,868,[20] an extremely small fraction of the total of all funds received for deposit during those years. As reported in January, 1934, only two mutual savings banks had failed during the depression of 1932. When they closed, the combined deposits of those two banks were about 9 million dollars, or 0.44 of 1 per cent of the total deposits of all savings banks in Massachusetts. The losses actually suffered by the closings were, of course, much less than 0.44 of 1 per cent of all deposits.

Under the temporary plan for Federal deposit insurance, members were liable for an assessment of one-half of 1 per cent of their deposits of less than $2,500, and the Corporation was authorized to make an additional assessment of one-half of 1 per cent if additional funds were needed during the operation of the Temporary Deposit Insurance Fund.

[20] Mass. Sen. Doc. No. 100 (1934), pp. 23-26.

As members, the savings banks of Massachusetts would consequently have been subject to maximum assessments of 14 million dollars -- a sum greater than the total of all deposits involved in the failures in the depression of 1932 and greater than the losses realized in all the years of their history. It, therefore, seemed undesirable for the savings banks to join an insurance plan which might prove so expensive for them, even though the maximum assessment might not be levied.

There were other reasons involved in the unwillingness of Massachusetts to have its savings banks become members of the Federal Deposit Insurance Corporation. The Federal insurance system was established primarily for commercial banks and it was believed that provisions relating to mutual savings banks were not relevant. Furthermore, membership in the Federal Deposit Insurance Corporation required eventual membership in the Federal Reserve System, whose services are designed chiefly for commercial rather than savings banks. The Mutual Savings Central Fund corporation served as a reservoir of credit for the savings banks of Massachusetts and membership in the Federal Reserve System seemed to offer little advantage. Massachusetts therefore organized its own system of deposit insurance for savings banks.[21]

The Deposit Insurance Fund of Massachusetts was established in 1934 as a part of the Mutual Savings Central Fund and for the purpose of insuring all savings banks. The Central Fund corporation was authorized to assess each member not less than one-fourth of 1 per cent and not more than 1 per cent of deposits in order to obtain insurance funds.[22] These funds are held separate from the other assets of the corporation.

[21] Subsequent to the organization of the Massachusetts Deposit Insurance Fund these various objections were met by changes in the provisions relating to mutual savings bank members of the Federal Deposit Insurance Corporation. Mutual savings banks were no longer required to become members of the Federal Reserve System and the mutual savings banks were insured under a separate fund, with lower assessments. Nevertheless, the Massachusetts deposit insurance system was maintained.

[22] Only the minimum assessment of one-fourth of 1 per cent was made until the enactment of Chapter 149 of the Acts of 1939, which provided for an annual assessment of one-sixteenth of 1 per cent of deposits on behalf of the Deposit Insurance Fund.

Upon the initiative of the Bank Commissioner, the corporation may temporarily take over the operation of a bank or it may liquidate the bank. The corporation may also extend assistance to banks through loans, purchase of assets, or payments to cover the difference between the book value and the market value of assets.[23] Earlier provisions had related only to the taking over of banks and to liquidation. The further authority for the corporation to assist banks in order to reduce risk and avert threatened loss was an important additional function.

When a bank is taken over and liquidated, the corporation pays to the depositors the full amount of their deposits plus interest accumulated from the date of the last dividend to the date of discontinuance at a rate not greater than 3 per cent. The payment must be made within three years. For such payment the corporation may use the money of the Deposit Insurance Fund if the assets of the bank are not adequate to make the payment.

The Deposit Insurance Fund was not called upon during the first years of its existence. Later, however, it did extend assistance to member banks.

By the establishment of the Central Fund and the Deposit Insurance Fund, the state of Massachusetts provided its savings banks with both a central reservoir of readily available credit, somewhat similar to that provided by the Federal Reserve System for its members, and a deposit insurance organization, functioning much as the Federal Deposit Insurance Corporation does, to assist weak banks in strengthening their position and to guarantee deposits if liquidation proves necessary.

4. Safety Experience

The mutual savings banks of Massachusetts have been extraordinarily safe institutions. The Bank Commissioner stated in 1918 that "although the mutual savings banks of Massachusetts alone now have total resources of $1,132,563,108, in a period of nearly thirty years, only seven savings banks have been closed by the bank commissioners with any loss to depositors, and the losses, when compared with the vast amount of deposits received and returned during that period, are of course infinitesimal."[24]

[23] Mass. Acts 1938, c. 125.

[24] Mass., *Annual Report of the Commissioner of Banks*, Part 1, 1918, p. ix.

In the years prior to the thirty years referred to by the Bank Commissioner, there had been a number of failures. From 1876 to 1878 real estate values, which had been greatly inflated at the close of the Civil War, underwent a serious decline. Since Massachusetts savings banks invested heavily in loans on real estate, the deflation of the 1870's led to difficulties in many banks and from 1875 to 1880 there were thirteen failures.[25] In view of the fact that these were years of severe financial difficulty and strain, the number of failures does not seem unduly high.

In the depression years following 1929 the mutual savings banks built an enviable record. As indicated in the discussion of deposit insurance, few banks closed and the losses sustained were small.

Thus throughout the many years during which they have operated, mutual savings banks have provided a high degree of safety to depositors. Losses suffered through the failure of savings banks in Massachusetts have been extremely small. Both the legal regulations concerning investments and the supervision of banks by the Commissioner of Banks have done much to insure the general soundness of the banks. In addition, specific means to prevent loss have been established in the form of the guaranty funds of the individual banks, the Mutual Savings Central Fund, and the Deposit Insurance Fund.

25 *Ibid.*, 1885, p. xvii.

Chapter IV

COMPETITION FACED BY THE SAVINGS BANKS

In preceding chapters of this study the community setting of the Northampton savings banks was described and the development of the banks themselves was traced by following changes in the major items of investment and in deposit liabilities. In this chapter and the following one, some of the factors influencing the development of the savings banks will be discussed. First among these influences was the competition which the banks met as institutions for the attraction of savings funds and as agencies for the extension of mortgage loans.

A. SAVINGS INSTITUTIONS

Mutual savings banks were among the earliest institutions organized for the care of small savings. These banks were the first type of savings institution to appear in Northampton, although from the early years there were, of course, other channels through which individuals could put their savings to work. Always there has been the possibility of investment in property and, to an increasing extent, the opportunity to invest in securities issued by various governments and private enterprises. Security investment, however, has been of a rather different nature from the accumulations placed in savings institutions since such investment has been primarily in the hands of wealthier individuals or of the various financial organizations. The motives involved in security investment have probably been more closely connected to the desire for income than the incentives leading to the use of savings institutions, whose clients are more likely to be concerned with the accumulation of small savings for a definite consumer expenditure or for unexpected emergencies.

Aside from direct investment, there have been many agencies other than mutual savings banks in which individuals of Northampton could place their small savings. Chief among these has been the cooperative bank, or building and loan association.

The commercial banks have also held savings in their savings departments, and earlier in the form of time deposits. In addition a postal savings office was opened in Northampton soon after the Postal Savings System was organized. The total assets of the mutual savings banks and of the cooperative bank, the savings deposits of the national banks and the trust company, and the deposits in the postal savings office are shown on Chart 37. Each of these will be discussed below in greater detail.

Certain other outlets for the savings of Northampton have been available but it is not possible to find the degree to which they were actually used. Savings may well have been sent outside of the city to other banks, mutual savings, cooperative, and commercial, but such bank deposits have probably been small. Insurance companies have been another important, and increasingly important, agency for absorbing savings. Data concerning the policies of life insurance companies are not segregated, however, in such a way that it is possible to estimate for a given locality the amount of savings invested in this form.

1. Northampton Cooperative Bank

Although cooperative banks were authorized in Massachusetts many years earlier, a cooperative bank was not organized in Northampton until 1889. This bank, the Northampton Cooperative Bank, continued as the sole representative of that type of institution throughout the remainder of the period under study.

One of the fundamental purposes of the cooperative bank, known sometimes as a building and loan association or a savings and loan association, is the encouragement of thrift through a plan of regular monthly savings. Subscribers to shares promise to pay to the bank one dollar monthly for each share to which they have subscribed until the shares reach their matured value of $200. Thus the savers incur a kind of obligation to put aside a certain amount regularly. Unmatured shares also furnish the means by which borrowers from the bank accumulate funds with which to repay the principal of loans from the bank.

In more recent years the cooperative banks of Massachusetts have been permitted to issue matured share certificates and paid-up share certificates upon which dividends are paid. These

Chart 37

GROWTH OF SAVINGS IN NORTHAMPTON, 1876-1938

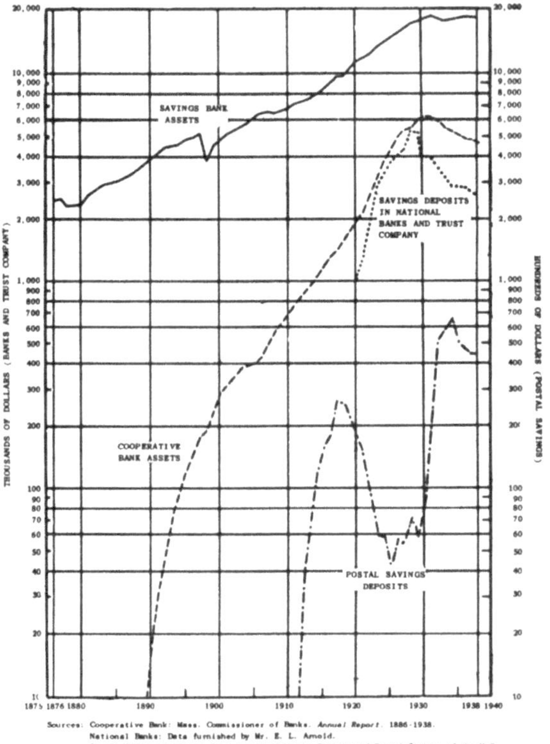

Sources: Cooperative Bank: Mass. Commissioner of Banks. *Annual Report*. 1886-1938.
National Banks: Data furnished by Mr. E. L. Arnold.
Postal Savings Deposits: Data furnished by the Division of Postal Savings of the U.S. Post Office Department.
Savings Banks: Computed from data in the annual reports of the Commissioner of Banks.
Trust Company: Mass. Commissioner of Banks. *Annual Report* 1920-1929.

allow borrowers and others to leave accumulated savings in the cooperative banks.

Growth of the assets of the Northampton Cooperative Bank, as shown in Chart 37, page 154, was rapid and without interruption until 1931. Thus until 1930 it was absorbing an increasing proportion of total savings, as indicated by the chart. By 1908 it was larger than the Florence Savings Bank and within the next few years it had outgrown the Nonotuck Savings Bank. Although the cooperative bank grew more rapidly than did the mutual savings banks, its assets never reached more than about one-third the size of the assets of all savings banks.

The downturn in the assets of the Northampton Cooperative Bank after 1930 was sharper than in the case of the mutual savings banks, and the decline continued through 1938, whereas savings bank assets increased after 1933. This same contrast in behavior is found in the banks of the state as a whole.[1] The decrease accompanied a decline in dues and profits capital rather than a decline in the value of matured and paid-up share certificates. In other words, the drop in assets was not a result of the withdrawal of the relatively permanent investments in the cooperative bank but a result of the lower rate at which people were saving or were accumulating to offset the principal of their loans. To some extent the maintenance of the value of paid-up share certificates was a result of the conversion of unmatured shares into paid-up form by share-holders who could not continue their purchase of serial shares. The drop in assets may, also, be explained in part by a change in the form of real estate loans after 1935, for the cooperative banks were then permitted to make direct reduction mortgage loans.[2] These do not involve the double transaction of borrowing and of buying shares which is typical of the cooperative type of loan. The borrower, however, is required to own one or more shares in the bank. All of these various factors contributed to the decline of assets in the 1930's.

[1] Donald H. Davenport, *The Cooperative Banks of Massachusetts*, p. 1.
[2] Mass. Acts 1935, c. 191.

2. Savings Departments of the National Banks and the Trust Company

Just as there were three mutual banks in Northampton during most of the years from 1876 to 1938, there were three commercial banks during most of the period. Two of them existed throughout the entire period as national banks. The third, which was also a national bank, operated continuously until 1920, except for a few months following the temporary closing of the bank in 1898. It was converted into a state trust company in 1920, and it dropped out of existence in 1930.

Until 1920 the savings deposits of the Northampton national banks amounted to only a few thousand dollars. The National Banking Act had made no special provision for savings departments or for time deposits. It was not until the Federal Reserve Act of 1913 that a distinction was made between time and demand deposits of national banks, although in actual practice many national banks had received savings deposits before 1913.[3]

As compared with savings banks, national banks had an advantage in attracting savings since the size of their accounts was not limited and they could pay interest at a fixed rate. As indicated in the preceding chapter, the limit upon deposits in mutual savings banks was gradually raised to meet such competition and the savings banks were permitted to place deposits on interest monthly if they chose to do so.

Through policies followed, the national banks of Northampton indicated a lack of interest in savings accounts. They consistently paid a rate of interest on savings accounts one per cent less than that paid by the mutual savings banks. They did not solicit savings accounts but looked upon their savings departments as primarily services to commercial bank depositors and to the community as a whole. Nevertheless, as shown in Chart 37, page 155, their savings deposits together with those of the trust company grew rapidly from 1920 to 1928.

One factor of growth arose from the circumstance that in a locality, such as Northampton, where a considerable part of the population is foreign born or first generation native born, a bank which is called "national" is likely to be favored since

3 Ray B. Westerfield, *Money, Credit and Banking*, p. 1050.

its name gives a feeling of added security and of government backing. Another factor in the growth of the commercial banks was the convenience to depositors of transacting in one room all their business relating to both savings and checking accounts.

The drop in savings deposits of the commercial banks in 1930 was a result of the dissolution of the Hampshire County Trust Company, since the savings deposits of the two national banks increased from 1929 to 1930. The decline after 1931 can be explained in part by the policy followed by the banks. The deposits in mutual savings banks and the ownership of shares in cooperative banks are limited by state law but no maximum has been placed upon the size of deposits in national banks. Especially after 1929 the national banks realized the difficulties inherent in large accounts with the possibility of simultaneous withdrawals. They, therefore, set about reducing their large savings accounts. Members of the Federal Reserve System are, moreover, not permitted to hold corporate savings deposits that do not represent genuine "savings" accounts. Thus commercial bank policy itself contributed to the greater drop in savings deposits as compared with the cooperative and mutual savings banks.

The increase in importance of the savings deposits of national banks in Massachusetts as a whole followed much the same pattern that they followed in Northampton: an increase in importance as compared with mutual savings banks from 1919 to 1930 and a decline after 1930.[4] A similar decline in relative importance occurred in New York State.[5]

3. Postal Savings System

The Postal Savings System was established in the United States in 1910 and the first offices opened for business in January, 1911. The System was instituted to encourage thrift among the low income groups. In particular, it was believed that this agency would attract the savings of immigrants and those who hoarded because of their awe of banks or because of their fear

4 Donald H. Davenport, *op. cit.*, p. 1.

5 Earl B. Schwulst, "The Competitive Position of the Mutual Savings Bank," p. 8.

concerning the safety provided by private institutions. Sums as small as one dollar may be deposited in the Postal Savings System until the total deposit, exclusive of interest, amounts to $2,500. Interest is payable at the rate of 2 per cent a year but it is not compounded as it is in the banks. For the country as a whole, the Postal Savings System has never been large, as compared with other types of savings institutions. It grew slowly until 1918, after which there was little increase until 1930. Enormous growth occurred from 1930 to 1931 and total deposits remained at a high level thereafter. A study made of postal savings indicates that, from 1921 to 1930, the growth in deposits was correlated with bank suspensions.[6] The tremendous growth in 1931 was, of course, a consequence of a general distrust of banks.

The growth of postal savings in Northampton is shown in Chart 37, page 154. The scale used is different from the one used for the other institutions and consequently the relative size of postal savings is less than it would appear at first glance. At their peak in 1934 deposit balances reached only $64,000, which amounted to about 2 per cent of the savings deposits in the national banks. Here, as with the Postal Savings System for the country as a whole, three periods appear: rapid growth to 1917; then a decline to a lower level; and a great increase after 1930. In Northampton there were no runs on the savings banks during the 1930's and confidence was not shaken by serious uncertainties concerning the other banks, except for the Hampshire County Trust Company, which was taken over by the Commissioner of Banks in 1930.

4. Summary

After the first few years of the period under study the mutual savings banks faced competition of other institutions for savings. The other banks offered somewhat different appeals and grew at a more rapid rate than the savings banks until 1929. During the 1930's the trend was reversed and deposits in the mutual savings banks did not decline as rapidly as those in

6 Louise Sissman, "Development of the Postal Savings System," *Journal of the American Statistical Association,* XXXI (1936), 715-18.

other banks. The chief competitor of the mutual savings banks was the cooperative bank. Postal savings deposits in Northampton increased greatly during the down swing of the depression but they never reached a size comparable to the volume of savings in the various banks.

B. MORTGAGE LOAN AGENCIES

As shown in the preceding pages, the mutual savings banks of Northampton faced considerable competition for savings funds, and in addition they met active local competition in the field of mortgage loans, which constitute the largest single class of investment made by the savings banks. The chief competitor engaged in making real estate loans in Northampton was the cooperative bank. However, certain other organizations also extended mortgage loans, such as the commercial banks and the trust company, Smith College, Smith Charities, insurance companies, the Federal Land Bank, and banks from other communities.

1. Northampton Cooperative Bank

Since one of the chief purposes of the cooperative type of bank is the financing of home building or of home purchasing, the Northampton Cooperative Bank was perhaps the chief competitor of the savings banks in their mortgage loan business. After the first three years of operation, approximately 90 per cent or more of its assets were invested in loans on real estate. This overwhelming importance of real estate loans decreased during the depression, but at their lowest point, reached in 1938, real estate loans were almost 75 per cent of the assets.

The striking growth of the real estate loans of the Northampton Cooperative Bank is apparent in Chart 38, where the mortgage loans of the cooperative bank and the combined loans of the savings banks are shown. Although the cooperative bank loans at their peak of $5,680,000 in 1931 were only slightly more than half the total volume of savings bank loans, they grew much more rapidly than the loans of the savings banks. The cooperative bank loans exceeded those of the Florence Savings Bank in 1896 and those of the Nonotuck Savings Bank in 1908 but never reached the size of the loans of the Northampton Institution for Savings (Charts 9, 10, and 11, pages 28, 29, and 30).

Chart 38

VOLUME OF REAL ESTATE LOANS OUTSTANDING
in Northampton Banks, 1876-1938

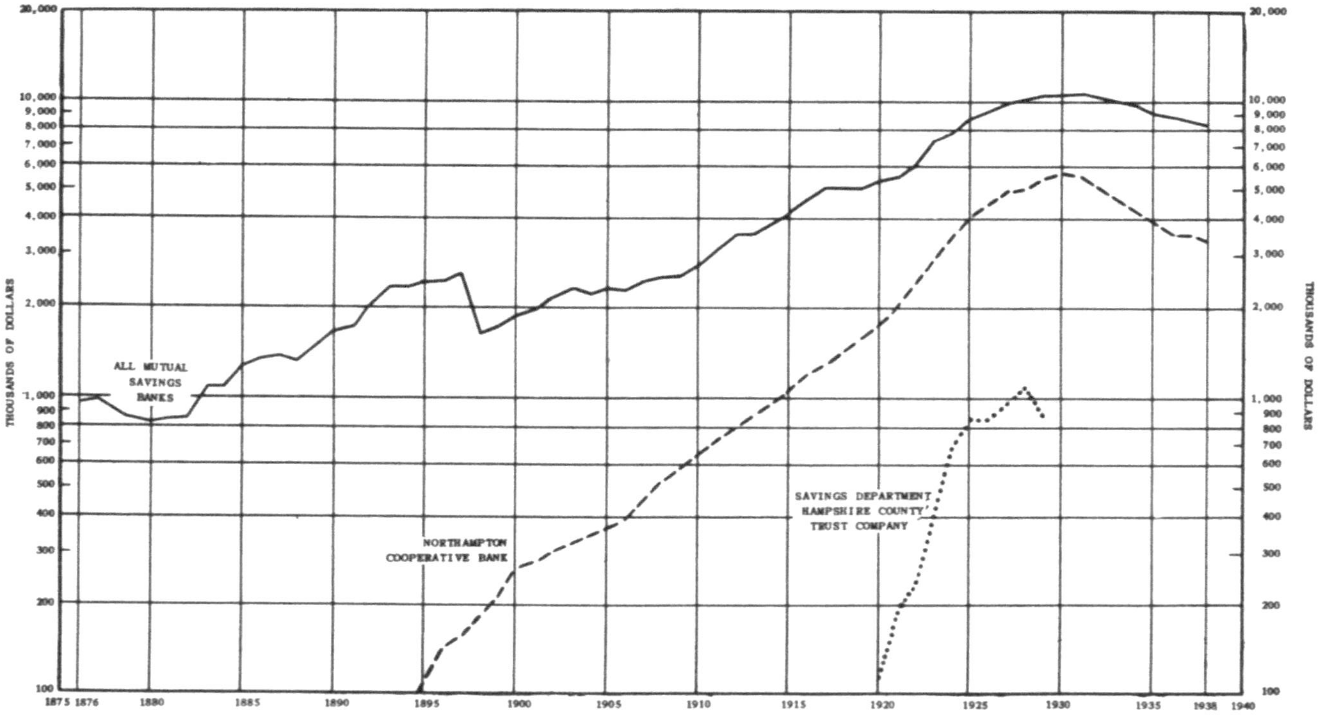

Source: Mass. Commissioner of Banks. *Annual Report*. 1876-1938. (Computed in part.)

Although the making of mortgage loans is a major objective in the cooperative type of bank as it is in the mutual savings bank, the loan contract is quite different. The cooperative type of loan involves both a promise to pay interest on the principal of the loan and the promise to purchase a certain number of shares in the cooperative bank. The shares are purchased by regular monthly payments of one dollar for each share subscribed. When the monthly dues paid in, together with accumulated profits on the shares, reach $200 a share, the real estate loan is thereby extinguished. This is quite different from the typical mortgage loan made by the Northampton savings banks, a loan payable on demand, or one day from date, with no contract requirement of amortization of principal. The loans of the cooperative bank, therefore, tend to turn over continuously whereas the loans of the savings banks may continue outstanding for many years -- or they may be repaid promptly if the borrower so wishes. To a considerable degree, the divergences in the loan contracts of the two types of banks disappeared in the later years when the Northampton savings banks were generally requiring amortization payments and when the cooperative bank was permitting monthly payments to be applied directly to the reduction of principal rather than waiting for the principal to be extinguished by the matured value of shares.

Loans of the cooperative bank also differ from savings bank loans in the maximum amount that can be loaned upon a given piece of property. Loans made by the savings banks cannot exceed 60 per cent of the value of the property[7] (40 per cent in the case of unimproved property), while cooperative banks may loan up to 80 per cent of the value of improved real estate (or 50 per cent of the value of vacant land). The cooperative bank, therefore, has an advantage over the savings bank in dealing with those purchasers or builders of homes who have only small funds available at the time of purchase or construction. The larger percentage allowed the cooperative banks has been justified upon the basis of the strict requirement that regular monthly payments be made towards the retirement of the principal of the loan.

[7] By an act of 1937 savings banks were permitted to make loans up to 70 per cent of the value of the underlying property if the terms of the note required quarterly amortization payments at the rate of 3 per cent a year.

2. National Banks and the Trust Company

The commercial banks were not primarily interested in making loans on real estate. Such mortgage loans as the national banks held were usually the result of other loans which had reached a precarious state and were converted into mortgage loans for added security. Thus, the national banks were not in a true sense competitors of the savings banks but were so only incidentally and inadvertently. However, the making of real estate loans was part of the normal business of the Savings Department of the Hampshire County Trust Company and a large proportion of its funds were invested in mortgage loans. As shown in Chart 38, page 160, the amount of such loans increased rapidly from 1920 to 1928.

3. The Trustees of the Smith Charities

An unusual type of organization, known as The Trustees of the Smith Charities, was incorporated in 1849 in accordance with the will of Oliver Smith.[8] The bulk of the estate was left for

[8] The will itself is of some interest. Most of the estate was set aside in three funds. One fund was to be used for the establishment of an agricultural school in Northampton. The school was to consist of a model farm, an experimental farm, a workshop for the making of agricultural implements, and a school of industry for the poor. The second fund was for the use of the American Colonization Society in transporting colored persons from the United States to the Colony of Liberia or to any other suitable colony and in furnishing them with supplies upon their arrival. The third and largest fund was to be used in assisting indigent boys, female children, young women, and widows. The boys were "to be bound out in good and respectable families, where they shall receive a good common school education, and be well instructed and brought up in the business of husbandry, or such mechanical trade or employment as may be considered by said Trustees most beneficial or useful for them." The boys were eligible to apply for a loan of $500 for a term of five years and if they were deemed worthy and paid their interest regularly the loan would be cancelled without payment of the principal. The indigent girls were, also, to be bound out, preferably to the families of farmers, in order that they might "be brought up in the habits of sobriety, industry, and morality -- and be furnished with all the necessary instruction to enable them to superintend the affairs of the household." Such girls were to be eligible for a "marriage portion" of $300. Indigent young women were also to be eligible for a "marriage portion" of $50. Indigent widows with children were to be given not more than $50 in any one year.

The unsuccessful contesting of this will in Northampton in 1847 was famous throughout the Connecticut Valley, in part because the will was defended by Daniel Webster.

the benefit of certain charitable activities. The will largely restricted expenditures of these charities to the income received from the funds. The principal of the chief fund was to be invested in "good and safe bonds, secured by good and sufficient mortgages on real estate." If such investment seemed unsafe or impracticable, investment could be made in bonds of the United States, New York, Massachusetts, Maine, New Hampshire, Connecticut, and Vermont, or in the bonds of the cities of New York, Boston, and Albany.

In actual practice the Smith Charities has seldom held Federal, state, or city bonds and when such securities were owned they did not constitute a large part of the assets. The Smith Charities has invested primarily in loans on real estate. The loans amounted to about $800,000 in 1876 and by 1938 they had increased to $1,800,000. They have extended to an area somewhat larger than Northampton, including the eight towns [townships] mentioned by Oliver Smith in his will. Some of the loans are on urban real estate but most of them have been secured by farm property. No attempt has been made to require amortization of loans. Although there is, of course, no legal restriction on the size of loans in relation to the value of the real estate, for many years the Smith Charities has followed the policy of loaning a maximum of 50 per cent of the value.

4. Federal Land Bank

Another mortgage loan agency operating in the Northampton area is the Federal Land Bank of Springfield, which cooperates with the Northampton National Farm Loan Association. The Federal Land Bank, established under the Federal Farm Loan Act of 1916, provides long-term credit for farmers. Thus the bank did not come into as direct competition with the savings banks as with the Smith Charities, which loaned primarily to farmers.

Credit extended through the Federal Land Bank was used to a large extent for the refinancing of farm debt. The peak year for Land Bank loans in Northampton occurred in 1933, when many creditor institutions were pressing farmers for settlement of their mortgage loans.

Two types of loans have been made in Northampton. The first consists of those extended through the local association. The application for a loan is appraised by the local association and after its approval, the funds are advanced by the Land Bank. The borrower is required to subscribe to one $5 share in the local association for each $100 borrowed, and the shares are retired upon the extinction of the loan. The contract provides for amortization of the principal, commonly over a period of twenty or thirty-three years. Loans are granted upon the security of a first mortgage and are limited in amount to 50 per cent of the appraisal value of the land and 20 per cent of the value of improvements. The interest charged must not exceed by more than 1 per cent the rate received by the Land Bank on its most recent issue of bonds. From 1918 to 1938 the contract rate varied from 6 per cent to 4 per cent.[9] In Northampton slightly less than one million dollars of such loans were made between 1918 and August, 1939. Of these about $650,000 were still outstanding in 1939.

The other type of loan is the Land Bank Commissioner loan authorized in 1933 to provide emergency relief to farmers. The amount of such a loan plus all prior debts secured by the property was limited to a maximum of 75 per cent of the appraised normal value. The loans could be based upon either a first or a second mortgage, and the rate of interest was set at 5 per cent.[10] Almost $300,000 of such loans were made in Northampton between 1933 and August, 1939.

5. Smith College and Other Organizations

Part of the endowment of Smith College (named after Sophia Smith, niece of Oliver Smith) has been invested in mortgages on real estate. The amount, however, has not been large; about $100,000 was so invested in 1886 and about $200,000 in 1910.

9 Congress granted relief to borrowers from the Land Banks through temporary reductions in interest rates. Regardless of the contract rate, the interest on loans made through national farm loan associations was reduced to 4.5 per cent a year for installments payable between July 11, 1933, and June 30, 1935 and 3.5 per cent on installments payable between July 1, 1935, and June 30, 1944.

10 The rate of interest was temporarily reduced by Congress to 4 per cent a year on all interest payable after July 22, 1937, and prior to July 1, 1940, and 3.5 per cent for all payments after June 30, 1940, and prior to July 1, 1944.

After the latter date the amount of such investment declined until in the 1930's only about $30,000 or $40,000 was loaned on mortgages.

From time to time, banks located outside of the community have made loans on real estate located in Northampton. This was true of some of the Boston and Springfield banks in the 1930's, when they had surplus funds to invest and when they occasionally extended loans on selected business properties in Northampton.

A few loans, likewise, were extended by insurance companies. Most of these were based upon business property since insurance companies have extended loans on homes only in more recent years.

6. Summary

Thus, direct competitors of the savings banks were not as numerous in the mortgage loan field as in the attraction of savings deposits, although there were several institutions engaged in making loans on real estate. The loans of the Federal Land Bank and of The Trustees of the Smith Charities were large in total amount but they were farm loans and thus offered slight competition. Because of the adequacy of funds available through these agencies, there has been little need for the savings banks to extend into the farm loan market. In the case of the Northampton Cooperative Bank, however, there was direct competition in the home loan field, in which savings banks have concentrated, and the greater rapidity with which the mortgage loans of the cooperative bank expanded indicates that the bank presented serious competition. The volume of loans made by other agencies was too small to affect the savings banks greatly.

Chapter V

OTHER FACTORS INFLUENCING THE DEVELOPMENT OF THE SAVINGS BANKS

In the preceding pages the effect produced on the savings banks by competing institutions was pointed out and in this chapter several other factors influencing the course of the banks will be discussed. The effects of interest rates charged and dividends paid by the savings banks and by their competitors, legal restrictions concerning the receipt of deposits and the investment of funds by the banks, and changes in the level of prosperity in Northampton will be examined.

A. INTEREST RATES

Although theoretical discussions center around a single rate of interest, it is generally recognized that market rates differ greatly at a given time. This may result from slowness in the movement of funds. If there were no hindrance to the substituting of one kind of loan for another, lenders would substitute as soon as a higher rate of interest made it profitable to do so and differences in interest rates would disappear. There are hindrances, however, to substitution and to the equalization of rates. Both the uncertainty concerning future interest rates and the lender's evaluation of those risks and the uncertainty concerning the ability and willingness of the borrower to meet his obligation, together with the expenses involved in the shifting of funds, hinder the substitution of loans.[1] On the side of the borrower there are similar hindrances in the possibility of future changes in interest rates and the trouble and cost involved in renewing loans or holding balances.

In addition to these hindrances to the equalization of rates, institutional elements may cause divergences between interest rates in different parts of the total loan or investment market. Commercial banks, for example, favor short-term or intermediate-term securities and lower yields on such investments may cause

[1] Karin Kock, *A Study of Interest Rates*, chap. ii.

no movement of their funds into the long-term market. Insurance companies and savings banks have ordinarily preferred relatively long-term investments and have shifted few funds into the short-term market even when short-term rates greatly exceeded the yields elsewhere available to them. Such preferences arise in part from the nature of the obligations of the various institutions and in part from the fact that it may be relatively costly for an investor or investing institution to enter a loan market with which it is not familiar. Special treatment under Federal and state tax laws and the inclusion of securities in the lists of investments legal for savings banks and insurance companies have increased the demand for certain kinds of investments and those investments therefore continue in spite of a low rate of return. The failure of funds to move from one market to another may therefore result from such factors as legal restrictions on investments, tax exemption provisions, the nature of the investor's obligations, and the character of the customary loan business of the investor.

In actual practice then we do not find a single rate of interest and a single market but we find many markets and many rates. Seeming divergences from the theory which says that interest is the stimulus bringing forth funds and the deterrent to investment may be caused by the lack of mobility of funds from one market to another. Furthermore, some rates are governed by custom and remain relatively stable through all kinds of conditions.

In view of the attention given to interest rates in economic theory, it is important to give consideration to the economic implications of changes which occurred in the interest rates received by the mutual savings banks of Northampton and the interest paid by them to depositors. Discussion of the interest received will come first, followed by that of the interest paid.

One of the questions which arise in connection with the first part of this discussion involves the effect produced upon bank assets by changes in interest rates received. This question concerns the influence of the rate charged by the banks upon the volume of real estate loans and the effect of varying rates upon the distribution of assets among different types of investments. Further questions arise concerning the factors which influenced the level of rates charged by the banks on their loans, the only rates over which they had any degree of control. Such factors might involve the desire for unity of action among the savings banks and the pressure of competing loan agencies.

In connection with the rate of dividends paid, the problem arises as to its effect in attracting or repelling savings. Here again lie the questions as to whether or not the banks recognized a certain mutual concern in pursuing identical policies and to what extent the banks were affected by the level of return elsewhere available to depositors.

All these are important questions to the economist, the banker, and the bank client. Although the questions, of course, cannot be answered here conclusively, it is hoped that some suggestions may be made concerning the directions in which the answers lie.

1. Interest Rates and the Assets of the Banks

a) Interest Charged on Mortgage Loans

(1) Mutual Savings Banks. At the beginning of the period under study, rates charged by the mutual savings banks of Northampton were declining. They continued to decline until about 1890, after which they remained at approximately the same level until the increase in rates at the conclusion of the War of 1914. Mortgage loan rates remained relatively stable from the war period to 1932, when the depression initiated a decline.

The movements of the interest rates may be seen on Charts 39, 40, and 41, pages 169, 170, and 171. Until 1907 the only rate reported by the Bank Commissioner was the rate received on all outstanding loans on real estate and on personal security, together with a few small items, such as railroad notes and loans to counties, cities, and towns. Beginning with 1907, the Annual Report separates the rates charged on outstanding loans on personal security and those received on real estate loans. During the earlier period the loans based upon non-mortgage security were large enough to have a substantial effect upon the average; after 1907, an average of the combined loans would be dominated by mortgage rates. The vertical lines on Charts 39, 40, and 41 show the range of interest rates on all loans from 1876 to 1906 and on mortgage loans from 1907 to 1938. Except in years when

Chart 39

AVERAGE ANNUAL RATE OF INTEREST CHARGED ON OUTSTANDING LOANS

Florence Savings Bank, October 31 of Each Year, 1876-1938

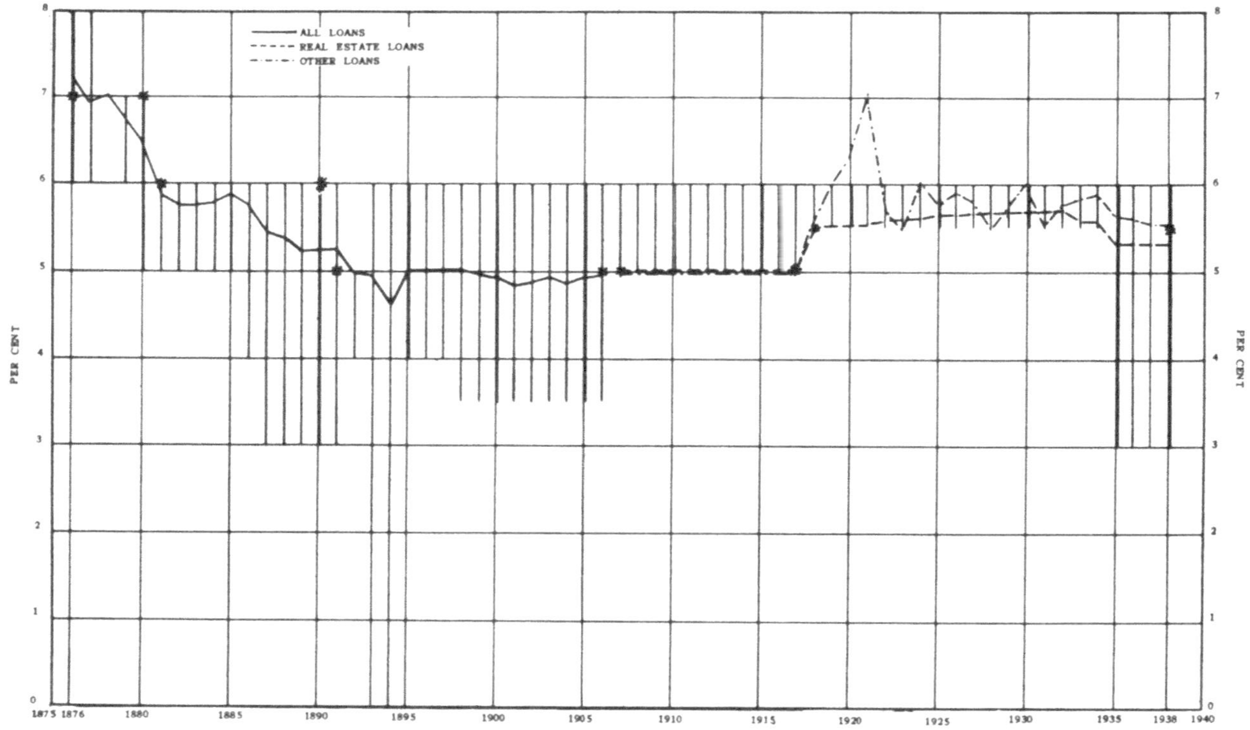

Source: Mass. Commissioner of Banks. *Annual Report*. 1876-1938. (Computed in part.)

Chart 40

AVERAGE ANNUAL RATE OF INTEREST CHARGED ON OUTSTANDING LOANS

October 31 of Each Year

Hampshire Savings Bank, 1876-1897

Nonotuck Savings Bank, 1899-1938

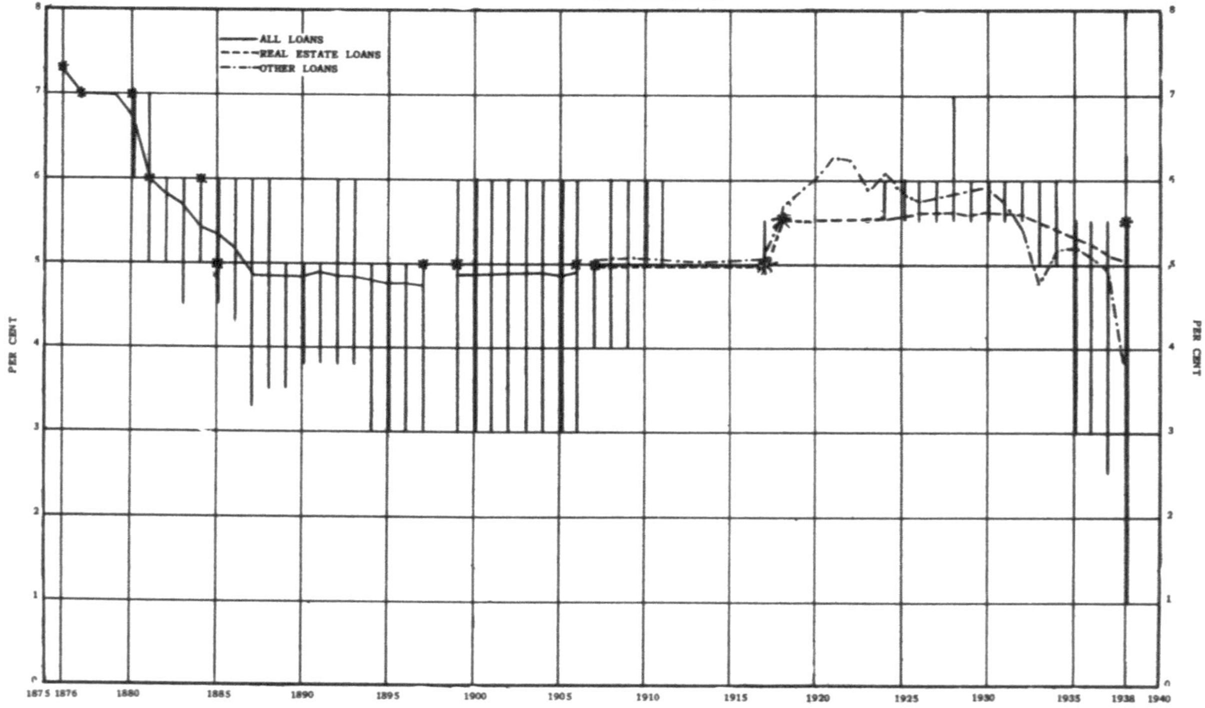

Source: Mass. Commissioner of Banks. *Annual Report*. 1876-1938. (Computed in part.)

Chart 41

AVERAGE ANNUAL RATE OF INTEREST CHARGED ON OUTSTANDING LOANS
Northampton Institution for Savings, October 31 of Each Year, 1876-1938

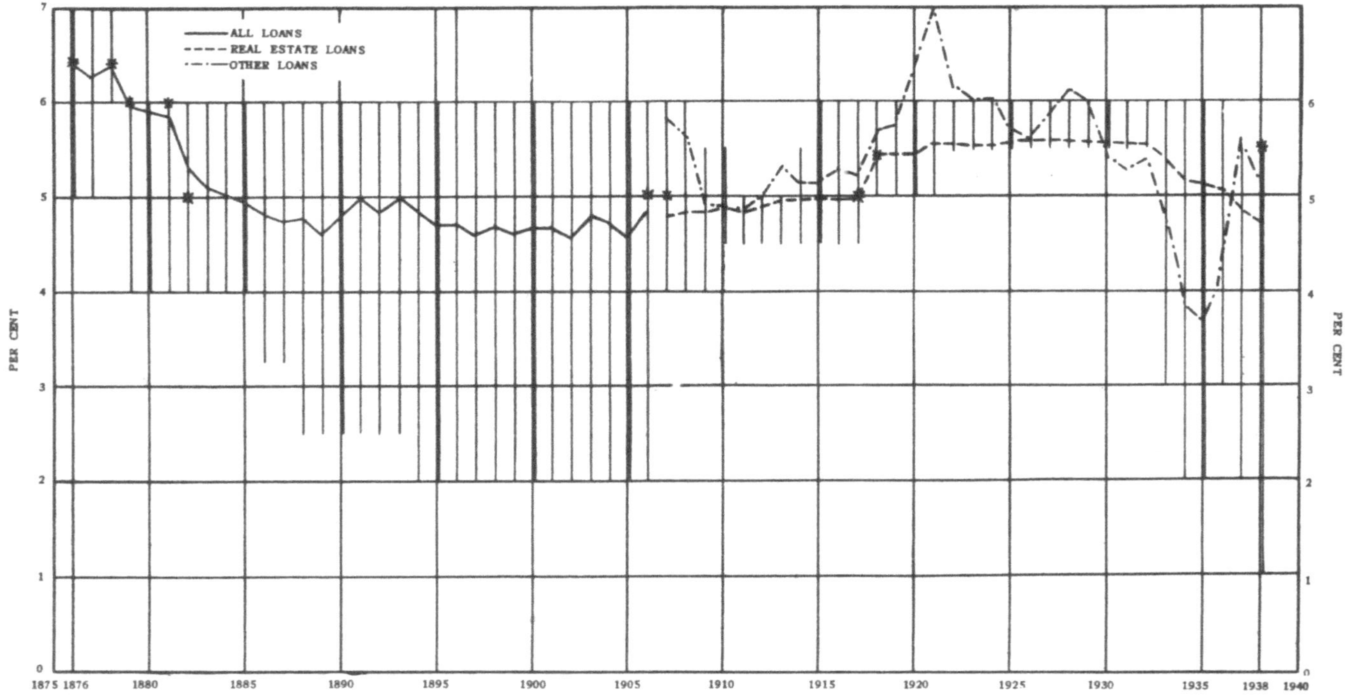

Source: Mass. Commissioner of Banks. *Annual Report*. 1876-1938. (Computed in part.)

the average was changing considerably, rates charged on loans were highly concentrated, however, around the prevailing, or modal, rate. Changes in this rate are indicated by asterisks on the charts.

Until 1892 the rates showed considerable variation between the three banks, and even after 1892 there was frequently a difference of about one-fourth of 1 per cent between the average rates. The rate charged by the Hampshire Savings Bank in 1876 was higher than the average in either of the other banks; each and every one of its loans bore 7.3 per cent interest. In 1877, the rate on all of its loans dropped to 7 per cent, which remained the prevailing rate until 1881. From 1879 to 1881 the average dropped sharply from 7 per cent to 6 per cent and continued to decline rapidly until it had fallen to less than 5 per cent in 1887. For the next ten years the average remained at about the same level.

In the 1870's, the loans of the Florence Savings Bank bore interest rates almost as high as those of the Hampshire Savings Bank. Although the prevailing rate on loans was 7 per cent from 1876 until 1881, the average rate received in 1876 was more than 7 per cent and some funds were loaned at a rate as high as 8 per cent. The average declined sharply after 1876 and by 1881 it had dropped below 6 per cent. Although from 1881 to 1890 most loans were paying 6 per cent, so many loans bore lower rates of interest that the average was considerably lower. On the last day of October, 1891, most loans were bearing 5 per cent interest, and this remained the prevailing rate until 1918.[2]

In the years preceding 1900, the average rate charged by the Northampton Institution for Savings was usually less than that charged in the other two banks. From 1877 through 1880 the prevailing rate at the other two banks was 7 per cent; at the Northampton Institution for Savings the prevailing rate in 1876 was 6.5 per cent and in 1879 it dropped to 6 per cent, or 1 per cent less than at the other banks. Although the other banks dropped their prevailing rate to 6 per cent in 1881, the rate

[2] The average rate did not deviate far from 5 per cent except in 1894. Aside from a small sum on which no interest was paid, the lower end of the range of rates charged in 1893 and 1894 was 4 per cent.

at the Northampton Institution for Savings fell to 5 per cent in 1882. Throughout most of the ten year period from 1876 to 1885 there was thus a differential of 1 per cent in the prevailing rates. However, because of the large number of loans made at rates other than the prevailing ones, the difference between the average rate charged by the Northampton Institution for Savings and those charged by the other banks was less than 1 per cent.

The drop in interest rates during the late 1870's and the early 1880's was caused by the more conservative loan policy adopted by the banks as a result of the decline in real estate values from 1876 to 1880. The banks acquired considerable amounts of real estate by foreclosure, as indicated in Charts 15, 16, and 17, pages 38, 39, and 40. Because of foreclosures and generally depressed conditions in the real estate market, the banks adopted a more conservative policy with respect to mortgage loans. In accordance with this policy and as a result of the generally low level of interest rates, the banks lowered the rate of interest charged. In addition there were doubtless concessions made upon distressed loans which the banks were trying to retain in good standing through reduced rates.

The downward movement of interest rates after 1876 reflected other interest rates and general investment conditions. Wholesale commodity prices displayed a downward trend in the 1870's and the general movement continued, with interruptions, until almost the close of the century. The depression and stagnation of business was felt throughout the whole country in the late 1870's. Business was poor, investors were cautious, and demand was therefore concentrated, to a considerable degree, on the highest grade securities. Bond prices were high and yields low. In the following years an increased volume of funds was available for investment. Retirement of the Federal debt was carried forward and funds were thereby released for investment. Savings bank deposits were growing and foreign investment in the United States was resumed. Thus large funds were seeking investment opportunities and at the same time business confidence was increasing; bond prices were therefore generally rising. The low rates of interest continued although there was considerable uncertainty concerning the resumption of specie payments and the relative places of gold and silver in the monetary system. Although there was great extension of railroad mileage and expansion of industry in the last twenty years of the century, large funds were available for investment and the tremendous volume of financing was therefore achieved without bringing higher interest rates. Thus the decline and continued low level of interest rates charged by the Northampton savings banks somewhat paralleled changes in rates elsewhere in the economy.

From 1900 to 1918 the average interest rates charged by Northampton banks remained almost unchanged, except that in the case of the Northampton Institution for Savings a slight increase occurred. Thus by 1917 all three banks were charging 5 per cent on almost every one of their mortgage loans.

Although interest rates charged by the Northampton banks showed little change from 1900 until the war, the yield on long-term bonds was generally rising during those years. At the opening of the century the settlement of the currency question by the adoption of the single gold standard, rising commodity prices, and large prospective profits from railroad and industrial consolidations contributed to the general optimism. Investors were turning away from low yield railroad bonds to second grade railroad bonds and to the securities of utility and industrial companies. Stock prices were high and, with some interruptions, there was much activity on the stock markets. In spite of the general prosperity and rising bond yields, the interest charged by the Northampton banks showed little increase in the years before 1918.

In 1918 the three Northampton banks increased the rate charged on most of their loans from 5 per cent to 5.5 per cent and this remained the prevailing rate through 1938. However, after 1932 the average for all loans fell considerably below 5.5 per cent because of the large number of loans at less than the prevailing rate. The lowering of the interest charge sometimes took place because a loan exceeded the maximum percentage of the value of the property and the bank was therefore requiring a reduction in the principal. To prevent foreclosure, the banks in other cases made concessions to borrowers who were good risks but were temporarily unable to pay the higher rates. Other low interest loans originated in the sale of property which the banks had acquired through foreclosure.

The movement of interest rates in Northampton after 1918 was to a considerable extent the counterpart of changes in yields on long-term bonds. The peak in rates on long-term bond issues was reached about 1921 or 1922 and yields remained high thereafter, although a gradual decline took place. After 1930 an interruption in the downward movement occurred, but yields declined again in 1933 and continued at low levels until 1938. The general low level of interest rates in the 1930's resulted from both the scarcity of new security issues and the lack of demand for funds because of business uncertainty and from governmental policy which favored low rates in order to induce business revival through expansion of the volume of credit.

Thus in the early years of this study the interest rates charged by the Northampton savings banks declined from about 7 per cent to 5 per cent. The decline reflected conditions in the local real estate market and the level of yields on other long-term investments. The rates charged by the banks remained at the 5 per cent level until 1918, when they rose to 5.5 per cent. The higher rates were maintained through the prosperous years when the real estate market was active and bond yields high. The depression of 1932 brought a decrease in real estate values and bond yields, and the average rate of interest charged by the Northampton banks likewise experienced a sharp decline. In the case of one bank the rate dropped to 4.75 per cent and the rates at the other banks fell to 5.04 and 5.33 per cent. Although there was some divergence in the early years, the banks in the later years maintained identical prevailing rates, apparently recognizing a mutual interest in pursuing similar policies.

(2) Other Mortgage Loan Agencies. The decline of interest rates in the savings banks following 1876 was somewhat paralleled by a decrease in the rates charged by the Smith Charities. There the rate was lowered from 7 to 6 per cent in October, 1876, and from 6 to 5 per cent in 1882. The rate remained unchanged from 1882 to 1938.

In the early years the interest rate charged by The Trustees of the Smith Charities was lower than the rates charged by the savings banks, especially the Hampshire and Florence banks. In

1887, however, the average rate of the Hampshire Savings Bank dropped below 5 per cent, the rate then charged by the Smith Charities. The rate at the Florence bank did not fall to 5 per cent until after 1891. During many of the years in the 1890's, however, the situation was reversed, since the rate charged by the Smith Charities was slightly higher than the average charged by all or some of the savings banks. Beginning with 1918 the prevailing rate on real estate loans at savings banks exceeded the rate at the Smith Charities by one-half of 1 per cent, and the average rates exceeded the rate at the Smith Charities, except in one bank in 1937 and 1938.

Since the Smith Charities did not have funds currently coming into the organization, except for income, the amount available for investment or reinvestment during the year was less than at the savings banks, which were receiving new funds. This softened any effect that the lower rate might have been expected to have upon the savings banks.

Because the Smith Charities dealt with farm mortgages primarily and the savings banks extended loans chiefly upon city real estate, competition between them was indirect for the most part. In addition, a difference of one-half of 1 per cent may be so small that it is ignored by the borrower of small sums.

Interest charges at the Northampton Cooperative Bank likewise differed from the rates charged by the savings banks, although it is impossible to know the effective rate of interest charged by the cooperative bank. While interest charges are stated for loans outstanding in October of each year, these rates cannot be directly compared with those charged by the savings banks or by the Smith Charities. The requirement that a borrower buy shares through monthly payments is almost equivalent to a requirement of periodic payments to reduce the principal of the loan. Interest payments on the original amount of the loan continue, however, throughout the life of the loan. If the interest charged on a loan were the same as the rate of profit paid upon shares, the nominal rate paid on the original amount would be the same as the effective rate paid on the original amount less the share values. Since the rate of profits in actual practice is less than the interest charged on loans, the nominal rate understates the effective rate paid.[3] Both the nominal rate and the differential between the rate charged borrowers and the rate paid to them in their capacity as share-buyers is shown in Chart 42, page 178.

The effective rate on cooperative bank loans was further increased above the nominal rate by the system of premiums permitted by law. Applicants for loans were allowed to bid for the privilege of receiving a priority upon available funds. In 1892 the highest premium received by the bank was 70¢. The rate fluctuated considerably and in 1902 the highest premium was only 10¢. Thereafter new loans were granted by the cooperative bank without the use of premiums.

The nominal rate of interest received by the cooperative bank was consistently higher than that charged by the savings banks. In 1896 the average rate was 6.5 per cent, or more than 1.5 per cent higher than the average rate then being charged by the savings banks. In 1903 and in subsequent years new loans were extended at an interest rate of 6 per cent and the average rate declined to 6 per cent in 1905. Even so, the cooperative bank was charging 1 per cent more than the savings banks were then charging their borrowers. Furthermore, if the differential between the interest paid to the bank and the interest received upon shares is taken into consideration, the difference in rate paid by a borrower at the cooperative bank and by a borrower at the mutual savings banks was even greater. Since the cooperative bank maintained the same nominal interest rate from 1905 to 1938, the difference between its rate and the rate charged by the savings banks was lessened by the rise in savings bank rates in 1918.

3 A borrower who had previously received a loan of $1,000 at the cooperative bank would have been paying 6 per cent on $1,000 in 1910 even though he had already paid $600 for the purchase of shares looking toward the cancellation of the principal. On those shares he would have received profits at the rate of 5.5 per cent a year. Thus the effective rate paid by the borrower was slightly higher than 6 per cent. The same borrower at a savings bank would have paid 5 per cent on $400, the unpaid balance on the principal. The cooperative bank might well point out, however, that its borrowers were forced to retire their debt and the borrower from the savings bank would quite possibly never have saved the $600 to apply to the principal of his loan.

Chart 42

ANNUAL RATE OF INTEREST CHARGED ON REAL ESTATE LOANS

Northampton Cooperative Bank, 1896-1938

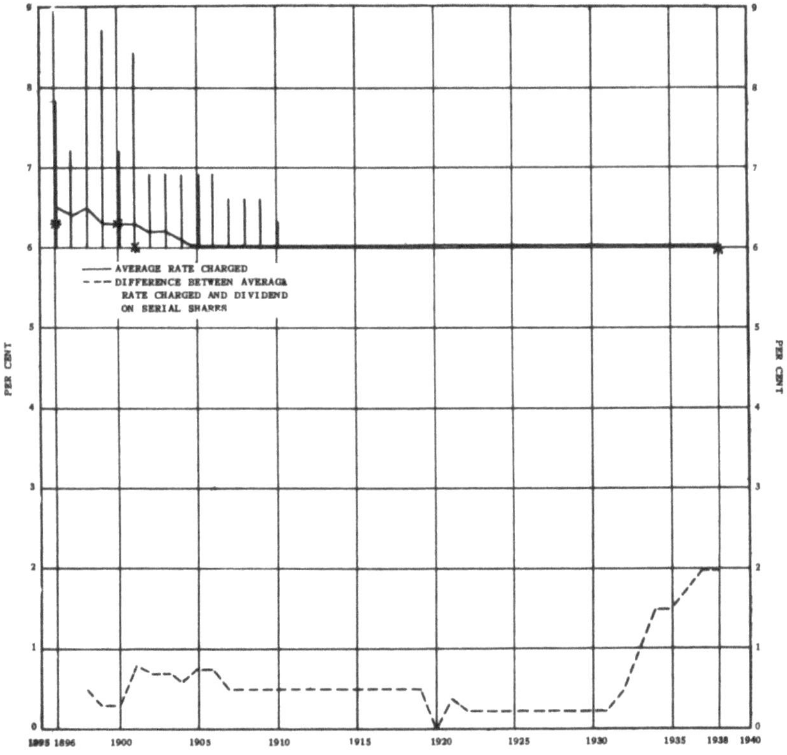

Source: Mass. Commissioner of Banks. *Annual Report*. 1896-1938. (Computed in part.)

After 1910 the prevailing rate charged by the cooperative bank was the universal rate for all mortgage loans, and the average rate therefore did not decrease after 1932 as it did at the savings banks. The effective interest charges of the cooperative bank actually increased after 1932 since the nominal rate remained unchanged and the rate of profits distributed dropped considerably. Thus we see one institution in which both the level of interest rates and the direction of movements in rates differed greatly from the interest charged by the other chief mortgage loan agencies, the savings banks and the Smith Charities.

It may be, as suggested earlier, that differentials in the interest expense involved in borrowing may be too small in the eyes of the prospective borrower to determine the place where he will finance his loan. Another element in connection with the cooperative bank is the fact that it is permitted to loan as much as 80 per cent of the value of the mortgaged property. Those with only small amounts of cash may find it necessary to borrow from the cooperative bank rather than from the less expensive savings banks or Smith Charities, each of which loaned a smaller percentage of total value. That such was actually the case is indicated by occasional movement of loans away from the cooperative bank after the principal had been reduced sufficiently to make it possible to borrow from one of the other institutions. Cooperative banks furthermore have made a special appeal to those with small savings and they have advertised the advantages of their plan whereby the principal of a loan is systematically reduced. They may thus have created a special following which ignored small differences in interest expense.

The rates of interest charged upon mortgage loans by the national banks would be a minor factor in the Northampton situation since such loans were small in total amount and were undertaken primarily as measures for refinancing loans made upon another basis.

The real estate loans of the Savings Department of the Hampshire County Trust Company were all extended at a rate of 6 per cent. Although this was slightly higher than the cost of a savings bank loan, the loans of the trust company expanded rapidly to something over one million dollars.

The rates of interest of the various Federal agencies seem to have had slight effect upon the mortgage loans of the savings banks. The rates charged by the Federal Land Bank were for many years lower than those charged by the savings banks. The loans were made primarily to another type of clientele, however, so that they did not directly affect the savings banks.

In Springfield and in Boston, important centers for Northampton, the mutual savings banks in the 1930's reduced their interest rates to 5 per cent. This reduction was caused, at least in part, by the competition of insurance companies. In Northampton, however, insurance company loans were not large enough to have any real effect. There were occasional sorties by Boston banks into the Northampton territory; they came in, looked over the choicest real estate, and then made it possible for the owner to obtain funds at 4.5 per cent. Because the Northampton banks could not meet this competition without lowering the prevailing rates on all loans, such occasional competition had no widespread effect.

Thus, during most of the years included in this study, different rates were received by mortgage loan agencies existing side by side. The rate at the Smith Charities was usually the same or less than the rate charged by the savings banks, and the rates received by the cooperative bank and by the trust company were higher than the rates at the savings banks. Unlike the mutual savings banks, none of these institutions, except the cooperative bank in the early years, extended loans at rates other than the rate established at that institution. Loans made by other agencies varied in rate but their volume was so small that they had little effect upon the loans of the savings banks.

b) Relation between the Volume of Real Estate Loans and Differences in Interest Rates

Since interest charges varied from one Northampton institution to another, it might well be expected that the differences in interest rates would bring divergences in the rate of growth of loans in the various institutions. However, no such simple relationship between high interest charges and a low rate of growth in the volume of loans, or between low charges and a high rate of growth, occurred.

Differentials in the interest charged by the savings banks apparently did not cause divergences in the rate of expansion of loans. Although the average rate charged at the Hampshire Savings Bank was usually higher than that at the Northampton Institution for Savings, its loans constituted an increasing part of its total assets from 1880 to 1897 and the percentage of assets so invested was higher than in the Northampton Institution for Savings (see Charts 12 and 14, pages 32 and 34). From 1881 to 1892 the Northampton Institution also invested an increasing proportion of assets in loans. The Florence Savings Bank, whose rate was almost as high as the average rate of the Hampshire bank from 1876 to 1882 and was higher than the rate in either of the other two banks for a number of years after 1882, showed a generally downward movement in loans as a percentage of total assets (see Chart 13, page 33). In the later years the savings banks established identical prevailing rates for mortgage loans, and the average rates showed relatively little divergence until after 1932.

If we consider the actual number of dollars loaned on mortgages, we find that the loans of the Hampshire Savings Bank, which charged the highest or next to the highest interest rates increased most regularly and rapidly from 1878 to 1897 (see Charts 9, 10, and 11, pages 28, 29, and 30). However, after 1890 the average rate charged by the Hampshire bank did not differ greatly from the average at the Northampton Institution for Savings. Although, from 1883 to 1900, the Florence Savings Bank maintained the highest interest charges of any of the savings banks, its loans on real estate continued to increase rapidly from 1883 to 1885, declined slowly from 1885 to 1894, and grew rapidly thereafter.

Although both the Northampton Cooperative Bank and the Hampshire County Trust Company consistently charged a higher rate of interest than the savings banks, their mortgage loans increased more rapidly, as shown in Chart 38, page 160. The narrowing of the difference in rates in 1918 seemed to have no effect upon the relative growth of the cooperative bank and the mutual savings banks. Thus, the higher rates charged by the cooperative bank and the trust company apparently did not adversely affect the growth of their loans, although the greater decline in the mortgage loans of the cooperative bank after 1931 may have been influenced by the increasing differential between its rates and those at the mutual savings banks.

Since the loans of the Smith Charities and the Federal Land Bank were extended upon other types of real estate than that mortgaged to the savings and cooperative banks and the trust company, it would not be expected that the lower rates of interest charged would directly influence the volume of loans.

During the period covered by this study the differences in interest charges at various institutions seemed to have little or no effect upon the volume of loans extended by the several institutions. If the differentials had effects, they are hidden by other factors. A slight difference in rate apparently was a minor consideration in determining the bank from which a borrower would obtain a loan. The volume of loans was more directly affected by the loan policy of the bank and by the total amount of funds available.

c) Interest Rates and the Distribution of Assets between Loans and Investments

Interest rates, both rates obtained on loans and yields received on bonds, would be expected to influence the manner in which the total assets of the savings banks were distributed between loans and investments, and yields would also enter into the determination of the broad groups of bonds purchased by the banks. In the following discussion the returns available through different uses of funds will be indicated in order to determine the extent to which the investments of the savings banks were influenced by comparative rates of return.

Other factors than the current rate of return, of course, enter into the investment decision. The volume of bonds and stocks available on the market and legal for savings bank investment presents a limiting factor, and the banks' estimate of the future course of events in a given industry, such as the railroad industry, also affects the decision as to where funds will be placed. In addition, the variation of price from par value influences the security purchases of the savings banks to a greater degree than with other types of investors. The savings banks, in general, carry securities on their books at par value, cost, or market value, whichever is lowest, although the reduction to market value in the case of depreciated securities may be very slow. Furthermore, even when realized, the appreciation of securities is not available for distribution as dividends.

In 1876 savings bank investments were limited in scope and confined largely to certain railroad bonds, bank stock, and public funds. By statute, investment in railroad securities was restricted to first mortgage bonds and this practically precluded the purchase of railroad obligations since few were at that time secured by first mortgages.[4] The consolidation of railroads and the development of railroad lines through the use of leases in the 1880's withheld many railroad bonds from the list of investments legal for Massachusetts savings banks.[5] Although the bonds of an increasing number of railroad companies were made legal for investment in the latter part of the nineteenth century, investment was chiefly confined to roads serving the New England area. Thus, in spite of the fact that the highest grade railroad bonds were selling at prices which yielded a rate equal to or higher than the rate of return on loans by the savings banks, there could be little shifting of bank assets into this field.

Bank stock during 1877 and 1878 was not looked upon with favor since conditions had been so bad that the liability of stockholders acted as a deterrent to the marketability of stock.[6] Although both the Northampton Institution for Savings and the Hampshire Savings Bank owned bank stock in 1876, their investment in this type of security showed little or no increase in the following years (see Charts 24, 25, and 26, pages 66, 67, and 68).

Investment in public funds seemed sound but yields were too low to make such securities attractive to the banks. Notes of cities and towns were considered a satisfactory kind of investment in 1878,[7] except that the yield of municipal bonds, as indicated in Dr. Macaulay's index,[8] was considerably lower than

4 Mass., *Annual Report of the Board of Commissioners of Savings Banks*, 1877, p. 370.

5 *Ibid.*, 1887, p. xii.

6 *Ibid.*, 1878, p. 374.

7 *Ibid.*, 1878, p. 375.

8 Frederick R. Macaulay, *Some Theoretical Problems Suggested by the Movements of Interest Rates, Bond Yields and Stock Prices in the United States since 1856*, pp. A172–A175.

the return possible through direct mortgage loans. The rates at which United States Treasury bonds were being issued during these early years were so low that it was not possible for the savings banks to invest in them and receive a return sufficient to maintain their dividend rates.[9] Investment in public funds by the Northampton Institution for Savings was, therefore, decreasing from 1879 to 1890 and little was so invested by the other two banks.

By 1900, legal restrictions concerning railroad bonds had been eased with respect to the requirements concerning the security of a first mortgage, the leasing of lines, and the location of roads. Thus the way was opened for large investment by the savings banks.

The banks increased their investment in railroad bonds after 1900 even though the rate of return was slightly lower than that on mortgage loans. If the banks were to invest not more than half of their deposits in loans (considered a normal standard and indicated as a maximum by the Bank Commissioners in 1878[10]), these investments were about the best ones available. Bonds and notes of the city of Northampton and of cities and towns within the state, which constituted the public funds held by the Northampton savings banks, were yielding only 3 or 3.5 per cent. As public funds matured they were reinvested in other kinds of securities, particularly railroad bonds, which bore a better rate.

During the first World War the savings banks invested heavily in United States Treasury bonds and they continued to hold the bonds for several years after the conclusion of the war. As they withdrew funds from investment in Treasury bonds, they purchased railroad securities and to some extent the public utility bonds which had been added to the legal list by the act of 1926. In the late 1920's the yield on the highest grade public utility bonds was slightly higher than the yield on the same grade of railroad bonds, and the utilities as a class were considered excellent investments.

From 1920 to 1930 the average yield of bonds and stocks owned

9 Mass., *Annual Report of the Board of Commissioners of Savings Banks*, 1878, p. 374.

10 *Ibid.*, 1878, p. 374.

by the savings banks varied between 4.5 and 5 per cent, as compared with a yield of about 5.5 per cent for mortgage loans (see Chart 43, page 186). The yield of bonds and stocks, however, is exaggerated to the extent that it is based upon book value and in so far as securities were bought above par value the yield would therefore be reported as higher than the market yield. However, since such a marking down to par value would have been charged to surplus, perhaps this is as significant a yield as the rate of return on the actual amount invested.

After about 1930, railroad bonds were yielding a slightly higher rate than were similar high grade utility bonds, and the Nonotuck and Florence savings banks were slightly increasing their investment in railroad securities. Although prospects for railroads as a group were not bright at this time because of the many roads operating under receivership or undergoing reorganization, the top grade securities continued to be well thought of. The Northampton Institution for Savings decreased its investment in both railroad and public utility bonds after 1930 and invested increasing amounts in Treasury bonds, which were low in yield, and in bank stocks. The savings banks considered bank stock a good type of investment with which to hedge against rising interest rates since commercial banks had by that time placed themselves in a sound position and their earnings would increase substantially as soon as any rise in interest rates took place.

Although the rate of return to be received from real estate loans was much higher than the return from security investments in the 1930's, the demand for loans was small and consequently the volume of mortgage loans made by the savings banks either decreased or remained unchanged during those years. The availability of greater funds for investment led to some increase in security investment by the Northampton banks and it led to a state-wide interest in the restatement of legal requirements to permit a broadening of the field of investment.[11]

The effect of the rate of return upon the distribution of assets among different uses may, thus, be offset by many factors. In the early years covered by this study, the security invest-

[11] Mass., *Annual Report of the Commissioner of Banks*, Part I, 1937, p. iii.

Chart 43

AVERAGE ANNUAL RATE OF RETURN ON AMOUNT INVESTED IN BONDS AND STOCK

Northampton Savings Banks, 1911-1938

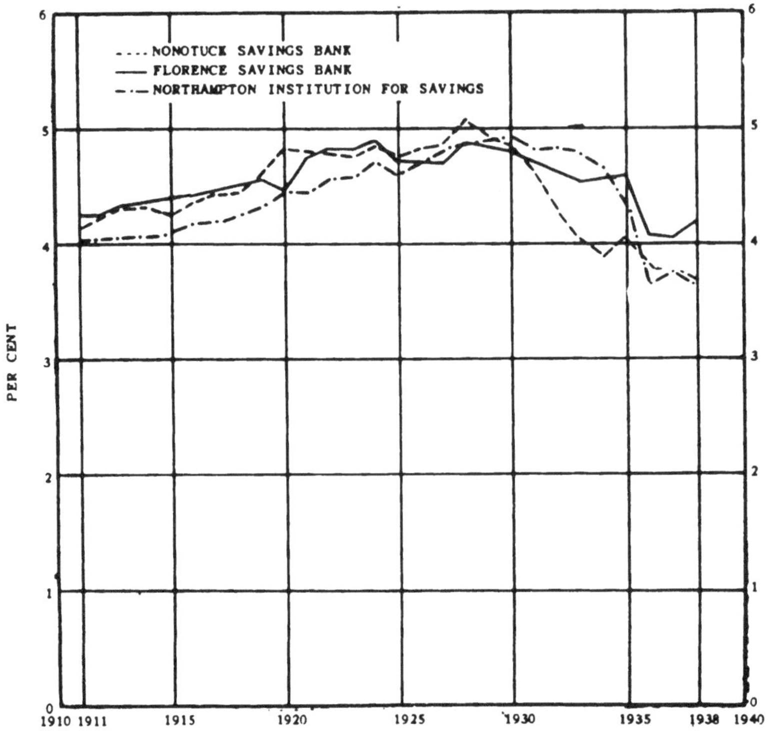

Source: Mass. Commissioner of Banks. *Annual Report* 1911-1938.

ments of the savings banks were so limited that the banks were forced to place a large part of their funds in mortgage or other direct loans. In the later years bank policy established a maximum of 50 or 60 per cent of assets for the total volume of mortgage loans and thus the banks invested in bonds and stock even though such investment led to a lower rate of return than that obtained on loans. In spite of the high prospective return on mortgage loans in the 1930's as compared with other uses of funds, the banks did not increase their mortgage loans because of the lack of demand for such loans and because of the caution engendered by the decline in real estate values. Within the limits of the legal list of investments, however, the banks shifted funds according to the rate of return anticipated on high grade securities. Thus the rate of return was one element determining the investment of assets but other elements, such as the demand for real estate loans, anticipations of the banks concerning the future of real estate values, the availability of high grade securities, the desire to keep a balance between loans and investments, and the preoccupation of the banks with the safety of their funds, entered into the distribution of assets.

2. Interest Rates and the Deposits of the Banks

a) Rates of Dividends Paid

(1) Dividends Paid by Mutual Savings Banks

(a) Legal Regulation. Since the savings banks are mutual organizations, legal regulations have been established to insure that the earnings of a savings bank are actually distributed to the depositors. Other restrictions concerning earnings and dividends have aimed at protecting the depositors from over-large dividends which might impair the position of the bank.

The law provided in 1876 that the income of savings banks was to be divided after reasonable expenses and after contributions to the guaranty fund. Ordinary dividends were to be paid every six months at a rate not greater than 2.5 per cent. This limit of 5 per cent a year was maintained throughout the period under study. Dividends were not to be paid on deposits of less than three months' standing. No dividend was to be declared if the net profits over and above the guaranty fund for the six months preceding the dividend date were not more than 2 per cent of the deposits.[12] This was soon changed to 1.5 per cent, that is, dividends were not to be paid if the net profits for six months were less than 1.5 per cent of the total deposits.[13]

In 1908, the law provided that ordinary dividends were to be declared from income remaining after reasonable expenses of management, state taxes, and additions to the guaranty fund had been deducted from income earned and collected during the preceding six months, except that the banks could appropriate from the undistributed earnings remaining after the declaration of the preceding semi-annual dividend. The total dividend declared in any twelve months, however, was not to be larger than the net income collected during that period, except by special permission.[14] Banks were later allowed to pay dividends for periods of not less than one month from income earned and collected during the preceding dividend period.[15] An act of 1933 authorized the payment of dividends at intervals of not less than three months. Furthermore no dividends were to be paid at a rate greater than 4 per cent a year unless the maximum semi-annual amount had been set aside for the guaranty fund.[16]

In addition to the ordinary dividends provided for by law, the banks have been permitted to declare extra dividends. In 1876 it was provided that once every three years when the net profits, above the guaranty fund and the dividends declared, were 1 per cent of those deposits which had remained in the bank for at least one year, the net profits were to be divided among depositors whose deposits had remained there for the preceding year. The extra dividend was to be paid to depositors in proportion to the amount of the dividends declared on their deposits during the preceding three years.[17] In 1888, the distribution of extra dividends was made optional, that is, the law said such net profits <u>may</u> be divided rather than <u>shall</u> be.[18]

12 Mass. Acts 1876, c. 203, secs. 14 and 15.
13 Mass. Acts 1880, c. 150.
14 Mass. Acts 1908, c. 590, sec. 60.
15 Mass. Acts 1919, c. 326, sec. 1.
16 Mass. Acts 1933, c. 334, sec. 17.
17 Mass. Acts 1876, c. 203, sec. 16.
18 Mass. Acts 1888, c. 355.

The regulations concerning extra dividends were changed in 1896. Once every three years if, after the payment of ordinary dividends, the net profits accumulated, including the guaranty fund, amounted to 11 per cent of the deposits which had remained in the bank for the preceding year, such profits in excess of 10 per cent were to be divided among the depositors in the same manner as before.[19] Later extra dividends of not less than one-fourth of 1 per cent were to be paid whenever the guaranty fund and undivided profits amounted to 10.25 per cent of deposits and the extra dividends were to be paid on deposits of six months' standing. Thus the earnings would be more nearly distributed among those whose deposit funds had earned the profits. The payment of extra dividends was not to reduce the guaranty fund and the accumulated profits below 10 per cent.[20] When the maximum amount allowed in the guaranty fund was increased to 7.5 per cent, these requirements concerning dividends were also altered. A limit of 15.25 per cent was substituted for 10.25 per cent and 15 per cent for 10 per cent in the above requirements.[21]

(b) Dividends Paid by the Savings Banks. Although the rate of dividends paid by the Northampton mutual savings banks was stable for long periods of time, it dropped sharply in the first years included in this study, remained almost unchanged for many years, was high in the 1920's, and dropped in the 1930's. Five distinct periods occur in the rate of dividends: 1876-80, 1881-99, 1899-1919, 1919-32, 1932-38. These are apparent in Chart 44, page 190, in which the semi-annual dividends for each bank are shown.

In the years from 1876 to 1880, the rate of dividends declined sharply in each of the three banks. At the time of the first semi-annual dividend payment in 1876 both the Northampton Institution for Savings and the Florence Savings Bank declared a dividend of 3 per cent, or a dividend at the annual rate of 6 per cent. The rate paid by the Hampshire Savings Bank was slightly lower. By the time of the first dividend payment in 1881 each of the banks had reduced its dividend to 2 per cent, or 4 per

19 Mass. Acts 1896, c. 231.

20 Mass. Acts 1908, c. 590, sec. 63.

21 Mass. Acts 1933, c. 334, sec. 19.

Chart 44

DIVIDENDS PAID

Semi-Annual Rate, 1876-1938

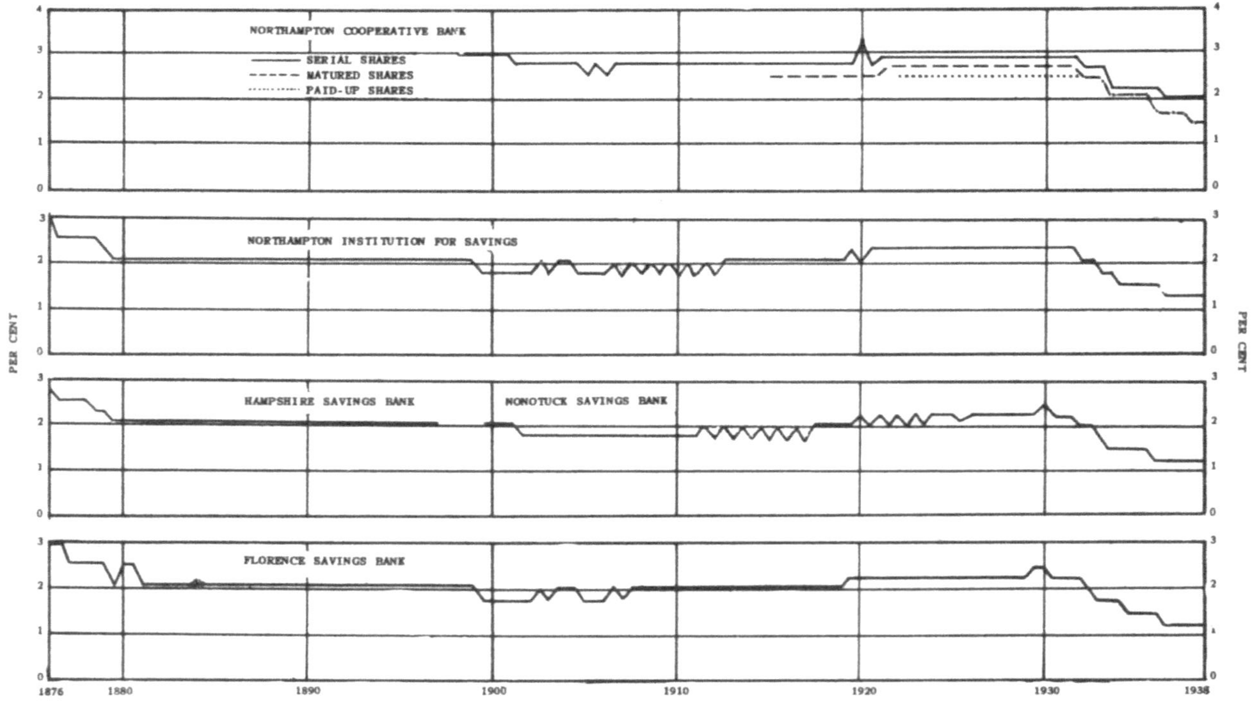

* An extra dividend of 1 per cent was also paid.

Source: Mass. Commissioner of Banks. *Annual Report*. 1876-1938.

cent a year. During these years following 1876, the interest rate charged on loans was declining from about 7 per cent to 6 per cent (see Charts 39, 40, and 41, pages 169, 170, and 171).

From 1881 until 1899, the annual rate of dividends remained at 4 per cent in each of the banks. During the early part of this period the interest rate received on loans was declining but throughout the remainder of the period the interest charge remained about 5 per cent, or 1 per cent greater than the annual rate of dividends.

The semi-annual dividend rates were slightly lower from 1899 until 1919 than in preceding years, varying between 1.75 per cent and 2 per cent. During this time the interest charged upon mortgage loans was generally 5 per cent, with only slight deviations from that rate.

The dividend rates at the Florence bank and the Northampton Institution for Savings rose in October, 1919, and at the Nonotuck bank in June, 1920, and they remained 2.25 per cent, semiannually, for most of the years until 1932. The rise in the dividend rate was foreshadowed by the increase which occurred in the rate charged on loans in 1918. At this time interest rates and bond yields were high and the savings banks were feeling the competition of United States bonds which their depositors were buying. The banks, therefore, believed it necessary to increase their rate of dividends and to do so they raised the prevailing rate on their loans.

The drop in the semi-annual dividend rate began in 1932, or perhaps in 1930, and carried the rate as low as 1.25 per cent by 1936. Dividends thus fell before the average rate received on real estate loans showed any real drop. The decline of rates charged on loans on personal security had already begun, however, and the current return on security investments was lower. The reaction of the dividend rate was thus prompt, not lagging behind rates of return as it did in 1919. Dividend rates might be expected to lag behind increases in the rate of return since dividends are declared out of the earnings of the preceding six months. The reaction of the dividend rates in the 1930's was extremely severe for it involved a reduction in rates of almost 50 per cent.

Although the dividend payments were similar in the three banks and always kept at about the same level, the rates were far from identical for the same years. At least in the more recent years the attitude of the Bank Commissioner has apparently been that it is undesirable for banks in the same community to maintain different dividend rates[22] and the banks themselves have taken much the same attitude. Differences in dividend rates may draw deposits from one bank to another; if so, the bank with lower dividends is forced to liquidate some of its assets. In the later years, of course, the desirability of attracting increases in deposits was lessened by the difficulty in finding suitable uses for additional funds.

Throughout the period included in the study, dividend rates promptly reflected changes in the rate of return on the loans and investments of the banks. This would be expected because of the legal requirement that dividends be paid out of the actual earnings of the preceding year. Changes in the dividend rate usually reflected the approximate size of the change in the interest rate received by the banks but in the years after 1930 the drop in dividend rates was more severe.

(2) Interest Paid by Other Savings Institutions

In the effort to observe the effect of interest rates upon the deposit funds of the savings banks, it is necessary to compare the rate of dividends received by savings bank depositors with the rate which they would have received if their savings had been placed in other institutions in Northampton.

The rate of dividend paid by the Northampton Cooperative Bank is shown on Chart 44, page 190. In accordance with its function of encouraging habits of thrift and regular savings, the cooperative bank paid a higher rate on serial shares, which represented new savings, than it paid on accumulations invested as lump sums in paid-up and matured shares. By law the bank was required to pay at least as high dividends upon the serial shares as upon the other two classes.

The rate of dividends paid by the cooperative bank upon serial shares was consistently higher than the dividend rate of the savings banks. The differential varied from 1 per cent semi-

22 Mass., *Annual Report of the Commissioner of Banks*, Part I, 1933, p. iii.

annually in the earlier years to five-eighths of 1 per cent in the 1920's. After 1933 the differential was for the most part three-fourths of 1 per cent. Even the lower rates paid upon matured and paid-up shares were consistently higher than dividends in the savings banks. Since the cooperative bank maintained a higher rate of interest on its loans than did the savings banks and since almost all its assets were invested in this relatively profitable form of investment, the cooperative bank could afford to pay higher dividends.

The interest rate paid by the Hampshire County Trust Company upon its savings deposits was 4.5 per cent a year, the rate then being paid by the savings banks. The national banks maintained an interest payment on deposits in their savings departments equal to 1 per cent less than the annual rates being currently paid by the mutual banks.

The interest paid on deposits in the Postal Savings System was lower than in any of the banks, except the national banks in the later years, for it was held at an annual rate of 2 per cent simple interest.

The monetary incentive to save, thus, varied widely in the savings institutions of Northampton. Until the 1930's the lowest rate was paid on postal savings deposits, which were never large in amount. The national banks, which did not wish to stimulate savings deposits, consistently paid a lower rate than that paid by the savings banks, but the rate paid by the trust company was the same as that of the savings banks. Throughout its existence the cooperative bank paid a higher rate upon its shares than the savings banks paid their depositors.

b) Relation between the Interest Rate and the Amount on Deposit

(1) Effect of the Differences in Dividend Rates

If the differentials between the dividend rates of the mutual savings banks are compared with new deposits (exclusive of dividends) and withdrawals made during the year or the number of accounts opened and closed, it is not possible to discern any effect of the differentials upon the comparative popularity of the banks. Although the dividends paid by the Florence Savings Bank were frequently higher than the dividends paid by the other banks, the difference seemed to have little or no effect upon its growth as compared with the others. The existence of a rate differential did not seem to bring a faster rate of growth than occurred when there was no differential. Although we might well expect that any long continued variation in dividends might affect the comparative rate at which the banks grew, the rate differentials that did occur were perhaps not maintained long enough to impress the savers as real and permanent differences. The mutual savings banks, furthermore, do not guarantee any rate of interest but, as their name "mutual" suggests, the profits of the period are simply distributed as dividends. Therefore the depositor cannot know exactly the rate at which future dividends will be distributed and the effect of differences in dividends may thus be somewhat vitiated.

The mutual savings bank deposits did not grow as rapidly as did the assets of the cooperative bank. The more rapid growth may be in part a consequence of the higher rate of profits distributed by the cooperative bank. However, the equally rapid growth of the savings deposits in the national banks with their lower rates of interest suggests that many factors other than the interest rate determine the particular institution in which people place their savings. Perhaps the interest rate plays a minor part in the decision concerning the place in which savings will be deposited. Convenience, familiarity, and the desire for or dislike of compulsion in regularity of savings -- all of these may outweigh the importance of the interest rate.

(2) Effect of the Level of the Dividend Rate upon the Growth of Deposits in the Savings Banks

The level of the dividend rate paid by the savings banks may well be compared with the growth of deposit balances to determine whether or not a high level of dividends stimulated growth of deposits in the banks and, conversely, whether or not a low level deterred the growth of deposits.

During the first five years included in this study the dividend rate was declining and the decline was accompanied by some decrease in the amount annually deposited in each bank. The drop in new deposits did not continue into the following years, however, when dividends were still falling.

The rise in the dividend rate in 1919 coincided with an increase in the amount deposited in the banks and the new deposits were likewise high during the following year. The increase over 1918, however, is in part explained by the withdrawal of the pressure of patriotism which caused people to divert their savings to the purchase of United States bonds and so to deposit fewer funds in the savings banks in 1918 than they otherwise would have deposited.

The dividends of the savings banks remained much the same through the 1920's and through the years when optimism and speculation were great and when many people with small funds were speculating in the security markets. Although the interest on savings deposits was a modest return for the times, the deposits of the savings banks continued to grow. The banks were not participating in the glorious expansion of the day but they more than held their own.

It has not been possible to trace the effect of the dividend rate upon the rate at which people are willing to save, as evidenced by the savings banks. The level of the rate of dividends is not directly and simply related to the volume of deposits. The rate of growth of the banks was much the same as the rate of dividends, suggesting that the banks grew primarily out of their own earnings. This is not an exact interpretation, however, since a large part of the deposits were withdrawn each year and other funds placed on deposit.

B. LEGAL REGULATION

In the preceding sections the discussion centered around the effects of interest rates as one factor influencing the development of the savings banks. Another element of great importance consists of the various legal regulations concerning the receipt of deposit funds, the use of these balances, and the distribution of earnings received upon the deposit funds.

Through various statutes, mutual savings banks have become institutions concerned primarily with the accumulation of small savings and with the provision of a high degree of safety for such sums. Furthermore, investment has been so restricted that savings bank funds have, to a large extent, been made available for financing the needs of the local community.

Changes in the restrictions profoundly influenced the course of the savings banks. Without the provisions making possible ever broader investments, the banks would have been severely hampered by inability to invest their increasing deposit balances. Without the raising of the limit on deposit accounts the savings banks would have been hindered in the building up of deposit funds. The effects of particular changes in regulations have been discussed elsewhere and here their importance is simply pointed out as one primary factor in affecting the development of the savings banks.

C. PROSPERITY OF THE COMMUNITY

The development of the Northampton savings banks has been affected by the competition of other institutions, by interest rates, and by the legal framework within which they operate, but the growth of the banks has also been dependent upon economic conditions in Northampton. The closeness of this connection must be recognized when half of the assets of the banks are invested in local mortgage loans and almost all of the deposit funds are placed in the bank by local citizens.

1. Mortgage Loans

The prosperity of the local community greatly affects any institution, such as a savings bank, which loans a large part of its assets on real estate located in the city. Without the continuing development of the Northampton community, the real estate loans of the savings banks could not have increased.

Activity in manufacturing in Northampton is indicated in Chart 2, page 7. From about 1897 to the first World War, Northampton industries were expanding, with some lessening of activity in 1900, 1904, 1907, and 1908. At the beginning of the war, Northampton industries expanded promptly and expansion continued after the United States entered the war. During the post-war years, manufacturing continued at a high level, but the silk industries, which had been an important part of the industrial life of Northampton, were not enjoying prosperity during these years. The mills changed ownership and some were permanently shut down.

Changes in building activity are indicated in Chart 45, page 198, where data of building permits are shown. Little building was carried on during World War I and by 1921 it was reported that Northampton was about one hundred houses short, in the class of houses renting from $25 to $45 a month. At that time there was considerable repairing and renovating but few new buildings were erected.[23] The number of permits issued for dwelling houses was at its peak in 1922 and it was high again in 1925 but thereafter it declined. The estimated cost of all building was high in 1923 and 1925, together with an additional high point in 1929. There are several institutions located in Northampton: schools; a college; state and county hospitals and a Federal veterans' hospital. These engaged in relatively large construction expenditures, not necessarily correlated with other business activity, and they were not financed by local credit agencies. The line of adjusted estimated cost in Chart 45 is an approximation of the amount of construction exclusive of these institutions.

In the first few years of the period covered by this study, the real estate loans of the savings banks were decreasing or growing slowly (see Charts 9, 10, and 11, pages 28, 29, and 30). These were years of uncertainty and real estate values were undergoing readjustment caused by the inflation of the Civil War years. A considerable degree of prosperity was enjoyed in 1880 and 1881; the decline of real estate loans in two of the Northampton banks halted and the rate of decrease diminished in the third. Although 1883 and 1884 were years of depression for the country as a whole, the real estate loans of the Northampton banks were increasing during those years. From 1886 to 1892, when business activity was high, with several mild recessions, the volume of real estate loans of the Northampton banks increased or remained relatively unchanged. Business in the community showed no pronounced improvement from 1893 until 1897, just as business in the country as a whole continued to be dull, and loans on real estate showed no great increase during these years.

From 1897 until the War of 1914, Northampton factories were expanding and enjoying more or less continued prosperity. During

23 *Springfield Republican*, September 14, 1921.

Chart 45

BUILDING ACTIVITY IN NORTHAMPTON, 1919-1938

Building Permits Issued

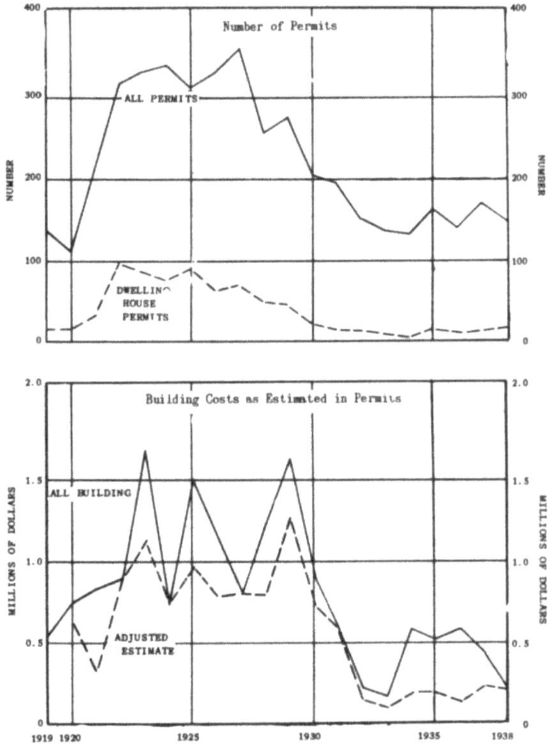

Source: Northampton (Massachusetts). Building Inspector. *Annual Report*. 1919-1938.

these years the mortgage loans of the banks were increasing, although not without exception. In 1908 and 1909 the growth of real estate loans was interrupted, reflecting the slackening of business in 1908, and again in 1913 there was a halt in the growth of real estate loans. During 1918 mortgage loans reflected the low activity in construction, but they expanded with the great increase in building that occurred soon after the conclusion of the war. The mortgage loans of the banks were increasing from 1922 to 1928, a period of high activity in construction and in business in general. With the lessened prosperity of the years from 1929 to 1933, loans showed little increase and then dropped as a result of the prolonged depression and the fall in the real estate market.

Thus the changes in the volume of mortgage loans in general reflected fluctuations in building activity and in the level of prosperity in Northampton, although the correlation is not perfect. The fact that many loans were outstanding for several years somewhat decreased the sensitivity of real estate loans to fluctuations in economic conditions.

2. Deposit Accounts

The prosperity of the community is reflected in the volume of savings deposits, as it is reflected by changes in the amount of mortgage loans made by the savings banks. Consideration of the effect of the level of prosperity involves the question of the motives which lead to the accumulation of surplus funds by individuals, although savings deposits constitute only one segment of total savings.

Many studies have been made of the pattern of consumer expenditures of different income groups. These budget studies, such as that conducted by the National Resources Committee in 1936, have established the fact that at any given time the proportion saved increases rapidly with increases in income. We should thus expect that changes in the prosperity of the Northampton community would lead to increased savings.

It has been further suggested recently that the volume of savings does not depend alone upon the size of income but that it is also a function of changes in income.[24] People tend to

[24] Mordecai Ezekiel, "Statistical Investigations of Saving, Consumption, and Investment," *American Economic Review*, XXXII (1942), 22-49.

follow habitual patterns of consumption and these patterns are less flexible than the savings pattern. Thus when incomes rise, people at first cling to their old habits of spending and the proportion they save increases greatly with the initial increase in income. As they become accustomed to the larger income, however, their expenditures for consumption increase and the margin of saving declines, although the margin is ordinarily higher than at the previous level of income. As compared with the static analysis in the budget studies, this tendency toward less flexibility in consumer expenditures would amplify the effect produced upon the volume of savings by income changes.

The motives leading to the accumulation of savings are varied. Provision for contingencies, such as sickness, unemployment, and loss, provides one incentive.[25] Anticipation of future needs, such as vacations and education, provides another stimulus. Saving may also be encouraged by the desire for independence, and the need for funds with which to carry on business enterprise.[26] Habits are strong and the thrift habit causes people to set aside funds even though their savings are for no such definite purpose as provision for an education or for old age.

In the Northampton savings banks, the opening of new accounts and the rate at which funds were placed on deposit reflected the degree of prosperity in the community, as indicated in Chapter III. Although the rate of return on savings accounts may affect the accumulation of deposit balances, little evidence of such an influence is apparent during the period studied. The amount of saving perhaps depends to a greater degree upon social habits, changes in income, and shifts in the distribution of income.

Deposits in savings banks do not, of course, reflect movements in total savings perfectly for they represent only a part of all savings and they are affected by shifts in the use of funds available for investment. This is indicated, in part, by Chart 37, page 155. Some of the savings funds which might have come to the savings banks were diverted to the other institutions shown. Although savings bank deposits were increasing during the period

25 Floyd F. Burtchett, *Investments and Investment Policy*, p. 390.

26 John Maynard Keynes, *The General Theory of Employment, Interest and Money*, pp. 107–10.

studied, from 1889 to 1929 a more rapid rate of expansion occurred in the savings placed in the cooperative bank and in the savings departments of the national banks and of the trust company. After 1929 and 1930, the savings banks enjoyed a shift in the distribution of funds among savings outlets, for their deposits failed to show the sharp downturn that occurred in the other banks.

Chapter VI

SUMMARY AND CONCLUSIONS

Although the increasing funds deposited in the mutual savings banks of Northampton from 1876 to 1938 were invested in an ever broadening field, mortgage loans throughout the years constituted the chief investment. On the whole, they made up about one-half of the assets. The loans, secured primarily by home mortgages, were small in size and were made chiefly to local residents. Although the loans were payable on demand, they were usually outstanding for a number of years. An apparent weakness in the loan situation consisted of the failure of borrowers to reduce the principal of their loans; in the later years the banks attacked this problem by making informal amortization agreements with borrowers.

The amount invested in mortgage loans by each of the banks showed almost continuous growth except for the decreases resulting from the deflation of real estate values in the late 1870's and in the 1930's. Growth was especially rapid in the years from 1910 to 1917 and from 1922 to 1927. These were years of prosperity and considerable activity in residential construction.

Foreclosures were important only during the deflation from 1876 to 1878 and in the 1930's, when the real estate market again underwent a serious decline. In this later period real estate acquired through foreclosure by the several banks reached a high point varying from 14 to 22 per cent of the value of outstanding loans and exceeding the value of the guaranty funds.

The loans based upon security other than real estate mortgages consisted chiefly of corporate notes and notes secured by stocks and bonds, by co-signers, and, in more recent years, by passbooks. The amount invested in this non-mortgage type of loan was large in the years prior to 1900, at times almost reaching the volume of real estate loans. After 1900, loans based upon personal security decreased in importance although the actual amount invested in this manner either showed little decline or increased. This decline relative to total assets resulted from the centralization of ownership of much of the business of Northampton and from the increased use made by local citizens of the services of the financial centers.

For the most part, movements in the volume of real estate loans and changes in loans on other security bore an inverse relationship. Loans on other security constituted a temporary use of funds awaiting opportunity for permanent investment in real estate loans or bonds. Furthermore, while real estate loans fluctuated with the degree of prosperity, other loans were often high when business was dull because people then borrowed upon their securities instead of sacrificing them in a low market.

In addition to their investment in direct loans, savings banks have been permitted to invest in certain bonds and bank stock. In 1876 the banks could invest in a rather narrow group of securities consisting of the obligations of certain governmental units in New England, the state of New York, and the United States, the bonds of certain railroad companies serving New England, and the stock of banks doing business in Massachusetts. With the economic expansion of the country and the development of the security markets, investment in a wider range of bonds was authorized. After 1876 the three groups were greatly broadened to permit investment in obligations of units of government throughout the United States, in securities issued by an increasing number of railroad corporations, and in the stock of banks located in New England. Bonds of street railway companies were added to the legal list in 1902, and this public utility group was later expanded to include many bonds of telephone, gas, electric, and water companies.

Public funds held in the early years were composed primarily of notes and bonds of cities and towns in New England. Investment in United States Treasury bonds occurred during World War I and the banks continued to hold Treasury bonds for a number of years after the close of the war. During the depression years of the thirties, the banks again increased their holdings of Treasury bonds. In the early years the banks invested in public funds in part simply because of the lack of other investment opportunities. As more and more bonds were made legal for investment, the banks placed a smaller proportion of their assets in public funds, except for the period of the first World War and the years following 1929. Investment in public funds was generally discouraged by the small yield on both Treasury and municipal issues.

Railroad bonds made up the largest single class of security held by the Northampton banks. The Northampton Institution for Savings invested as much as 35 per cent of its assets in railroad bonds in 1909 and, at their peak, railroad bonds constituted 20 per cent of the assets of the Nonotuck and Florence banks. During most of the years railroad securities were a favorite group in the investment market and the yield was generally higher than that on public funds. The banks were increasing their holdings of railroad securities in the early years of the twentieth century, but the increase ceased during the years of Government operation of railroads. In the 1920's investment in railroad securities rose again and then leveled off from 1926 to 1934. Thereafter the other two banks slightly increased their investment but in the Northampton Institution for Savings the holdings of railroad bonds decreased.

In the nineteenth century the Northampton banks invested a considerable portion of their assets in bank stock. The Hampshire Savings Bank, which held almost no other securities, invested as much as 40 per cent of its assets in bank stock from 1876 to 1879. The other banks invested in stock to a smaller degree. From 1895 to 1925, bank stock either remained unchanged in amount or decreased, and it constituted but a small percentage of assets. After 1926 investment in bank stock was increasing but it was still small relative to total assets.

The savings banks were authorized to invest in certain bonds of public service corporations, first the bonds of street railway companies and then the bonds of telephone companies and of electric, gas, and water companies. As public utility bonds were made legal, the banks invested heavily in them and investment increased especially rapidly after 1926.

The bond portfolios of the banks were analyzed for certain years in terms of the ratings made by Moody's Investors Service. From the standpoint of investment rating as indicated by Moody's Service, public funds were the most satisfactory class of securities. This is to be expected from the large proportion of

Treasury obligations owned by the banks. Railroad bonds, which were the largest class of investment, suffered during the first World War but recovered during the prosperous twenties. In the years following 1929 the investment standing of railroad bonds, many of which the banks had held for a long period of time, was greatly injured and by 1938 little improvement had occurred. Public utility bonds showed a somewhat better standing than railroad obligations during the depression years. This was in part a reflection of general investment conditions and in part a result of the more rapid turnover of the securities issued by public utility companies.

The bond portfolios were also examined with respect to the scattering of maturities over time. From 1911 to 1938 the holdings became less concentrated in long-term issues. By 1938 a considerable part of the bonds was to mature within five years and a large part within ten years. Changes in the distribution of maturities resulted from bank policy and from investment in public funds and in public utility bonds, which were generally of shorter maturity than railroad securities.

Since one of the purposes of mutual savings banks is to make capital available to the local community, the assets of the banks were examined to ascertain the degree to which investment had been confined to Northampton and to the New England region. Through loans, which were extended chiefly to local borrowers, about one-half of the assets of the banks were utilized within or near the city of Northampton. In addition, many other investments of the savings banks were placed in businesses serving primarily the New England region. Bank stock owned by the Northampton banks was entirely confined to the stock of institutions located in Massachusetts. As savings banks were authorized to invest in the bonds of companies serving wider and wider areas, the proportion of bonds invested in companies which served primarily the New England area declined in relative importance. Nevertheless, when assets are considered as a whole, most of the funds of the savings banks were made available for use in New England.

The total amount on deposit in Northampton savings banks grew almost continuously throughout the period included in this study but the deposit accounts continued to represent accumulations of small savings. The occasional decreases in the amount due depositors or the lowering of the rate of growth reflected lower business activity in Northampton.

As was the case with the total amount due depositors, the number of accounts in the savings banks and the average size of deposit balances grew throughout the period. However, deposit accounts were small in average size, ranging in 1938 from less than $600 to slightly more than $700. This was to be expected by reason of the fact that the size of deposits in Massachusetts savings banks was legally limited in order to make sure that the banks were patronized by the small savers for whom the banks were established and also to reduce the danger of concentrated withdrawals. The service rendered to small savers by the banks was further borne out by an analysis of deposit receipts. According to this analysis, which was made at five year intervals from 1889 to 1914, about three-fourths of the number of deposits received during the year were items of fifty dollars or less. The public has also been concerned that the savings banks should well serve the needs of women, and in the classification of deposits made at five year intervals it appeared that some 40 per cent of the number of deposits made during the year were made by women and girls. Thus the banks have served the groups whose needs were given special recognition in legislation governing the operation of savings banks.

Although deposit accounts in the Northampton banks showed great activity, the degree of activity declined through the years included in this study. The number of accounts opened and the number closed each year were decreasing percentages of the number of accounts on the books of the banks on the thirty-first of October in each year. In the later years the number of accounts opened during the year amounted to about 8 or 9 per cent of the number of open accounts and a similar percentage was closed. No definite trend appeared in the percentage relationship between the amount deposited each year and the amount due depositors on the thirty-first of October or in the relationship between the amount withdrawn during the year and the balance on deposit. However, in the later years the average percentages were somewhat lower than in earlier years. From 1926 to 1938 the amount deposited during the year in the three banks varied from approximately 16 per cent to more than 18 per cent of deposit balances, and the amount withdrawn was a slightly higher percentage, being about 19 per cent of the total amount due depositors.

The activity of deposit accounts reflected fluctuations in general business activity. When business was good, the number of accounts opened was usually high and the amount deposited during the year was large. The closing of accounts and the making of withdrawals was not so responsive to changes in business.

Depositors in Massachusetts savings banks have been effectively protected from loss. Safety has been achieved through careful regulation of investments, by the requirements concerning the accumulation of reserves, and through the establishment of central funds. Each bank is required by law to accumulate and maintain a guaranty fund, or surplus, which is ordinarily more than adequate to absorb losses through the depreciation of securities and through bad debts. Because of the magnitude of losses of this kind after 1929, the size of the guaranty fund was increased. The Mutual Savings Central Fund of Massachusetts was established in 1932 to advance funds to banks in need of cash. Advances can be made upon the security of various kinds of collateral, including mortgages, which constitute such a large part of the collateral held by the banks and which are ordinarily extremely difficult to liquidate. The Deposit Insurance Fund, which was established in 1934 as part of the Mutual Savings Central Fund, insures the deposits of the mutual savings banks and stands ready to take over the operation of any bank in order to avert threatened loss. Thus, adequate supervision and regulation of the banks, together with a tradition of conservative banking, has made the savings banks of Massachusetts such secure institutions that losses suffered by depositors have been extremely small. In Northampton, itself, one savings bank was closed in 1898 because of the misuse of funds which had been made possible in part by the lack of simultaneous examinations by state and national authorities, and the ultimate loss to depositors was about 21 per cent.

Both as mortgage loan agencies and as savings institutions the savings banks of Northampton faced local competition. Among institutions for savings, the chief competitor was the Northampton Cooperative Bank, organized in 1889. Later a Postal Savings Office was established in Northampton and the national banks opened savings departments. Deposits in mutual savings banks grew less rapidly than the savings placed in the cooperative bank and in the savings departments of the national banks and the trust company. Nevertheless, total deposits in all savings banks continued to exceed the savings in either the cooperative bank or in the savings departments of the other banks. After 1929 the savings bank deposits showed a smaller decline than did the savings in the other institutions. Postal savings deposits were comparatively small at all times.

As mortgage loan agencies the savings banks competed with the cooperative bank, which extended loans upon the same type of real estate, and later the savings department of the Hampshire County Trust Company. The loans of each of these banks increased more rapidly than did those of the savings banks. Other loan agencies were of less importance to the savings banks. The Trustees of the Smith Charities and the Federal Land Bank of Springfield were primarily concerned with farm mortgage loans and therefore did not compete directly with the savings banks. Loans extended by other agencies, such as Smith College, the national banks in Northampton, banks from other communities, and insurance companies, were small in total amount.

The interest rates charged on mortgage loans by the Northampton savings banks and by their competitors were examined to determine their effect upon movements in the volume of mortgage loans. In the early years there were differences between the prevailing rates charged by the several savings banks but, in the later years, rates were the same. Other mortgage loan agencies charged rates differing from those at the savings banks. However, the higher rates at the cooperative bank and at the trust company did not seem to deter the expansion of their loans for they grew more rapidly than those of the savings banks. Differentials in interest charges, therefore, seem to have been a minor consideration to borrowers on home mortgages. The greater growth of mortgage loans in the cooperative bank may have resulted from the cooperative bank's privilege in loaning a larger percentage of the value of the mortgaged property than the savings banks and from the requirement by the cooperative bank that monthly payments be made towards the retirement of the principal of the loans.

Differences between interest rates on mortgage loans and yields on bonds were only one element in determining the distribution of funds between loans and investments. The interest rate received upon mortgage loans was relatively stable; thus, when bond yields declined, the difference between the two rates of return was enlarged. It was not always possible, however, to expand mortgage loans at such times because of the depressed condition of the real estate market and the lack of demand for real estate loans. Furthermore, bank policy usually restricted the amount invested in mortgage loans to 50 or 60 per cent of assets. On the other hand, differences in the yields on high grade securities in various fields of investment did cause the shifting of funds from one field to another, for example, from railroads to public utilities.

The dividend rates of the savings banks and the rates of interest paid by other savings institutions were investigated to observe whether or not the growth of deposits in one institution was stimulated by a higher rate of return on deposits there. The growth in funds placed in the cooperative bank, where the rate paid on shares was higher than the dividend rate paid by the savings banks, exceeded the growth of the savings banks; but the increase in deposits in the savings departments of the national banks, where the interest paid was lower, also exceeded the growth of deposits in the mutual banks. Thus, the interest rate was not the most important element determining the institution in which savings were placed. Other factors, such as convenience and the desire for a plan of regular savings, outweighed the importance of the interest payments.

No relationship was observed between the level of the interest rate and the volume of savings placed in the savings banks. While an increase in the interest rate may increase the total volume of savings, no support for this relationship was apparent in the development of the Northampton mutual savings banks. It must be recognized, of course, that the volume of deposits is a result of both the total amount saved and the shifting of savings between various alternative investments.

The development of the mutual savings banks was closely connected with the prosperity of the local community. The growth of mortgage loans, most of which were based upon property located in Northampton, depended upon the rate of building construction, the condition of the real estate market, and the general level of business activity in Northampton. Likewise, the increase in the balances on deposit in the savings banks reflected changes in the level of income in the community. When business was good, the amount deposited during the year and the number of new accounts were usually high and, conversely, when business was poor, the opening of accounts declined and the amount deposited fell.

BIBLIOGRAPHY

Books and Pamphlets

Böhm-Bawerk, Eugen v. Capital and Interest. Translated by William Smart. London: Macmillan & Co., Ltd., 1890.

Bogart, Ernest Ludlow. War Costs and Their Financing. New York: D. Appleton & Co., 1921.

Burtchett, Floyd F. Investments and Investment Policy. New York: Longmans, Green & Co., 1938.

Carson, William J. Savings and Employee Savings Plans in Philadelphia. Industrial Research Department, Wharton School of Finance and Commerce, University of Pennsylvania, Research Studies XVII. Philadelphia: University of Pennsylvania Press, 1932.

Clark, Evans, editor. The Internal Debt of the United States. New York: Macmillan Co., 1933.

Clark, John Bates. The Distribution of Wealth. New York: Macmillan Co., 1899.

Davenport, Donald H. The Cooperative Banks of Massachusetts. Publication of the Graduate School of Business Administration, XXV (April, 1938), Business Research Studies, No. 20. Boston: Graduate School of Business Administration, Harvard University, 1938.

Davenport, Herbert Joseph. The Economics of Enterprise. New York: Macmillan Co., 1913.

Fetter, Frank A. Economic Principles. Vol. I, Economics. New York: Century Co., 1915.

Hannay, Agnes. A Chronicle of Industry on the Mill River. Smith College Studies in History. Vol. XXI, Nos. 1-4 (October, 1935-July, 1936). Northampton, Massachusetts: Department of History of Smith College.

Harold, Gilbert. Bond Ratings as an Investment Guide. New York: Ronald Press Co., 1938.

Hart, Albert Bushnell, editor. Twentieth Century Massachusetts (1889-1930). Vol. V, Commonwealth History of Massachusetts. New York: States History Co., 1930.

Keynes, John Maynard. The General Theory of Employment, Interest and Money. New York: Harcourt, Brace & Co., 1936.

Klimm, Lester Earl. The Relation between Certain Population Changes and the Physical Environment in Hampden, Hampshire, and Franklin Counties, Massachusetts, 1790-1925. Philadelphia: University of Pennsylvania Press, 1933.

Kirshman, John Emmett. Principles of Investment. 2d edition. New York: McGraw-Hill Book Co., Inc., 1933.

Kock, Karin. A Study of Interest Rates. Stockholm Economic Studies, No. 1. London: P. S. King & Son, Ltd., 1929.

Livermore, Shaw. Investment, Principles and Analysis. Chicago: Business Publications, Inc., 1938.

Macaulay, Frederick R. Some Theoretical Problems Suggested by the Movements of Interest Rates, Bond Yields and Stock Prices in the United States since 1856. National Bureau of Economic Research, No. 33. New York: National Bureau of Economic Research, 1938.

Marshall, Alfred. Principles of Economics. 8th edition. London: Macmillan & Co., Ltd., 1920.

Meade, J. E. The Rate of Interest in a Progressive State. London: Macmillan & Co., Ltd., 1933.

Noyes, Alexander Dana. Forty Years of American Finance. New York: G. P. Putnam's Sons, 1909.

———. The War Period of American Finance 1908-1925. New York: G. P. Putnam's Sons, 1926.

Sherman, Franklin J. Modern Story of Mutual Savings Banks. New York: J. J. Little & Ives, 1934.

Smith Charities. Annual Report, 1876-1938.

Smith, Oliver. Last Will and Testament as approved and allowed by the Judge of Probate for the County of Hampshire, Commonwealth of Massachusetts, on December 9, 1846. Privately published. Obtained by the author from The Trustees of the Smith Charities.

Thomas, Brinley. Monetary Policy and Crises. London: George Routledge & Sons, Ltd., 1936.

Thon, Robert W., Jr. Mutual Savings Banks in Baltimore. Johns Hopkins University Studies in History and Political Science, Series LIII, No. 3. Baltimore: Johns Hopkins Press, 1935.

Thorp, Willard Long. Business Annals. Publications of the

National Bureau of Economic Research, Incorporated, No. 8. New York: National Bureau of Economic Research, Inc., 1926.

Welfling, Weldon. Savings Banking in New York State. Durham, N. C.: Duke University Press, 1939.

Whitney, Caroline. Experiments in Credit Control. Studies in History, Economics and Public Law, No. 400. New York: Columbia University Press, 1934.

Westerfield, Ray B. Money, Credit and Banking. New York: Ronald Press Co., 1938.

Periodicals and Newspapers

Caplan, Benjamin. "Reinvestment and the Rate of Interest," American Economic Review, XXX (September, 1940), 561-68.

Cassel, Gustav. "Keynes' 'General Theory,'" International Labour Review, XXXVI (October, 1937), 437-45.

Commercial and Financial Chronicle. Yearly review, 1875-1894.

Curtis, Myra. "Is Money Saving Equal to Investment?" Quarterly Journal of Economics, LI (August, 1937), 604-25.

Ellsworth, P. T. "Mr. Keynes on the Rate of Interest and the Marginal Efficiency of Capital," Journal of Political Economy, XLIV (December, 1936), 767-90.

Ezekiel, Mordecai. "Statistical Investigations of Saving, Consumption, and Investment," American Economic Review, XXXII (March, 1942), 22-49 and XXXII (June, 1942), 272-307.

Friend, Irwin. "Ezekiel's Analysis of Saving, Consumption, and Investment," American Economic Review, XXXII (December, 1942), 829-35.

Fulcher, Gordon S. "Annual Savings and Underspending of Individuals, 1926-1937," Review of Economic Statistics, XXIII (February, 1941), 28-42.

———. "Saving of Individuals in Relation to Income," American Economic Review, XXXII (December, 1942), 835-40.

Hampshire Gazette (Northampton, Massachusetts), passim, 1920-1938.

Hawtrey, R. G. "Alternative Theories of the Rate of Interest. Three Rejoinders, III," Economic Journal, XLVII (September, 1937), 436-43.

Heilbroner, Robert L. "Saving and Investment: Dynamic Aspects," American Economic Review, XXXII (December, 1942), 827-28.

Hicks, J. R. "Wages and Interest: the Dynamic Problem," Economic Journal, XLV (September, 1935), 456-68.

Husband, William H. "Interest Rates for Home Financing," American Economic Review, XXX (June, 1940), 272-84.

Keynes, J. M. "Alternative Theories of the Rate of Interest," Economic Journal, XLVII (June, 1937), 241-52.

Knight, Frank H. "The Quantity of Capital and the Rate of Interest," Journal of Political Economy, XLIV (August, 1936), 433-63, and XLIV (October, 1936), 612-42.

Landauer, Carl. "A Break in Keynes's Theory of Interest," American Economic Review, XXVII (June, 1937), 260-66.

Lerner, A. P. "Mr. Keynes' 'General Theory of Employment, Interest and Money,'" International Labour Review, XXXIV (October, 1936), 435-54.

________. "Saving Equals Investment," Quarterly Journal of Economics, LII (February, 1938), 297-309.

Long, Clarence D., Jr. "Long Cycles in the Building Industry," Quarterly Journal of Economics, LIII (May, 1939), 371-403.

Lutz, F. A. "The Structure of Interest Rates," Quarterly Journal of Economics, LV (November, 1940), 36-63.

Millikan, Max. "The Liquidity-Preference Theory of Interest," American Economic Review, XXVIII (June, 1938), 247-60.

Moody's Manual of Investments, American and Foreign. 1911, 1914, 1919, 1922, 1929, 1932, 1938.

Neifeld, M. R. "True Effect of Depression on Savings as Shown by Elimination of Interest," Annalist, XXXVII (April 3, 1931), 635-36.

Ohlin, Bertil. "Alternative Theories of the Rate of Interest. Three Rejoinders, I," Economic Journal, XLVII (September, 1937), 423-27.

________. "Some Notes on the Stockholm Theory of Savings and Investment." Economic Journal, XLVII (March, 1937), 53-69, and XLVII (June, 1937), 221-40.

Riggleman, John R. "Building Cycles in the United States, 1875-1932," Journal of the American Statistical Association, XXVIII (June, 1933), 174-83.

Robertson, D. H. "Alternative Theories of the Rate of Interest, Three Rejoinders, II," Economic Journal, XLVII (September, 1937), 428-36.

Shaw, E. S. "False Issues in the Interest-Theory Controversy," Journal of Political Economy, XLVI (December, 1938), 838-56.

Sissman, Louise. "Development of the Postal Savings System," Journal of the American Statistical Association, XXXI (December, 1936), 708-18.

Springfield (Massachusetts) Republican, September 14, 1921, and October 18, 1922.

Steiner, W. H. "Activity of Mutual-Savings-Bank Deposits," Journal of Political Economy, XLV (December, 1937), 789-803.

Steiner, W. H. and Others. "Cooperative Banking for Savings Banks," The Bankers Magazine, CXXXII (May, 1936), 409-17.

———. "Deposit Insurance for Mutual Savings Banks," The Bankers Magazine, CXXXII (June, 1936), 524-30.

Welfling, Weldon. "Some Characteristics of Savings Deposits," American Economic Review, XXX (December, 1940), 748-58.

Government Publications

Massachusetts

Bureau of Statistics of Labor. Census of Massachusetts. 1875, 1895, 1905, 1915.

Commissioner of Banks. Annual Report. 1875-1940. (Published by the Commissioner of Savings Banks, 1875; by the Board of Commissioners of Savings Banks, 1876-1905; by the Bank Commissioner, 1906-1919.)

Commissioner of Corporations and Taxation. Annual Report. 1875-1940.

———. Aggregates of Polls, Property, Taxes, etc. 1875-1940. (Compiled by the Secretary of the Commonwealth, 1875-1907; by the Tax Commissioner, 1908-1918).

Decennial Census. Compilation by the Secretary of the Commonwealth. 1925, 1935.

Department of Labor and Industries. Annual Report on the Statistics of Manufactures. 1907-1921.

Department of Labor and Industries. Statistics of Manufactures. 1920-1938.

Documents of the Senate and House of Representatives

House Doc. No. 1280 (1908).

House Doc. No. 1262 (1922).

House Doc. No. 1275 (1923).

House Doc. No. 1167 (1933).
Senate Doc. No. 503 (1922).
Senate Doc. No. 100 (1934).
General Court. Acts and Resolves. 1876-1939.

Northampton

Building Inspector. Annual Report. 1917-1939.

United States

Bureau of the Census. Census of Population. 1940.
Comptroller of the Currency. Annual Report.

Unpublished Material

Evans, Helen. "The Economic Development of the Connecticut Valley." Unpublished Master's thesis. Smith College. 1930.

Freeman, Phyllis Maud. "Industrial and Labor Developments in the City of Northampton, Massachusetts, 1898-1930." Unpublished Master's thesis. Smith College. 1931.

Schwulst, Earl B. "The Competitive Position of the Mutual Savings Bank." Address delivered on May 4, 1938, before the 18th Conference of the National Association of Mutual Savings Banks.

Whitbeck, Sterling R. "The Investment Trends of Massachusetts Savings Banks since 1900." Unpublished thesis submitted in partial fulfillment of the requirements of the Graduate School of Banking of the American Institute of Banking. New Brunswick, New Jersey. 1939.

Much information was obtained from the following persons then associated with the listed organizations:

Mr. Homer C. Bliss and Mr. Percy F. Spencer, Florence Savings Bank;

Mr. Sterling R. Whitbeck, Nonotuck Savings Bank;

Mr. Edward T. Heaphy and Mr. Ralph E. Harlow, Northampton Institution for Savings;

Mr. E. L. Arnold, First National Bank of Northampton;

Mr. A. P. Cushman, Northampton National Bank and Trust Company;

Miss Fenton, Northampton National Farm Loan Association; Mr. George S. Swift, The Trustees of the Smith Charities.

Data concerning the Postal Savings Office of Northampton was furnished by the Division of Postal Savings of the United States Post Office Department.

INDEX

Bei Fragen zur Produktsicherheit wenden Sie sich bitte an:
If you have any questions regarding product safety,
please contact:

Walter de Gruyter GmbH
Genthiner Straße 13
10785 Berlin
productsafety@degruyterbrill.com